Aesthetics and Video Games

Bloomsbury Aesthetics

Series Editor:
Derek Matravers

The Bloomsbury Aesthetics series looks at the aesthetic questions and issues raised by all major art forms. Stimulating, engaging and accessible, the series offers food for thought not only for students of aesthetics, but also for anyone with an interest in philosophy and the arts.

Available from the series:

Aesthetics and Architecture by Edward Winters
Aesthetics and Film by Katherine Thomson-Jones
Aesthetics and Literature by David Davies
Aesthetics and Morality by Elisabeth Schellekens
Aesthetics and Music by Andy Hamilton
Aesthetics and Nature by Glenn Parsons
Aesthetics and Painting by Jason Gaiger
Aesthetics and Photography by Dawn Wilson
Aesthetics and Music by Andy Hamilton
Philosophy of Painting by Jason Gaiger
Aesthetics and Emotion by Cain Todd and Joerg Fingerhut
Aesthetics and Nature by Glenn Parsons
Aesthetics of Care by Yuriko Saito
Aesthetics and Glamour by Carol S. Gould
Architectural Aesthetics by Edward Winters
Aesthetics and Morality by Elisabeth Schellekens
Aesthetics and Design by Jeffrey Petts

Aesthetics and Video Games

Christopher Bartel

BLOOMSBURY ACADEMIC
LONDON • NEW YORK • OXFORD • NEW DELHI • SYDNEY

BLOOMSBURY ACADEMIC
Bloomsbury Publishing Plc
50 Bedford Square, London, WC1B 3DP, UK
1385 Broadway, New York, NY 10018, USA
29 Earlsfort Terrace, Dublin 2, Ireland

BLOOMSBURY, BLOOMSBURY ACADEMIC and the Diana logo are trademarks
of Bloomsbury Publishing Plc

First published in Great Britain 2025

Copyright © Christopher Bartel, 2025

Christopher Bartel has asserted his right under the Copyright,
Designs and Patents Act, 1988, to be identified as Author of this work.

For legal purposes the Acknowledgments on pp.viii-ix constitute
an extension of this copyright page.

Cover design: Louise Dugdale
Cover image © Hector Roqueta Rivero / Getty Images

All rights reserved. No part of this publication may be reproduced
or transmitted in any form or by any means, electronic or mechanical, including
photocopying, recording, or any information storage or retrieval system, without
prior permission in writing from the publishers.

Bloomsbury Publishing Plc does not have any control over,
or responsibility for, any third-party websites referred to or in this book.
All internet addresses given in this book were correct at the time of going to
press. The author and publisher regret any inconvenience caused if addresses
have changed or sites have ceased to exist, but can accept no responsibility
for any such changes.

A catalogue record for this book is available from the British Library.

A catalogue record for this book is available from the Library of Congress.

ISBN: HB: 978-1-3501-0483-9
PB: 978-1-3501-0482-2
ePDF: 978-1-3501-0484-6
eBook: 978-1-3501-0485-3

Series: Bloomsbury Aesthetics

Typeset by Newgen Knowledge Works Pvt. Ltd., Chennai, India
Printed and bound in Great Britain

To find out more about our authors and books visit www.bloomsbury.com
and sign up for our newsletters.

*To Jennifer and Evalyn
for all the games we play*

Contents

Acknowledgments		viii
1	Aesthetics	1
2	Three Attitudes of Play	19
3	Goal-Seeking Aesthetics	49
4	Narrative Aesthetics	81
5	Dollhouse Aesthetics	117
6	The Aesthetics of Moral Choice	151
7	But, Is It Art?	185
Notes		207
References		221
Index		233

Acknowledgments

This book is the result of many conversations with colleagues, students, and friends about video games and why we play them. Thanks first to Derek Matravers, the editor of this book series, who casually asked me if I wanted to write a book about aesthetics and video games while we were standing outside a pub in London. I tried to keep my cool when I said, "Yeah, sure, sounds fun." Actually, I was ecstatic to have been asked.

My colleagues are people who I deeply admire, and I have learned so much from our conversations and correspondences. Some of our conversations were formal conference talks, others were just short comments delivered as we waited between sessions, and sometimes we just talked about what I'm up to at the moment over a drink. All of your friendly advice and patient listening has been deeply appreciated. Thanks to Angela Black, Renee Conroy, Anthony Cross, Alexandre Declos, A. W. Eaton, Javier Gomez-Lavin, René Jagnow, Emily Lacy, Morgan Luck, Aaron Meskin, Shelby Moser, Karim Nader, C. Thi Nguyen, Mark Nunes, Jem Page, Stephanie Patridge, Elisabeth Schellekens, Jonathan Weinberg, Rissa Willis, and Nick Wiltshire. I am immensely grateful to Antony Aumann, Brandon Polite, Nathan Wildman, Sarah Worth, and Michel-Antoine Xhignesse for very kindly (and charitably) reading draft versions of chapters of this book. Thanks also to my departmental colleagues—especially Anna Cremaldi, Rick Elmore, Mathew Foust, Jack Kwong, and Randy Reed—for many talks over the years on this project and for giving me the time during a research leave to finish it.

Parts of this book have been presented at conferences, departmental seminars, and invited guest lectures in my colleague's classes. Audience members at these talks provided many helpful comments and questions. I would thank each of you by name, but I am very bad at note-taking during my talks. Thanks to the audience members of Elisabeth Schelleken's departmental research seminar at Uppsala

University, A. W. Eaton's graduate class at the University of Illinois, the American Philosophical Association Central Division Meeting (2022), the American Society for Aesthetics Annual Meeting (2023), and the Southern Aesthetics Workshop (2023). A very special thanks to Enrico Terrone's graduate reading group at the University of Genoa who read the penultimate draft of the book.

I have had too many conversations with too many students, to name them all, who have shaped my thinking about video games. Some of those conversations happened so many years ago that I doubt the student would remember it now. But I remember and I still appreciate it. Thanks to Taylor Dobson for pushing me to think about video games philosophically in the first place; to Annabella Del Ciotto for their enthusiasm and insight, and for talking me through the joys of *Animal Crossing*; and to Maxwell Butterworth, who challenged me to rethink the scope of dollhouse play. The students in my Philosophy and Video Games classes offered numerous comments, examples, and insights over the years that challenged and inspired me. Thank you especially to Abby Branco, Dagan Danevic, Jacq Dozier, Jack Faullin, July Harris, Christopher Harrison, Tyler Holbrook, Connor Kusilek, Christian Moeller, Josh Russell, Macy Sutton, and Anna Wilson.

Finally, thank you to Jennifer Courtney-Bartel for her support and encouragement, and for letting me hog the TV. And to Evalyn Bartel, whose play and playfulness inspired some of the key insights of this book. Now that I've finished writing it, we can finally get back to our farm in *Stardew Valley*!

1

Aesthetics

Dragon Age: Origins (*DA:O*) was the game that really changed the way that I thought about video games. Prior to playing *DA:O*, there were things that I expected from video games and things that I didn't. I expected the obvious things: that they should be fun, exciting, and challenging. But *DA:O* convinced me that games could be more. I think the reason why *this* game had such an effect on me partly has to do with the game itself, but it also has a lot to do with me. (And incidentally, that is the main theme of this book.) To see why, it helps to know how I got into video games.

There are many "entry points" into gaming, just as there are many different reasons to stay. But there are some entry points that are very common for many people. My story is similar to lots of people of my generation.

The first games I ever played were arcade cabinets that I found in bars, restaurants, and my local laundromat in the late 1970s and early 1980s. I played *Pong*, *Q-Bert*, and *Centipede* while we were waiting for our food to be served or waiting for our clothes to dry. Then my parents bought an Atari 2600. I spent my weekends and summers playing *Pac-Man*, *Frogger*, and *Missile Command* in our basement. However, my favorite game of that generation was *Pitfall*. It seemed to tell a story, however minimal it was. My friends and I were so excited to see what challenges or treasures might be waiting on the next screen. A few years later, my family had bought the fancy new Nintendo Entertainment System. I became hooked on *Super Mario*

Bros., *Punchout*, and *Kung Fu*. And I continued playing arcade games like *Rampage* and *Paperboy*. My local mall had a small arcade tucked away in a far corner where I spent hours pouring quarters into *Indiana Jones and the Temple of Doom*.

However, by the time I entered middle school in the mid-1980s, I had been introduced to *Dungeons & Dragons* (*D&D*). That effectively killed my interest in video games. The games I had simply weren't as rich, detailed, and exciting as a session of *D&D*. Playing *The Legend of Zelda* sometimes scratched that itch, but I would gladly drop my control pad for a d20 if I had the chance.

By the time I had reached high school, I had other interests taking me away from video games. My friends and I had formed a punk band. From that point on, I was too pretentious to play games at all. I got all the way through college and a brief music career without owning another console, or a TV for that matter. (As I said, *pretentious*.) Still, I found time to play arcade games when I could. Near my college in Boston, there was a pizza shop on Boylston Street that had a *Mortal Kombat* cabinet. If I had $5, I would buy two slices of pizza and a bottle of Coke for $4.50 and then I would pump the remaining two quarters into *Mortal Kombat*. More often, I would play pinball. The studio that my band practiced out of had *Attack from Mars*. We played that more than we practiced.

When I got to graduate school, I had a lot of time to myself. So, I began developing an interest in video games again. I bought a second-hand N64 and, a few years later, a GameCube. My love of *D&D* led me to *Baldur's Gate* on PC. I didn't have anyone at this point in my life to play *D&D* with. Yet, *Baldur's Gate* was able to offer me a well-defined campaign with pre-generated companions. I spent so much time campaigning with Minsc and Boo. It was fun, but the gameplay often felt slow. When I finished graduate school and got myself a real job, I celebrated by purchasing a PlayStation 2. Naturally, I was drawn to *Baldur's Gate: Dark Alliance*. I felt that this improved on *Baldur's Gate* by offering faster-paced gameplay, but it is a straightforward hack-and-slash.

I upgraded my console to a PlayStation 3 specifically because I wanted to play *Dragon Age: Origins*. This, it seemed to me, solved both problems. The gameplay was fast enough, but it still demanded some thoughtful strategizing. But there was more to *DA:O* than that. I had long thought of video games as a weak substitution for *D&D*. Video games could have fun gameplay, but little in the way of a story. The storytelling of *DA:O* felt rich in comparison to anything I had played before. The game allows the player to choose an avatar from a few different races, and the player can choose the avatar's gender as well. The origin story of the main avatar changes depending on what race and gender you choose. And interestingly, I found that this choice also changed the way that I thought about my character's motivation. I didn't know that video games could do that. In the world of *Dragon Age*, elves had suffered a long period of enslavement at the hand of humans. When I played as an elf, my interactions with the world were colored by tones of racism. Similarly, playing as a female character reoriented my attitude toward my interaction with the gameworld.

I expected games to be shallow and frivolous, one-sided devices that could only deliver on gameplay, like pinball machines made out of pixels. But *DA:O* showed me that games can offer unique forms of storytelling too. There is an aesthetic richness to video games that is not neatly boxed in by only one aspect. *Dragon Age: Origins* inspired me to explore further, to see what other aesthetic possibilities were available.

This book is motivated by the belief that the widespread appeal of video games has something to do with their aesthetic value. Video games are fun and challenging, but they can also be beautiful, frightening, cute, sad, elegant, and awe-inspiring. They can evoke emotion. They can tell complex stories. Really good video games produce a feeling in players that is electrifying. And really bad video games are disappointing because they fail to produce that feeling. The best way to explain these kinds of values is to look at video games as aesthetic objects.

The central claim of this book is that the aesthetics of video games has as much to do with the player as it has to do with the game itself. The aesthetic values that players find in video games depend on the kind of attitude that the player takes toward playing the game. There are three distinct attitudes that players take when they play video games. I call these the *goal-seeking attitude*, the *narrative attitude*, and the *dollhouse attitude*. Each of these attitudes has a distinctive impact on the player's aesthetic experience. There are certain qualities of games that appeal to one attitude or another, while there are other qualities that can be aesthetically transformed when players take different attitudes toward their play. The aesthetics of video games must account for how the game is crafted alongside the player's attitude toward their play.

But, what is "aesthetics"? Whether or not gamers find any aesthetic value in video games depends, of course, on what counts as "aesthetic." This will be the subject of this chapter. To introduce this topic, I think there are two general issues we can think about. First, we should think about what kind of a philosophical explanation we can hope for. In Section 1, I introduce the philosophical debate over aesthetics very generally. A *philosophical approach* to aesthetics should aim to explain *why* we find certain things aesthetically appealing and other things not. However, that is obviously very hard to do. So hard, in fact, that many theorists think it is hopeless. For some theorists, the only way to study aesthetics is to provide a detailed account of what kinds of things people find aesthetically valuable. We can think of this as the *sociological approach*: we can catalog and describe various kinds of aesthetic practices, but we cannot explain why those practices work. This kind of approach to the aesthetics of video games is very common in media and game studies, and it is certainly an academically valuable way to go. However, I think we can say some things about *why* we value certain things. I hope to prove that with this book.

In Section 2, I defend a broad understanding of the concept of *the aesthetic*. There are certain experiences that are unique to video games. But one could question whether those experiences are "aesthetic experiences." The definition I will use is this: "aesthetics" refers to apparently intrinsic properties that are valued for their own sake. Aesthetic enjoyment is one of the basic pleasures of life. And importantly, we appreciate objects aesthetically because doing so is itself worthwhile and enjoyable. We do not appreciate objects aesthetically as a means to some other end. Aesthetic appreciation is an end in itself. When looking for the aesthetics of video games, we should look for properties intrinsic to the game that are valued for their own sake. I take this definition to be broad enough to encompass many possibilities without narrowing our sights too much. By adopting a broad understanding of "the aesthetic," we can take current aesthetic practices around gaming at face value and see how they develop. What I particularly want to avoid is deciding in advance what counts as "aesthetic" only to find that what gamers value about video games falls outside of our definition. Instead, I want to look and see what gamers value about a video game for its own sake before drawing limits on the aesthetic.

1 What Is Philosophical Aesthetics?

This book is about what makes video games aesthetically enjoyable. In particular, I am interested to know what is aesthetically distinctive of video games. I know that sounds like a tall order, but it can be done. Before we can explain the aesthetics of video games, we first have to be clear about what kind of explanation is possible.

I would love to give you a list of criteria for what makes video games aesthetically good, which you could then just use like a checklist. But that isn't possible. When we think about what a diverse collection of things falls under "video games"—which would include first-person shooters, hidden-object games, cozy games, farming games, match-three games, deck-building games, battle royale games, massively multiplayer online role-playing games (MMORPGs), and numerous other genres—there is no one thing that clearly makes video games aesthetically good. Intense battles make first-person shooters fun, but they would be completely out of place in a café management game. Instead, there are many possible things to aesthetically value in video games; some aesthetically valuable elements of a game are incompatible with other aesthetically valuable elements, and no video game can do everything.

Video game critics and theorists often talk about "aesthetics" in a narrow sense. If you think that the "aesthetics" of the game is just the way that it looks, perhaps also the way that it sounds, then you are taking a narrow approach to aesthetics. People who take a narrow approach will often talk about gameplay, the story, and the aesthetics of a game as three separate things. There might be interesting connections to form between them—like when the look of a game is reflected in its story—but ultimately these are distinct things. It is understandable why many people think of these as three different things. After all, in large game studios, you will find different teams of specialists for mechanics, story development, and art design. The word "aesthetics" as we know it today evolved out of a philosophical debate about the nature of sense perception beginning with Alexander Baumgarten and arrived at the more familiar sense that we use today from David Hume (1757) and Immanuel Kant (1790), a sense that links *aesthetics* to *art*. So, it is not unreasonable to think that the art design team are the people who are responsible for the aesthetics of a video game.

However, this narrow sense of "aesthetics" doesn't really match what players, critics, and game designers actually do. It might be tempting to maintain the narrow sense of "aesthetics" by thinking that storytelling in video games becomes an aesthetic object only because it is a visual form of storytelling, like cinema. But that would obviously ignore the fact that novels and poems are aesthetic objects too, and their aesthetic properties are not dependent on visual aspects. Some might be willing to concede that storytelling in video games is part of their aesthetics, but that only expands the realm of aesthetics somewhat. What about gameplay? Fans and critics of games often describe gameplay in aesthetic terms. Gameplay can be satisfying or clunky, battles can be exciting or disappointing. The idea that gameplay is itself a source of aesthetic value has been growing in recent years (Kirkpatrick 2011; Nguyen 2020; Robson and Tavinor 2018). With this book, I want to examine where we can look for aesthetic value in gameplay, but that requires that we expand our understanding of aesthetics.

A broader conception of "aesthetics" holds that there are many kinds of aesthetic values and that many different kinds of objects can be sources of aesthetic value. This means two things. First, that "aesthetic values" are more diverse than the traditional focus on beauty. Beauty has long been regarded as the quintessential aesthetic value and has occupied a central place in discussions of aesthetics for much of its history (Zangwill 1995). However, it is not the only aesthetic value worth talking about, even if it is one of the most prized. We should also be able to talk about what makes something dainty, dumpy, garish, joyful, disgusting, and incoherent, to name a few. Second, a broader conception of aesthetics also accepts that the objects that can hold our aesthetic interest are not limited to traditional art. Works of art are not the only things that have aesthetic value. We can also talk about the aesthetics of food, flower gardens, and landscapes, as well as events, like sports matches, a long drive, or a quiet morning breakfast at your favorite café. Video games can certainly be objects of aesthetic attention, and we can find more aesthetic value in them than just beauty.

It is very common for people to think that "aesthetics is subjective." In one sense, this is true; but this idea is often misinterpreted. Many people interpret "aesthetics is subjective" to mean that aesthetics is really just a matter of individual opinions and there can be no true claims about aesthetics that are not made from some individual perspective. What is beautiful to me might not be beautiful to you, and there is no sense in having arguments about aesthetics beyond the recognition that we might disagree. To say that aesthetics is subjective is to deny that there is anything true or objective about aesthetics. This belief is partly what motivates the sociological approach to aesthetics—if there are no general truths about what is aesthetically valuable or why, then all we can do is just catalog what people happen to like.

Many philosophers in the analytic tradition take a more nuanced view of the notion of subjectivity, one that is informed by the theories of Hume and Kant. On the Humean-Kantian view, aesthetics is subjective in the sense that we must judge the quality of an object by appealing to our sense perception. Aesthetic judgments cannot be deduced from logical principles. If they could, then I should be able to infer what aesthetic properties any object has so long as I have a complete and accurate description of it. And that is impossible (Sibley 2001). To know what aesthetic qualities an object has, I have to see for myself. But crucially, *seeing for myself* doesn't automatically mean that aesthetics is just a matter of individual preference or opinion. It could also be the case that, when I see for myself, I come to verify what aesthetic quality an object really has, just as anyone else who sees for themselves can do. Of course, aesthetic judgments are subjective in a weak sense—I have to see for myself—but according to Kant, they nonetheless have an interesting universal validity.

This debate about the subjectivity of aesthetics often makes me wary because my own view on the matter is conflicted. On the one hand, I think Kant's idea of "universal validity" promises too much. At the same time, I resist the idea that aesthetics is just about individual preferences and opinions because I think that view robs artists (and musicians, game designers, and other creators of aesthetic objects) of their skill to know how to get certain aesthetic responses from their audiences. Of course, no artist can know with absolute certainty how their work will be perceived and interpreted by their audience. But artists are not just taking a shot in the dark either. Artists tend to be people who are embedded in their own communities and they tend to be active fans of the artforms that they work in. Through experience they come to learn what are the expected aesthetic norms of their community. If they are particularly astute, they can even learn to recreate the qualities that members of their community aesthetically admire.

For my part, I don't think that I can prove to you (or to anyone else) that aesthetics is universally valid in the way that Kant thought. But I also don't think I have to. Instead, all that matters to me is that we acknowledge that there are two parts to aesthetics: the object and the subject. Objects really do have properties to them—properties that cause aesthetic experiences for individuals—but it isn't possible to say what an individual's experience of those properties might be like without also specifying who the subject is and how they think about things. My view of aesthetics follows that of Elisabeth Schellekens (2006). On her view, objects have certain properties objectively, but one's aesthetic experience of those properties depends on certain psychological features of the subject. Two subjects who possess the same relevant psychological features can be expected to respond to the object in similar ways, while two subjects who possess different psychological features would naturally respond to the object differently. Schellekens' view allows us to acknowledge the differences between subjects and the diversity of our aesthetic responses, while still maintaining an objectivity about properties. Artists can learn to anticipate how audiences will respond to their work, but doing so means understanding your audience as well as understanding your artform. Video games are crafted with certain expected qualities in mind too. The way in which players aesthetically experience a game depends in part on how the game was designed and also on who the player is and what attitude they bring to their play.

We can offer more than a sociological account of the aesthetics of video games. The kind of account I hope for is one that can explain how individual elements of games impact players while also accounting for the fact that not all players are the same. I believe the attitudinal account that I offer in this book takes one important step toward that goal.

2 What Is the Aesthetic, Philosophically?

When a new aesthetic practice arises, theorists typically seek to explain it by using familiar existing theories from similar practices. In debates over the aesthetics of video games, we can see theorists attempting to scrutinize games from the perspective of preexisting aesthetic practices. For instance, theorists have sought to treat games as an extension of film (Gaut 2010; Wolf 2001) or as kinds of fiction (Robson and Meskin 2016; Tavinor 2009). This sort of approach makes a fundamental assumption about the nature of the aesthetic—that the boundaries of "the aesthetic" are already defined well enough by these existing theories. However, the creation of a new aesthetic practice may force us to reconsider the boundaries of the aesthetic. Games offer new elements that may be of aesthetic relevance—like interactivity, embodiment, and game mechanics (Aarseth 1997; Juul 2005, 2013; Kirkpatrick 2011; Nguyen 2020)—that cannot be understood by looking through the lens of film, literature, or visual art.

Games can be criticized in a number of ways, many of which seem to have little to do with aesthetics. For instance, from the perspective of *game design*, we may question whether a game's rules are fair or whether its challenges are well balanced. While I will later argue that many of these aspects of game design are in fact part of the aesthetics of games, this point is not obvious at the outset. At least initially, it seems true that some aspects of game design are more concerned with playability than aesthetics. Of course, this assumes that we know what we mean when we say "aesthetics."

Philosophers often use the term "aesthetic" to describe any number of things: some philosophers talk about aesthetic *properties*, some talk about aesthetic *judgments*, and some talk about aesthetic *experiences*. In each of these cases, theorists have sought to identify what exactly makes some properties, judgments, and experiences distinctively *aesthetic* ones. The first thing to notice about each of these phrases is that they purport to denote special kinds of properties, judgments, and experiences. For instance, when we describe an experience as an "aesthetic experience," we are implying that aesthetic experiences are distinctive in some way that marks them out as different from non-aesthetic experiences. Our task is to figure out how they are distinctive.

While all of these philosophical terms are useful, I will mainly focus on aesthetic experiences. Doing so is not to imply that experiences are the primary concern of aesthetics. Rather, I will focus on aesthetic experiences because I believe that doing so would best fit the way that video game criticism is typically written. It is uncommon for video game critics to talk about aesthetic properties or judgments. However, it is extremely common for video game critics to talk about what it is like to play a game—that is, to talk about their experiences.

So, what is distinctive about aesthetic experiences? Philosophers have had a lot to say about this topic, too much to review fully here.[1] Instead, some broad points will do. Philosophical debate over the nature of aesthetics can be traced far back in the history of Western philosophy. Both Plato (see his *Ion*, *Symposium*, and *Republic*) and Aristotle (see his *Poetics* and *Rhetoric*) had things to say about aesthetics. However, the major themes of the debate today take their cues from two ideas that emerged in the eighteenth century about the distinctive nature of aesthetic judgments: that they are *immediate* and *disinterested* (Shelley 2017). On the first point, aesthetic judgment is *immediate* in the sense that it is not something that one reasons out. Aesthetic judgments are not made by logical inference. Just as in perceptual experience where the appearance of an object is not something that one must infer or reason out, so too in aesthetic experience do objects appear to us to be beautiful or ugly in themselves. For eighteenth-century philosophers like David Hume and Immanuel Kant, the challenge of aesthetics is not only to accept the immediacy of aesthetic judgment but also to avoid relativizing aesthetic judgments to individual subjectivity. On the second point, to describe aesthetic judgment as *disinterested* is to say that one appreciates the object in a way that is impersonal or unbiased by the individual's practical needs and concerns (e.g., Hume 1757, para. 21; and Kant 1790, §5). To judge something to be financially good, for instance, is to judge it to be good for me in a certain way—it serves to increase my financial gain. On some accounts, moral and political goodness are similarly self-interested judgments that are relative to the interests of an individual or a social group. But judging something to be aesthetically good—for instance, to describe a painting as "well composed," or a sculpture as "graceful," or a piece of music as "strident"—has nothing to do with any self-interested gains, or so the thought goes. Many philosophers have sought to maintain the eighteenth-century idea that aesthetic judgments are immediate and disinterested, though how those ideas are spelled out is open to debate.

A basic distinction between different theories of aesthetic experience is that some philosophers offer an *internal* account of aesthetic experience while others offer an *external* account (Shelley 2017: §2.4). Internal accounts tend to focus on psychological or phenomenological features that are internal to an aesthetic experience, the idea being that aesthetic experiences are distinct from non-aesthetic experiences because of some unique psychological feature of them. By contrast, external accounts focus on features of the objects perceived. The most recent defender of the external account is Noel Carroll (2006), who defends a theory he calls the "content-oriented approach." Central to Carroll's account is the idea that aesthetic experiences have "content," where the content of an experience is whatever object is the focus of one's attention.[2] To have an aesthetic experience is for the content of one's experience to include aesthetic properties among the represented properties of some object. Aesthetic properties would include things like the object's form, any expressive properties that it might have, and the ways in which the form and expressive properties might interact with each other (Carroll 2006: 89). One of the virtues of Carroll's content-oriented approach is that it places the value of aesthetic experience in objects themselves: the value of an aesthetic experience is to be explained by the value of the object's aesthetic properties. Another point in favor of the content-oriented approach, and of externalist theories generally, is that it is not dependent upon individuals and their subjective feelings. This is good, not only because it avoids relativizing aesthetics to subjectivity, but also because there seem to be some aesthetic experiences that are not associated with any particular subjective feeling. Carroll offers the following example: "One might take note of the angularity of Katherine Hepburn's body, her gestures, her facial structure, and her way of speaking and, in addition, realize how this all 'fits' with the 'edginess' that her characters are meant to project; and yet one may take no pleasure, nor suffer any other affect while doing so" (ibid.: 72). In other words, one can notice the aesthetic quality of some object without feeling anything in particular toward that quality, and yet such experiences still seem to be aesthetic experiences.

While externalist theories offer some benefits, they also come with some high costs for us. The trouble with locating aesthetic qualities in external objects is that there are certain aspects of the evaluation and appreciation of video games that, strictly speaking, do not attribute aesthetic qualities to games themselves. Think of things like *immersion* and *flow*. Undoubtedly, these are qualities that figure strongly in the appreciation of video games, which offers prima facie reason to think that these are aesthetic qualities. Interestingly, however, these qualities are not a part of the content of any game. While we may be able to point to specific game contents that contribute to its beauty or its expressive quality, there is no part of a game's content where we can locate its immersive quality. If we wish to count experiences of immersion and flow as aesthetic experiences, which I think we should, then we likely should not adopt an external theory of aesthetic experiences.

Many philosophers have developed different sorts of internalist theories of aesthetic experience. The one thing that these philosophers share is that they seek to identify what is distinctive about aesthetic experience by examining the nature of the experience itself from a perspective internal to the individual. Aesthetic experience is ultimately a mental phenomenon, which is distinguished from other mental phenomena in some way. The question is, in what way? Some philosophers hold that aesthetic experience is distinguished by the particular psychological operations that underlie such experiences. For instance, Kant thought of aesthetic experience as the exercise of a faculty of taste. When one regards an object disinterestedly, an object of beauty will cause the subject to experience a "free play of the imagination," which the subject experiences with pleasure (1790: §9). For Kant, it is not the feeling of pleasure that characterizes an aesthetic experience. Rather, it is an aesthetic experience because of the specific psychological mechanism that gives rise to the pleasure.

Other philosophers have sought to distinguish aesthetic experiences from non-aesthetic experiences by referring to a distinctive subjective feeling. For instance, early in the twentieth century, John Dewey (1934) offered an affective-narrative account of the aesthetic. Many of our everyday experiences are unremarkable, fleeting, and lacking in any unified coherence. Other experiences are mechanical and predictable. These all are "enemies of the aesthetic" (1934: 47). By contrast, an aesthetic experience according to Dewey is an experience that possesses a sense of completeness and an identifiable emotional quality, one where the experience is consummated into a unified and distinctive whole. The kinds of experiences that Dewey identifies are certainly valuable experiences, and they are likely aesthetic experiences; but it is unlikely that Dewey's account exhausts the possibilities of aesthetic experience. The problem primarily is that experiences of disunity or incoherence can themselves be aesthetic experiences too (Kieran 1997).

The internalist approach to identifying aesthetic experiences that I favor could be described as an *attitudinal account* of aesthetic experience.[3] Aesthetic experiences are those where a person values an object in a particular kind of way. There are many ways that we can value objects that have nothing to do with aesthetics—like when we value objects as historical documents, as embodiments of one's culture, as investments, or as beneficial for one's health. To value an object aesthetically is to value some object for no other reason than because it is worthy of attention—or, to value the object for its own sake. As Gary Iseminger says, "Someone is appreciating a state of affairs just in case she or he is valuing for its own sake the experiencing of that state of affairs" (2006: 99). Perhaps you have a favorite coffee mug. There may be many things about that coffee mug that you might like—it holds a good amount of coffee, it is easy to wash, it was given to you by someone that you love. All of these are good reasons to value that mug, but none of these are aesthetic reasons. They are instead pragmatic and sentimental reasons. Alternatively, perhaps the thing you like about your mug is just the way that it feels in your hands. It feels almost as if it was designed to fit *your* hands. Perhaps the experience of holding a warm drink in your coffee mug is particularly satisfying. *That* is an aesthetic experience. It is an experience that you enjoy just for its own sake.

This is not to say that aesthetic experiences must always be pleasurable experiences. Pleasure is one kind of aesthetic experience;

beauty is another kind. But sometimes, perhaps oddly, we are fascinated by things that are ugly or disgusting. Car crashes are hard to look away from. We can even value an experience that we wish never to repeat. Darren Aronofsky's film *Requiem for a Dream* is a masterpiece, and I never want to see it again.

Aesthetic experience is a kind of valuing that Jerrold Levinson calls "endorsed satisfaction"—in some sense, one approves of having the experience because the experience is intrinsically worthwhile. Levinson characterizes endorsement as a "positive hedonic, affective, or evaluative response or reaction to the perceptual experience" (2013: 39). However, I think that is still a little too narrow. Some experiences can be absorbing, but I wouldn't describe them as positive or approving. When I was a child, a house down the road caught on fire. My entire neighborhood gathered around to watch. I remember being both terrified and fascinated. It wasn't *fun* or *enjoyable* to watch someone's home burn to ash. But it was also impossible to look away. That too was an aesthetic experience.

The attitudinal account of aesthetic experience has a number of virtues. First, aesthetic experiences are distinct from mere experiences—that is, merely sensing or merely noticing does not count as an aesthetic experience. I can notice the warmth of my coffee mug without thereby appreciating it. Second, this account of the aesthetic is broad enough to account for the aesthetic enjoyment of everyday objects (Saito 2007), and yet it is sufficiently narrow to pick out a genuinely distinct form of experience. Third, focusing on experience in this way allows us to recognize that some experiences fail to be *aesthetic* even when they are focused on the right sort of objects. It is possible to perceive a work of art coldly. For instance, highly trained musicians might analyze the formal structure of a musical work without valuing their experience of the music. Even though the musician's attention is focused on the music, and specifically to its musical form, possessing the right perceptual content does not make the experience an aesthetic one (*pace* Carroll 2006).

Finally, and importantly for us, the attitudinal account of aesthetic experience allows us to theorize about the aesthetics of video games without being beholden to traditional aesthetic qualities. Video games are unique. They share some features with film, fiction, animation, and comic books. But the aesthetics of video games is not restricted to only those qualities that video games share with these other artforms. The attitudinal account allows us to look at video games and ask, what qualities do players value for their own sake? For instance, video games are often valued for the sense of immersion that they provide. But why do we value immersion? My answer: we value it for its own sake. It is a fascinating and unique sort of experience, one that is rather different from our everyday experience. On my reading, then, *immersion* should be thought of as an aesthetic value and one that is specially valued in the aesthetics of video games. The attitudinal account will allow us to identify unique features of video games that are valued for their own sake without prejudging them because they do not overlap with other, older artforms.

3 Going Forward

Here is how the rest of the book will unfold.

In Chapter 2, I will examine in detail the idea of play attitudes. I will argue that philosophers of games have long held that games and play are partly defined by the player's attitude. Video games too require an *attitudinal* theory of play. There are three attitudes that players take toward video games: a goal-seeking attitude, a narrative attitude, or a dollhouse attitude. When we approach games as a challenge to be won or a puzzle to be solved, we are taking a goal-seeking attitude. This attitude is characterized by its acceptance of the built-in goals of a game, its use of means–ends reasoning, and the quantifiability of outcomes. When we approach games as stories, we are taking a narrative attitude. Some games have a built-in narrative—a story that the game designer wants to tell; however, all games have the right temporal structure to allow the player to develop their own story. Finally, when we approach games as toys that can be bent to our own will, we are taking a dollhouse attitude.

This attitude is characterized by its lack of means–ends reasoning, a de-emphasis on quantifiable outcomes, and the willingness of the player to project their own stories and goals onto the game. Each of these attitudes makes a distinctive contribution to the player's aesthetic experience, which will be detailed in three separate chapters.

In Chapter 3, we will examine the goal-seeking attitude. This chapter begins with a discussion of two influential philosophers in the history of the philosophy of games: Johan Huizinga and Roger Caillois. While Huizinga was somewhat dismissive of the idea that the joy of play could be fully described by its aesthetics, Caillois was more accepting of the idea that play could be valued aesthetically. Caillois offers a helpful taxonomy of kinds of play that I argue offers a helpful guide for where we can look for the aesthetic value of goal-seeking play. I argue that the aesthetic value of goal-seeking play comes from a number of sources. Drawing on the work of Mihaly Csikszentmihalyi and C. Thi Nguyen, I argue that goal-seeking play can induce "flow states" and also provides the right structure for "striving play." Finally, I argue that we derive aesthetic value from the uncertainty of play and that games are aesthetically valued for their rules and mechanics.

Chapter 4 turns to an examination of the narrative attitude. Stories can be told in many ways through video games, and many theorists have detailed many different ways that video games can produce valuable narratives. In this chapter, I first offer some clarification of what a "narrative" is. I argue that we can attribute a narrative to a game when we must explain what is happening in the game by referring to the relationships between the game's fictional characters and events. Next, I examine some key elements of storytelling: action, worldbuilding, lore, narrative structure, and cut-scenes. Finally, I argue that the interactivity of video games creates opportunities for an "aesthetics of consequences" and "narrative role-playing."

Chapter 5 is the most speculative chapter. Here, I argue that some players take a dollhouse attitude toward play, which is a free and imaginative form of play. Dollhouse play is more common than we might think; however, it is also a form of play in video games that is under-theorized. The primary forms of dollhouse play are dress-up, collecting, and "dollhouse role-playing." These forms of play show up in unexpected places. Every time we customize our avatars, collect objects in games for its own sake, and role-play our own stories and adventures, we are engaging in dollhouse play. I hope that, by drawing attention to the ubiquity of dollhouse play, we can better appreciate the role of formless play in video games.

Aesthetics is about valuing objects for their own sake. However, it is difficult to take aesthetic pleasure in an object that one finds morally or politically offensive. Many gamers, critics, and game theorists hold that moral judgments have no place in the appreciation of video games. In Chapter 6, I argue against this view. Instead, I argue that video games are value-laden already, that players employ their actual moral judgment when playing moral-choice games, and that moral judgments have a role to play in our aesthetic experience and evaluation of video games.

Finally, in Chapter 7, we will consider whether video games should count as "art." I will argue that the resolution to that question is actually less important than we might think, which is the reason why this chapter comes last. Once the concept of *art* is decoupled from the concept of the *aesthetic*, then we are free to go looking for the aesthetic value in video games whether we think of them as art or not, just as we have done in the earlier chapters of the book.

I love talking about video games and we will have a lot to talk about in this book. So, let's get to it!

2

Three Attitudes of Play

When my daughter was eight years old, she watched me play through *The Legend of Zelda: Breath of the Wild* (*BOTW*). She enjoyed the action and the story even more. She particularly loved the relationships between the four Champions. We cheered and celebrated when Gannon was finally defeated.

I spent many hours playing that game, building up Link to the point where he could feasibly defeat Gannon. While I experienced a lot that the game had to offer, I didn't, however, experience everything. I didn't "platinum" the game. But that's okay, I felt like I got what I wanted out of it. And I have lots of other games that I want to play.

Instead of totally putting down *BOTW*, though, I just handed my game over to my daughter. She was thrilled. She wasn't very good at the combat—she would just swing a sword wildly until her enemies were dead—which was fine, because Link had so many *hearts* that he could easily survive any encounter. If things got too rough for her, she could just run away. I was pretty pleased with myself too. I thought that this would be a great way for her to be introduced to this kind of combat. It was impossible for her to lose, so she wouldn't get too discouraged.

So, she carried on playing for a while. But, as I watched her play, I began to notice something: she *never* sought out any combat. Instead, she would spend her time catching horses, climbing mountains, collecting flowers, and cooking different foods. At one point, she completed all the missions needed for Link to buy a house. Then she decorated the house, hanging all of his best weapons on decorative weapon racks. Then—to my horror—she spent an hour walking around Link's backyard mowing the lawn with the Master Sword. *What a waste!*, I thought. *She isn't putting any of those good weapons to use! She isn't really playing the game!* What bothered me was that she wasn't trying to win anything or earn any loot. She was using Link as if he was just a doll, something to dress up and take on little imaginary adventures of her own making. *She's playing it wrong!*

And she was having a blast.

That was the moment when it hit me. The game that I treated as a competition was just a dollhouse to her. *And it worked perfectly well that way.* In fact, she discovered things about the game that I never noticed because I was so fixated on winning. My daughter discovered that you can ride not only horses but also wild deer (though you can't keep them). She discovered that you can buy a house and decorate it. She discovered lots of fun places where you can go shield surfing. She got a lot of enjoyment out of the game that I didn't. I only pursued quests and goals that led to my ultimate goal: defeating Gannon. I didn't want to keep Princess Zelda waiting, after all. But she discovered that it is okay to just have fun with it.

An aesthetic experience is the result of an interaction between a person and an object. When a player has an aesthetic experience of a video game, their experience is partly determined by features of the game that are intrinsic to it. We will talk about how features of games contribute to the player's aesthetic experience in later chapters. In this chapter, I want to focus on another facet of aesthetic experience: that the player's experience is also partly determined by matters that are intrinsic to the player.

We have defined "aesthetics" as valuing something for its own sake, but this does not happen in the abstract. Players interact with games from a particular situated position—physically, culturally, historically. These situational features of the player also have some impact on the player's aesthetic experience of a game. To offer one quick example, think about the relationship between a player's perception of a game's difficulty and their level of skill. Whether a game is *challenging* or *easy* has as much to do with the player as it has to do with the game itself. I cannot do justice to all the various situated features that contribute to the player's response here. Instead, my aim is to describe just one: the player's attitude toward their play.

I argue that we basically do three things when we play video games: we pursue goals, we engage with a narrative, and we play with dolls. These make up the three basic forms of play in video games—goal-seeking play, narrative play, and dollhouse play.[1] To be more accurate, I argue that each of these identifies a distinct kind of attitude that the player takes toward game playing. Goal-seeking play, narrative play, and dollhouse play are not genres or categories of games. They are psychological attitudes that the player takes. Players can freely switch from one to the other. Some games are designed to complement one specific attitude, while other games are designed to allow the player to choose how they wish to play. Players experience different aesthetic qualities depending on what attitude they take toward their play.

We will talk about the specific aesthetic impact that each of these attitudes offers in Chapters 3 to 5. In this chapter, I want to argue that three distinctive attitudes are involved in gaming and that an attitudinal approach is a good way to think about the aesthetics of video games. To do this, I will first examine some influential accounts of the nature of play and games. What we will find there is that, according to many theorists, it is not possible to account for play, and therefore to account for games, without referring to the player's attitude. Once that background is in place, we can then consider some more general points about the attitudes of play that are involved in gaming.

1 Philosophical Accounts of Play and Games

It is impossible to define "play" or "games" without referencing the player's mental state. On this point, theorists about games and play are nearly united. Where various theorists disagree is about the specific nature of the player's mental state. In this section, we will examine some influential accounts of the nature of play and games, paying specific attention to the role that the player's psychology makes in defining their activity. My aim here is to provide a representative sample of influential theories that figure strongly in the philosophy of games today, rather than to provide an exhaustive account of the history of theories of play and games.[2] This brief history will set up the main claims that I defend in Section 2.

Philosophers' and cultural theorists' interest in the theory of play and games has been on the rise over the past half-century. It is difficult to find much philosophical discussion of these topics prior to the twentieth century. It is possible to find brief mentions of games, sports, and even specific athletes in the writings of the ancient Greeks, though most of these consist of little more than passing references that serve as illustrative examples of some other philosophical concern. More often, games are mentioned by philosophers as a kind of diversion from more important issues. For instance, David Hume makes a passing reference to playing a game of backgammon as a way to distract himself from his academic pursuits (*Treatise* I.6.vii).

Contemporary accounts of the philosophy of games can be traced back to two groundbreaking works, by Johan Huizinga (1970, originally published 1938) and Roger Caillois (2001, originally published 1961). Huizinga's primary concern was to offer a sketch of the nature of play.[3] For now, we will narrowly focus on what they had to say about the role of the player's attitude.

Huizinga identifies four characteristics of play (1970: 26–32): it is a voluntary activity, separate from the everyday, bounded by artificial limitations, where certain rules are upheld, thus creating its own order. Huizinga holds that play depends on a special state of mind of the players. This is captured nicely by one of the most quoted parts of Huizinga's account, known as the "magic circle."[4] He says,

> All play moves and has its being within a playground marked off beforehand either materially or ideally, deliberately or as a matter of

course. Just as there is no formal difference between play and ritual, so the "consecrated spot" cannot be formally distinguished from the play-ground. The arena, the card-table, the magic circle, the temple, the stage, the screen, the tennis court, the court of justice, etc., are all in form and function play-grounds, i.e. forbidden spots, isolated, hedged round, hallowed, within which special rules obtain. All are temporary worlds within the ordinary world, dedicated to the performance of an act apart. (Huizinga 1970: 28–9).

Many games take place within a physical space that is marked off by special boundaries that indicate the area of legitimate play, either "materially or ideally." In boxing, legitimate play happens within the ring, and any punch that is thrown outside of the ring is illegitimate. However, the "magic circle" does not only refer to the physical space in which a game takes place. It also refers to a conceptual space, one where the player gives willing consent to abide by the rules of the game and accept as legitimate whatever outcome may follow. Boxers must wait for the bell to ring, signaling the beginning of a round, before they can throw a punch, and another bell signals that they must stop at the end of the round. This is not a physical boundary but a conceptual one.

Ultimately, what legitimizes play is the consent of the players. In traditional games and sports, play is sustained by the ongoing and active will of the players. For instance, when playing a board game, it is up to the players to enforce the rules. Or if a group of friends decides to play a casual game of soccer in the park, it is up to the collective will of the group to uphold the rules. The rules must be policed by the players themselves. Video games are different from traditional games in that the job of upholding the rules is automated by the computer (Juul 2005: 49). This difference aside, the player still willingly accepts the rules and challenges of the game.

Inspired by Huizinga, Roger Caillois (2001) also sought to explain where play comes from and how it gives shape to social behaviors. Caillois argues that games are a formalization of play, but play is the more fundamental category that needs to be explained (2001: 4). Caillois begins by offering an account of the characteristics of play. On Caillois' account, play has six characteristics (many of which overlap with Huizinga's four). First, play is *free* in the sense that it is not obligatory. If we were obligated to play, then play "would lose one of its basic characteristics: the fact that the player devotes himself spontaneously to the game, of his free will and for his pleasure" (ibid.: 6). Second, play is *separate* from the concerns of the real world. Spaces and times are set aside for play. Third, play is *uncertain* in the sense that one cannot determine the course of play or the outcome in advance. If one is merely following a predetermined set of directions, then one is not playing. "An outcome known in advance, with no possibility of error or surprise, clearly leading to an inescapable result, is incompatible with the nature of play" (ibid.: 7). Fourth, play is *unproductive*. It is easy to misinterpret Caillois here. He is not saying that play is wasteful or useless. Rather, he is saying that the purpose and value of play is not for the production of goods. If we looked at play from the perspective of someone who only cares about productivity, then play would appear to be a "waste of time, energy, ingenuity, skill" (ibid.: 5–6). But that is the wrong way to think about the value of play. Players expend considerable energy, but at the end of a game, players simply erase the score and start over again.[5] Finally, Caillois' fifth and sixth characteristics are that play is either *rule-governed* or it is *make-believe*. Some play is governed by rules that "suspend ordinary laws, and for the moment establish new legislation" (ibid.: 10). This is the case particularly when we play formal, competitive games. Other play is ungoverned by rules, as is the case with imagination games—like playing with toys, playing dress-up, or playing *House*. These are games that "presuppose free improvisation, and the chief attraction of which lies in the pleasure of playing a role, of acting *as if* one were someone or something else... [and] the sentiment of *as if* replaces and performs the same function as do rules" (ibid.: 8).

The attitudinal nature of play can be seen in a number of places in Caillois' account. It is in the free and voluntary nature of play: "One plays only if and when one wishes to" (ibid.: 7). It is in the "*as if*" sentiment of imagination games. It is in Caillois' point about the unproductive nature of play—play happens when one shifts from thinking of an activity as extrinsically valuable to thinking of it as intrinsically valuable. Finally, it can be seen in Caillois' discussion of the arbitrary nature of rules. Ultimately, the rules of a game are meaningless—there is no reason *outside of the desire to play the game* that necessitates following its rules. A cheater is someone who does not question the rules but attempts to take advantage of the other players' loyalty to them, while a nihilist is someone who refuses to play the game at all because they recognize the meaninglessness of its rules. In fact, the nihilist is correct, says Caillois.

> The game has no other but an intrinsic meaning. That is why its rules are imperative and absolute, beyond discussion. There is no reason for their being as they are, rather than otherwise. Whoever does not accept them as such must deem them manifest folly. (Ibid.: 7)

Bernard Suits (2014) offers a specific account of "game playing" that is narrower in focus than either Huizinga's or Caillois' accounts but one that highlights the attitudinal nature of game playing. In Suits' words, he defines game playing as "activity directed towards bringing about a specific state of affairs, using only means permitted by rules, where the rules prohibit more efficient in favor of less efficient means, and where such rules are accepted just because they make possible such activity" (2014: 36). Suits identifies four conditions for some activity to count as a game-playing activity, which he calls the *prelusory goals, lusory means, constitutive rules,* and the *lusory attitude*. A prelusory goal is a certain state of affairs that could be achieved independently. That state of affairs might be to cross a finish line, jump over a high bar, or arrange the pieces on a chessboard so that one's opponent is in checkmate. The prelusory goal is achieved by following certain sanctioned actions, called the "lusory means." These are designed to offer a challenge, which is achieved by selecting means that are less efficient than some other available option—these are the "constitutive rules." The easiest way to win at pole vaulting is to use a ladder to clear the bar. This would more efficiently achieve the prelusory goal—clearing the bar—than the sanctioned means of vaulting over the bar at the end of a long pole. But using these more efficient means would not count as pole vaulting. Players adopt less efficient means to make the task challenging. Finally, and importantly for us, players willingly adopt inefficient means to achieve the prelusory goal just because doing so makes the entire activity worthwhile, which is called the "lusory attitude." Echoing Caillois' point about the arbitrariness of a game's rules, we accept the inefficient and arbitrary means to achieve some goal just because doing so makes achieving the goal worthwhile. When we play games, the goals we pursue are not intrinsically valuable, and the means to achieve the goal are unnecessarily difficult. Yet, playing a game becomes a meaningful activity when, and only when, the player accepts the challenge for what it is.

Jesper Juul (2005) seeks to define "games" rather than "play." His account employs six conditions: "A game is [1] a rule-based system [2] with a variable and quantifiable outcome, [3] where different outcomes are assigned different values, [4] the player exerts effort in order to influence the outcome, [5] the player feels emotionally attached to the outcome, and [6] the consequences of the activity are negotiable" (2005: 36). For our purposes, the interesting condition is (5). Conditions (1) to (4) are formal conditions, meaning that they describe features of game playing that can be identified objectively by a dispassionate observer; while condition (6) is a social condition, meaning that the outcome of a game being attached to some external reward has more to do with the culture of the players than it has to do with the game itself. Condition (5) is neither formal nor social. It describes an individual, psychological feature of the player's attitude toward the game rather than a formal or social aspect of the game. As Juul notes, condition (5) follows from condition (4). Given that players expend considerable effort to influence the outcome of a game, they naturally feel some emotional investment in seeing the outcome go their way, even in games of chance where the player's influence on the outcome is quite minimal (ibid.: 40).

Ian Bogost (2016) tells a familiar story about domestic life that illustrates his account of play. In his story, Bogost is hurrying through a shopping mall running some dreadful errand. His aim is to get it over with and get out of the mall as quickly as possible. However, he is accompanied by his young daughter who has made a game out of trying to keep up with the fast pace of her father. In his description of the situation, his daughter has found a way to turn an otherwise unpleasant task into something fun. As he says, "my daughter's playful act interpreted her situation as much as my attempt to rush us through it did. While I was only focused on the goal, she managed to attend to the process" (2016: 92). The difference between Bogost and his daughter was a matter of attention—by attending to the activity itself, rather than the goal, she could turn the activity into a form of play. Ultimately, Bogost concludes that it is possible to turn anything into play—shopping, mowing the lawn, an academic career—by turning our attention to the process and its materials.[6]

Finally, C. Thi Nguyen's (2020) recent account of the value of games offers a key insight to the attitudinal nature of play. Nguyen spells out a detailed picture of how players take on different goals, shifting attitudes as the demands of play shift. Nguyen offers a rich theory that has a number of aims. He argues that games are an artform (2020: 1–3), that the medium of games is *agency* (ibid.: 14–15),[7] that games provide players with a "library" of different forms of agency (ibid.: 78–83), and that the motivational structure of games can be exploited in sometimes harmful ways (ibid.: 189–215). These claims are fascinating; however, I will briefly draw attention to one part of Nguyen's account of a player's psychology.

Nguyen identifies a fundamental distinction in what he calls two "modes of play" (ibid.: 8). Sometimes we play to win. When this happens, our purpose in playing is aligned with the goal of the game. Nguyen calls this "achievement play." At other times, we set aside the goal of winning in order to enjoy some aspect of the game. For instance, in an open-world video game, I might go looking for random encounters just because I like the battles. While winning these encounters provides some experience and loot, that might not be my motivation. My motivation is to enjoy the battle. In an odd way, winning the battle too quickly can be a disappointment. I might draw out the game, by perhaps playing on a higher difficulty setting or by using only suboptimal weapons and armor, thus making the battles longer, more exciting, and more dangerous. Nguyen calls this "striving play" (ibid.: 9). In striving play, my purpose in playing does not align with the goal of winning. Nguyen describes this as a "motivational inversion." He says,

> A striving player acquires, temporarily, an interest in winning for the sake of the struggle. ... In ordinary practical life, we pursue the means for the sake of the ends. But in striving play, we pursue the ends for the sake of the means. We take up a goal for the sake of the activity of struggling for it. (Ibid.: 9)

Striving play is very common. There can be many factors that interfere with, and supersede, our desire to win. For instance, imagine that you have invited a few friends over for a dinner party, and at some point, you pull out a party game (this is Nguyen's example [ibid.: 72]). During the first few rounds of the game, you play to win. However, you quickly realize that some of your friends have not yet grasped the rules. They are playing badly and making obvious mistakes. If your aim was to win, then you could easily crush your friends. But doing so would not be very enjoyable for them. You want your friends to have a good time, so instead of crushing them, you intentionally hold back. Doing so draws out the game longer and allows the others the chance to come to grips with the game's rules.

There are many cases where players handicap themselves in order to give weaker or inexperienced players a fighting chance. When parents play games against their children, the aim is not to crush them. The aim is to teach them how the game works, help them develop the skills to play well, and to enjoy spending time with them. When I play *Mario Kart 8* against my daughter, I impose additional rules and limitations on myself in order to extend our gameplay further. I will avoid sliding and drifting, which denies me a speed boost; and I do not use red shells on her, though green shells are fair game. I do this in order to draw the game out and to give her a reasonable chance to win. But importantly, adding these self-imposed restrictions does not mean that I'm not having fun. Instead, I'm still having loads of fun playing against her, even though I have to follow additional rules that she does not have to follow. The enjoyment comes from my *striving* to win.

The lessons that I take from these theorists are these. First, game playing is an activity that is formally similar to many other kinds of activities (like working, traveling, studying), but it can only be distinguished from these activities by referring to the player's mental state. For Caillois, the amateur player who seeks no extrinsic reward is *playing*, while the professional athlete who cares only about the prize money is *working*, but both might perform what are formally identical actions (2001: 6). Or think of Bogost's point that anything can become play by focusing on the process rather than the objective. Second, there are different ways of playing a game. An external observer watching you play cannot tell whether you are, for example, an achievement player or a striving player, or a professional athlete who is just working. From the outside, these all look the same. The difference between each is still an important one, but it is a difference that can only be described by referring to the players' attitudes. Finally, players can freely and willfully switch from *playing* to *not-playing*, or from *achievement play* to *striving play*, or from *playing* to *working*. "One plays only if and when one wishes to" (Caillois 2001: 7).

2 How We Play Video Games

When we play video games, we basically do three things: we pursue goals, we engage with a narrative, and we play with digital dolls. These make up the three basic forms of play in video games, which I call *goal-seeking play*, *narrative play*, and *dollhouse play*. Each form of play is, of course, more complicated, having many different and more specific kinds of play. For instance, goal-seeking play includes things like puzzles, team battles, and racing. Nonetheless, the distinction between goal-seeking play, narrative play, and dollhouse play is a fundamental one. Whenever you are playing a video game, you are either pursuing one of the goals given to you by the game, engaging with the game's story, or playing your own imagination game with a digital doll. Each of these makes a distinctive aesthetic contribution to the player's experience of the game. We will talk about specific details of each in the next three chapters. Here, I want to spell out what I mean in broad strokes.

Each of these forms of play has certain formal qualities that are associated with it, but the main difference between these forms of play is ultimately psychological. We saw above that many theorists have identified many psychological features of games. What I want to add to their ideas is the thought that video games in particular employ three different attitudes toward play and players choose how they want to play a game by adopting one of those attitudes. Let's first outline the main differences between each attitude of play.

Goal-seeking play is what we typically imagine when we think about playing a game.[8] When players take a goal-seeking attitude, they play a game with the intention to win. The game sets the player a challenge, the player accepts the challenge on its own terms, and they do what it takes to meet it. If the player is successful, then they are rewarded in the game. Goal-seeking play is distinctive in three respects. First, the goals and challenges are set by the game itself. It is the game that tells me that I have to collect a certain number of coins, or I have to beat my opponent to the finish line, or I have to find the solution to the puzzle. These are goals that are built into the game. The player then pursues these goals because they accept that achieving this goal is what it takes to win. Some in-game goals are *ultimate* while others are *ancillary*. In *Super Mario Bros.*, the ultimate goal is to rescue the Princess. Once this goal is reached, the game is over. An ultimate goal is whatever counts as beating the game. Ancillary goals are ones that help the player to achieve the ultimate goal, some of which are essential to achieving the ultimate goal and some of which are non-essential. Again, in *Super Mario Bros.*, I can rescue each of the toads in the other castles, but I do not have to. I can skip levels to get to the Princess faster. The toads are side-quests. While all side-quests are ancillary goals, we often must complete some side-quests in order to level-up enough to achieve the ultimate goal. The value of completing a side-quest is often part of its value toward completing the ultimate goal.

A further subtlety here is that many in-game goals feature a *compound reward system*. When I complete a side-quest, I do not receive just one reward, but a package of rewards. I get some experience points, some loot, maybe an unlockable item, or I might open up new dialogue options or storylines. This is helpful given that players are often motivated by different kinds of goals. Some players want to level-up quickly in pursuit of the ultimate goal, while other players want to explore the immersive world through the side-quests. Offering compound rewards thus gives each player a little of something that they want.

The second distinctive feature of goal-seeking play is that it is governed by means–ends reasoning. The player's choices in the game are determined by their reasoning about how best to achieve their goals. If I want to buy the best weapons, then I need to collect gold, which means that I should complete many side-quests. I do not complete the side-quests for their own sake. Instead, I pursue various side-quests because that is what I have to do to achieve my goal. Or, if I want to defeat this powerful foe, then I need to employ stealthy tactics. So, I seek out missions and battles that allow me to practice my stealth skills. The reason why I seek out these missions is, again, because I have determined that it is the best way for me to develop my skills, which will allow me to beat that powerful boss. My reasoning always follows this pattern in goal-seeking play: I accept a particular goal and then I figure out the best way of doing it.

Finally, goal-seeking play is distinctive for its quantifiability, which allows for comparison between players or between playthroughs. Because of the quantifiability of goal-seeking play, we can ask questions like: Who won? Who played the game best? Who collected the most achievements in the fastest time? Some games are easily quantified along a single metric. In classic *Tetris*, the only metric that matters is my score. However, other games feature compounded metrics. Just like the idea that rewards can be compounded, the quantifiability of goals can be too. Some games feature a *dominant* metric, even while other quantification metrics are available. In *Clash Royale*, the dominant metric is the trophy count. Players are placed into different leagues based on the number of trophies they have collected, and some clans require a minimum number of trophies to join them. In this case, the game is designed primarily around the trophy metric; however, *Clash Royale* offers other challenges that each have their own quantification metric. There are other games that quantify goals along a number of *variable* metrics, none of which are dominant or primary. In these games, the player can effectively choose which metric matters most to them. In *Stardew Valley*, there are many quantifiable measures of success, but the game does not tell the player that any one measure of success is dominant, or even necessary. In one playthrough, I could try to speed-run to finish the community center. In another playthrough, I can sell the community center to JojaMart. I can try to befriend as many of the villagers as I can. Or I can just devote myself to farming parsnips. The general point here is that the in-game goals are quantifiable and comparable, and players take a goal-seeking attitude when they are looking for metrics by which to measure their gameplay.

Narrative play is a very different attitude. When players engage with video games *as* narratives, the focus is not on winning or goal-seeking but is instead on appreciating the story and lore of the game's fictional world. What is distinctive here is the relationship between storyteller and audience. The game designer has a story to tell, and the player is their audience. In narrative games, the story is told through the cutscenes, action, worldbuilding, and lore that the game designer has developed. Players engage with the story in any number of ways. Sometimes the story unfolds directly, either in real time during an action sequence or during a cutscene. Other times, the player must uncover items or objects to engage with the story. In *Elder Scrolls V: Skyrim*, the player can find books and libraries throughout the world that fill out the history and lore of the world. Reading these books is voluntary, for the most part. The player does not have to read every volume in the library of Winterhold to complete the game. So, why would the player spend time reading digital books in an imaginary library? The answer is because they have adopted a narrative attitude to the game and they are enjoying the lore of Skyrim.

I have characterized the narrative attitude as a relationship between the game designer and the player, where this attitude is characterized by the player's openness to the game designer's story. Of course, video games are interactive fictions. In *Skyrim*, the player does not just passively learn about the world of *Elder Scrolls*, but they also contribute to the unfolding story. While the game designer is telling a story, they have sanctioned that certain plot points are dependent on the actions of the player. Sometimes that dependence is very minimal, like when the player's actions merely trigger predetermined narrative events. In other cases, the player's influence on the game is more substantial. But no matter what choices the player makes, the story still belongs to the game designer, the story still progresses in one of the ways that the game designer has sanctioned in advance.

Dollhouse play is subtly distinctive when compared to both goal-seeking play and narrative play. The kind of play I have in mind is when the player uses a video game in the same way that they might use a toy—that is, as an object that acts as a prompt to engage in one's own imaginative play. Examples of dollhouse play are things like customizing one's avatar, collecting and crafting objects for their own sake, and exploring. These forms of play need not be either goal-seeking play or narrative play. Dollhouse play is unlike goal-seeking play in that players do not pursue in-game goals; it does not employ means–ends reasoning, and it lacks quantifiable outcomes. In dollhouse play, there is nothing that the player *has* to do nor any achievements that constitute winning. Dollhouse play is also unlike narrative play in that the player is not bound to the story that was developed by the game designer. Instead, the player tells their own imaginative story using the video game as a toy. When players customize their avatars, collect objects for their own sake, and go freely exploring in a gameworld following only their curiosity, they are engaged in dollhouse play. In a sense, both goal-seeking play and narrative play are *prescriptive*: goal-seeking games prescribe what the player ought to value and valorizes the means of achieving its ends, while narratives in games prescribe the game designer's story. By contrast, dollhouse play is not prescriptive, it is *suggestive*. The game suggests what the player *can* do, but it makes no demands about what the player *must* do. The difference between my playing of BOTW and my daughter's playing of it, described at the beginning of this chapter, is that I took a goal-seeking attitude to the game while she took a dollhouse attitude.

What kind of activities are part of dollhouse play? While a full answer to that question requires some subtlety, the basic point is that some of the things that players do in a game are identical to what you would do if you were playing with a doll. There are three in-game activities that are unambiguously forms of dollhouse play. The first, and most obvious, is when we customize our avatars. In *Skyrim*, one of the first things that the player does is to create their avatar. There are many customization options. The player can choose their fantasy race and gender. Then there are many options available to change minor details about the avatar's body, hair, face, skin color, eye color, and so on. The first time I played *Skyrim*, I happily looked through all of the options and crafted my avatar to be exactly what I wanted. When I finished, I realized that I had spent two hours creating my avatar. Now, from the perspectives of goal-seeking play or narrative play, I was not pursuing any goal or engaging in the game's story. If those two attitudes were the only legitimate forms of play, then you could say that I spent two hours "not playing the game" while I was designing my avatar. But that is not how it felt to me. I was having fun!

The interesting thing about customization is that, effectively, all we are doing is playing dress-up with a digital doll. If you don't like the sound of that, then think of it this way: customization is just the act of making aesthetic choices in games that have no goal-seeking or narrative purpose. I didn't select the shape of my eyebrows in *Skyrim* because it provided me with some strategic advantage or because it opened up new storylines. I did it because I liked the way that it looked. And that is the essence of playing dress-up.

Another form of dollhouse play is collecting. Think about actual dollhouses: while children will actively play with a dollhouse, adults will often use a dollhouse only to display a collection. They might create a tableau in the rooms of their dollhouse with the intention that the scene is not to be touched or played with any further. It is a staged scene intended for display. Some gamers engage in similar in-game collecting practices. There are various cities and towns throughout the province of Skyrim where the player can acquire a house. You can then decorate the house. Some house upgrades can be purchased, which provide some moderate in-game benefits. The player can also display objects that they have collected during their adventures around their houses. Why would anyone bother to spend time doing this? I think the obvious answer is, because they enjoy it. Collecting objects to display in my house in *Skyrim* is neither goal-seeking play nor narrative play. Rather, the player collects and displays items in the game just for its own sake, and not for the sake of any other goal, just as a collector would play with a dollhouse.

How is collecting different from goal-seeking play? After all, the player has to have set themselves the *goal* to complete the collection. So, it doesn't seem all that different. However, in subtle and important ways, it is. The difference is that the player has selected the goal for themselves, the goal is not imposed on the player by the game. There are many games that include collecting missions. Every gamer who has played an open-world game is familiar with these kinds of missions—collecting all the bird feathers in *Red Dead Redemption*, or collecting all pieces of the Mongol armor in *Ghost of Tsushima*. When a player collects items in a game for the sake of unlocking an achievement, then they are engaged in goal-seeking play. The player is merely pursuing the goal because the game told them to. It is a means to achieving the end of platinuming the game. But the player who collects items in a game just because they want to—not because it gives them loot, an achievement, a strategic advantage, or a new storyline—is motivated by something very different from goal-seeking. For instance, in the *Final Fantasy* games, "chocobos" are birds that are large enough to be ridden like horses. Different types of chocobos are better suited to different types of terrain. Some areas of the world are inaccessible without possessing the right kind of chocobo. So, there is an in-game, goal-oriented reason to breed at least some types of chocobos. However, there comes a point in the game where it is no longer necessary to breed any more. The player who breeds every type of chocobo in *Final Fantasy VII*, not because they need them to complete the game but just because they want to, is engaged in dollhouse play.[9]

A third form of dollhouse play is role-playing, which can come in many forms. A basic form of role-playing is exploration, when the player freely explores a digital open-world following their own curiosity. Suppose that I set out to climb all the highest peaks in *Skyrim*. This is not a game-directed goal, I don't receive any special loot or experience for doing so, and climbing every peak is not required by the story. Instead, I do it just because I'm role-playing that my digital doll is on an adventure. Other games offer role-playing through simulations—like driving, flying, building, and farming. Just like collecting, some players take a goal-seeking attitude toward simulations. For instance, many of the *Grand Theft Auto* games include driving missions. The player must complete these missions to complete the game (and to learn how to drive). If the player pursues the driving mission only for the sake of completing the game, then they are taking a goal-seeking attitude. But other players engage in simulation as a form of role-playing, which substantially changes the player's orientation to the activity.

Dollhouse play is not unusual. Some games are designed primarily for dollhouse play. *Animal Crossing: New Horizons* is essentially a dollhouse, where the main play styles are dress-up, collecting, and exploring. Players collect outfits for their avatars and furniture for their dwellings. They collect fish, bugs, fossils, and works of art to display in the island's museum. They collect K.K. Slider's albums and hang the record covers around their houses. And players explore other players' islands and view other players' collections. While there are achievements to unlock and trophies to collect, many players are unconcerned about these game-imposed goals. Moreover, there is no narrative to engage with, apart from the initial premise that the player has won a getaway package for an island vacation. Other games are primarily designed for either goal-seeking play or narrative play, but they offer small elements of dollhouse play. Dollhouse play is sometimes momentary. When I customize my avatar in *Call of Duty: Black Ops III*, I am briefly engaging in dress-up. But when I am finished, I go back to my goal-seeking attitude and try to beat the game.

Of the three attitudes that I have identified, dollhouse play is the least understood and also the most derided. Games that are designed for dollhouse play are often dismissed as "not *real* games," and people who engage in dollhouse play are dismissed as not "real gamers." In the 2010s, a number of games started to appear on Facebook, like *FarmVille* and *CityVille*. These games are often called different things—mobile games (because many were designed to be played on a smartphone), social games (because many encouraged players to invite their friends to play), or "freemium" games (because many adopted the free-to-play payment method). I will refer to them as "casual games" because they are typically designed to be played in short bursts of time. Casual games have an interesting position in the gaming world. Commercially, they are highly successful. But they are widely hated by "real" gamers and game designers (Consalvo and Paul 2019). The hate that casual games receive is motivated by various concerns. Some hate is motivated by mere tribalism—"first-person shooters are real games, everything else sucks!" Much of the hate is motivated by the fear that the commercial success of casual games will lead developers to prioritize making more of them, which would take time and development money away from more traditional big-budget games. Some academics developed their own criticisms of casual games. Ian Bogost sought to satirize such games by developing his own game, called *Cow Clicker*. Here is Bogost's description of it:

> You get a cow. You can click on it. In six hours, you can click it again. Clicking earns you clicks. You can buy custom "premium" cows through

micropayments (the Cow Clicker currency is called "mooney"), and you can buy your way out of the time delay by spending it. You can publish feed stories about clicking your cow, and you can click friends' cow clicks in their feed stories. Cow Clicker is Facebook games distilled to their essence. (Bogost 2010)

Bogost describes his animosity toward "Facebook games" as having less to do with some undefinable worry about whether they are "real games" and more to do with the way that many of these games suck up our time by enhancing the compulsive aspect of video games while also lacking any real challenge (ibid.). Bogost is partly right here—gaming *can* lead to compulsion—but Bogost's worry about the lack of challenge seems misplaced. It is a common misconception that games are supposed to be challenging *by their essence*. Maybe the games that *you* like are challenging, but "challengingness" is not some essential feature of all games. Roulette is not challenging, neither is *Pass the Pigs*, nor are most drinking games. If games are supposed to *be* anything, then they are supposed to be *fun*. A challenge can make a game fun (though needless challenges can also make a game stressful or frustrating). But many games are fun even though they lack any challenge.

Juul offers a different characterization. Juul distinguishes between three types of games. The first two are familiar and intuitive: *games of skill* are tied to the player's personal ability, while *games of chance* are simply tied to luck. However, a third type could be called *games of labor* (2013: 73–4; Juul credits the term to Naomi Clark). These are games where the player is rewarded for repetitively performing "routine tasks," tasks that are easy to perform in themselves. The challenge that games of labor present comes from performing the task so often that the combined effort of each task eventually accumulates into a big outcome. Harvesting crops and gathering materials in *Stardew Valley* is easy, but harvesting and gathering enough crops and materials to reach the Fern Islands takes some dedication. The person who wins a game of labor is the one patient enough to grind it out for the longest time. I think Juul is also partly right here—many games are designed with particular types of play in mind—but Juul seems to make no space for games that lack goals, achievements, and outcomes. To put it another way, games of skill, with their goals and outcomes, are paradigmatic games for Juul. Games that do not valorize skill must still have something to do with goals and achievements, otherwise they cannot be games at all.[10] But, just as games do not necessarily need to be challenging, games also do not necessarily require achievements. *Proteus* is a video game where the player explores a pixilated colorful island. There are interesting plants and animals to discover, and occasionally small abandoned huts. The only thing that the player can do in the game is explore and take pictures. There are no achievements to unlock or goals to pursue. The player can take as much time as they wish to explore the island and take pictures. Maybe this game sounds incredibly boring to you, but my point is that *it is still a video game*.

To be clear, not all dollhouse games are casual games; and not all casual games are dollhouse games. However, the animosity toward casual games that arose in the 2010s often carries over to dollhouse games. Dollhouse games tend to lack a challenge, and they tend to be games of labor. So, if we were to agree with Bogost and Juul, then we would likely view games that encourage dollhouse play as *lesser than* games that encourage either goal-seeking play or narrative play. I suggest that we avoid seeing these attitudes hierarchically, as if one is closer to "the essence" of "real games" than any other. Each attitude is valuable and can be a legitimate source of aesthetic value. It is also worth noticing how common dollhouse play is—most gamers participate in dollhouse play to some degree. Even if you refuse to play games like *Animal Crossing* or *Stardew Valley*, I bet that you customize your avatar, sometimes collect things that you don't need, and go exploring in an open-world game just for fun. In those instances, you are playing with a doll.

3 Defending Attitudes

This rough description of each attitude will do for now. The next three chapters will examine the aesthetic value of each in detail. What matters for us here is the idea that goal-seeking play, narrative play, and dollhouse play are not genres of games or categories of games. They are psychological attitudes that the player takes. But, what exactly does that mean?

First, it means that *what* the player is doing is partly constituted by *how they think about it.* Imagine playing a game against a friend where you are taking the game very seriously while your friend is just playing around. I'm sure this is an experience that is familiar to nearly everyone. Maybe you are playing one-on-one basketball where you are seriously trying to score while your friend is taking silly shots. Or maybe you are playing *Mario Kart* where you are trying hard to win while your friend is just having fun on the course. In these cases, both of you are *playing the game*, but it feels like your friend isn't "really" playing. The difference between these two players has nothing to do with their actions or outcomes. Your friend is not cheating or even breaking any rules. And frustratingly, maybe your friend is winning, even though they are not taking it seriously. The difference between these two players really has to do with their different mindsets—one is playing to win while the other is being more "playful."

One attitude toward play is neither better nor worse than any other. Sure, it can be frustrating when two people playing together do not share the same attitude toward their play, but individually neither player is doing anything wrong. If your wish is to play a serious game of one-on-one basketball and your friend just wants to play around, then that is an understandable source of conflict and disappointment. But neither attitude toward play is "right" or "wrong." You might accuse your friend of not taking the game seriously, but your friend might just as well accuse you of taking it too seriously. "It's just a game, after all."

Additionally, players can freely switch from one attitude to another. Players are not locked into one attitude forever. I might craft some armor in *Elder Scrolls Online* because I need a specific kind of protection for an upcoming fight, but then I stop to dye the armor a different color. The armor's color has no impact on its use. So, while I take a goal-seeking attitude to crafting the armor, I take a dollhouse attitude to dying it. In this example, crafting and dying are two different actions associated with two different attitudes. In other cases, one and the same action could be performed from a goal-seeking attitude or from a dollhouse attitude. Perhaps one player crafts some armor because they are trying to unlock a blacksmithing achievement, while another player crafts the same armor just because they enjoy it. A passive observer would not be able to tell which player was pursuing a goal and which was not just by watching them play. And of course, it is not that *all* gamers make use of *all* three attitudes. Some gamers prefer one type of game—like competitive battle royale esports games. Others might steadfastly avoid certain types of games—like cozy farming games. This should not worry us. The fact that some gamers limit their interest in games to only one facet of what the medium can do is their choice. And these self-imposed limits certainly happen in other artforms as well. Consider film: someone who describes themselves as a "film buff" might really only like horror movies, or they might steadfastly avoid romantic comedies, or they might only know American films. Or consider music: some music aficionados might limit themselves only to black metal, or they might steadfastly avoid dance music. No one reasonably thinks that all film buffs need to like all genres of films, or that all music fans need to listen to all types of music. The same is obviously true of video games. I would go further and suggest that none of the three attitudes identified above are central or primary to gaming in some special way. It might be tempting to think that goal-seeking play is *really* what gaming is about, while both narrative play and dollhouse play are mere side-interests for some weirdos. I think that belief does not do justice to how diverse video gaming is. Some people get into gaming because they like interactive stories. Others get into gaming because they like exploring, decorating, and playing around. Again, the same is true of other artforms: no one reasonably thinks that there is one genre of films that is central to film, or one genre of music that is central to music—at least not without risking the accusation of snobbery.

My understanding of an "attitude" comes from a long tradition in philosophy of language about the nature of thought. There is no need to go into great detail on the history of this debate or the various technical points that philosophers have raised.[11] Broadly speaking, however, many philosophers have thought that *thinking itself* has two parts to it: there is the content of the thought and the thinker's psychological attitude toward that content. The "content of a thought" is basically whatever you are thinking about. Sometimes that content can be expressed in a simple proposition, like "tomorrow it will rain," or "my cat needs to see the vet." However, by itself, that propositional content is just a thought in my head. What I do with that content depends on my attitude. Attitudes that I could take toward these contents include *believing, doubting, fearing*, and *hoping*. If I *doubt* that "tomorrow it will rain," I might take certain actions, like water my garden and make plans to go camping. However, if I *believe* that "tomorrow it will rain," I might take other actions, like buy an umbrella and cancel my camping trip.

These examples are fairly simple—cases where one holds a single content in mind and takes some attitude toward it. When we play games, it is not that simple. The content of our thought is likely far more complex. It is not even clear that the content of our thought could be neatly captured in a proposition. But that complexity aside, the basic point is that what we are doing in a game, and how we value it, depends on the player's attitude. The attitude that I take toward my play determines what kinds of activities I pursue, how seriously I take my playing, and what value I might find in play.

An alternative suggestion would be that how we play video games has nothing at all to do with the player's attitude. Instead, the three kinds of play that I have identified are in fact broad *categories* or *types* of video games. The thought would go like this. Games are designed with the intention that they should be played a certain way. The game designer builds goal-seeking play, narrative play, or dollhouse play into the very fabric of the game. In a sense, the game designer has determined in advance what the player *ought* to do with the game. The player typically just follows the game designer's lead. If I am supposed to collect trophies and unlock achievements, then this functionality will be built into the game, and the player either chooses to play the game on its own terms or they choose not to play. What the player is supposed to do with a game is built into the code or the algorithm. So, whatever differences there are between goal-seeking play, narrative play, and dollhouse play are differences that can be found in the game itself. These differences have nothing to do with the player's psychology. Therefore, this talk about "attitudes" is unhelpful.

This thought is very common. There are many philosophers and game theorists who take this approach, believing that what we do with a game is governed by certain norms, that those norms are partly the results of the game designer's intentions, and those intentions are built into the game itself.[12] We can describe this as an *ontological approach*: that what we do with a video game is built into the very structure of the game. For example, Bogost (2010) and Juul (2013) each seem to adopt this kind of ontological approach to video games. For Bogost, "Facebook games" have certain essential qualities built into them—they are designed to be compulsive. For Juul, the difference between games of skill, games of chance, and games of labor is built into the demands that these games place on the player. Those demands are independent of the player's intentions.

Recently, Bettina Bódi has developed an account that focuses on the ways in which design elements in video games both afford and limit the player's agency in video games, one that aims to address "the seemingly simple question: what can the avatar do?" (2023: 43). There are affordances and limitations built into what the avatar can do. They are something that the game designer anticipates and expects with the aim of shaping and controlling the player's experience. These affordances and limitations give shape to the player's agency, which is the player's ability to make choices and to act within the gamespace. Bódi identifies four different dimensions of game design that impact and shape the player's agency. The "spatial-explorative" dimension accounts for the way that the player's avatar can move within a virtual space; the "temporal-ergodic" dimension focuses on time, which includes both the way that time constrains the player's actions as well as ways in which players might be able to manipulate time; the "configurative-constructive" dimension accounts for those games that offer the player some control over the design of their avatar and its environment; and finally, the "narrative-dramatic" dimension accounts for the ways in which the player's action may be constrained by a game's story.

Bódi's analysis of the different forms of agency parallels the account of games that I will offer here. That being said, there is a fundamental methodological difference between Bódi's account and mine. Bódi's account focuses on design elements and the choices that game designers make in advance of anyone's playing of the game to answer the question "what can the avatar do?"—that is, Bódi takes an ontological approach. My own account focuses instead on the player's side of things, taking an attitudinal approach. An importantly different question we can ask is, "what does the player do?" On my account, we must answer this question by looking at the player's motivation—what the player does can really only be understood against what motivates them to act.

Stepping back from Bogost's, Juul's, or Bódi's theories, I think there are additional general reasons to prefer an attitudinal account rather than an ontological account. One reason is that if we adopt an ontological account, then lots of games are hard to classify. What category of game is *Minecraft*? The ultimate goal is—apparently—to beat the Ender Dragon, but most players don't bother with that. Are those players therefore "playing it wrong"? That seems unnecessarily restrictive. Or, even better, exactly what category of game is *World of Warcraft*? It has no ending. It is really just a world of side-quests. These games are hard to classify because they clearly offer many different types of play, some goal-seeking, some narrative, and some dollhouse.

Another reason to prefer the attitudinal account is that game players can be very creative at finding ways to play how they want to. Regardless of the game designer's intentions, gamers will co-opt a game and do whatever they want with it. Gamers can be quite willful. For instance, *Stardew Valley* was ostensibly designed to be a noncompetitive farming game, yet some players speedrun it competitively. Regardless of how games are designed, players have their own agendas. Sometimes players act in ways that correspond to the designer's expectations and sometimes they don't. Players can be transgressive in their play, often playing *against* the designer's expectations. Instead of focusing on the way in which games are designed in advance of how anyone plays them, my starting point is to look at how players play, what motivates the in-game decision-making, and what aesthetic impacts those motivations may have. In fact, I think this sort of approach makes better sense of what is happening in transgressive play.

The most important reason to prefer the attitudinal account over the ontological account, in my view, is that the attitudinal account better helps us to understand what the player is doing. At any particular moment in a game, I am either working toward some goal, or engaging with the game's narrative, or merely playing with a digital doll. And the difference between these activities comes down to my attitude toward my gameplay, not the game designer's intentions or the ontological category of the game. Again, two players might perform the same action in a game for different attitudinal reasons. You might be clearing out the mines in *Stardew Valley* because you need to complete a mission (goal-seeking play), while I am clearing out the mines just because I enjoy doing so (dollhouse play).

This is not to say that games cannot be categorized. In this respect, we can actually have it both ways. Game designers surely anticipate the attitudes that players will adopt when playing their games. And they surely design games with certain play attitudes in mind. So, there is likely to be a tight connection between the game designer's intentions, the implied norms of gameplay, and the kinds of attitudes that players will take.[13]

Finally, it is worth noticing how games can be designed with just one attitude in mind, or they can be designed to treat one attitude as *primary* while some others are *secondary*, or they can be designed to be genuine hybrid games that aim to appeal to each attitude almost equally. First, consider those games that are designed to appeal to just one specific play attitude exclusively. *Tetris* is designed for goal-seeking play. There is no story to engage with, nor any opportunity to engage in dollhouse play. It resists being played any other way. *That Dragon, Cancer* is a narrative game designed to lead the player through a harrowing story. There is no winning the game and the player cannot deviate from the story to engage in their own imaginative play. Finally, *Proteus* is an experimental, artistic game that is designed entirely for dollhouse play. There are no goals that the player has to pursue and no story to engage with.

Other games are designed primarily for one attitude, but they contain elements of play that engage with the other attitudes. *Clash Royale* is primarily designed for goal-seeking play, but the player can engage in collecting and decorating activities. There are many objects available to collect: cards, banners, emotes, badges, and tower skins. Players can decorate their battle banner with badges and upgrade the appearance of their cards. The scope for dollhouse play is very limited in *Clash Royale*, but it is still there. Taking another example, *Calico* appears primarily to be a dollhouse game, one where the player ostensibly runs a cat café, making drinks, desserts, and sandwiches. By selling things in the café, the player earns money to decorate their café and buy new outfits. But there are goals too. Specifically, there is a main mission to open up all the pathways on the island, thus giving the player the opportunity to explore as much as they wish.

And finally, some games are hybrids in the sense that they are designed with multiple attitudes in mind, where it can be difficult to say that any one attitude is primary. *Skyrim* offers many goals to pursue, a rich narrative, and ample opportunity for dollhouse play. It would take hundreds of hours of gameplay for a player to experience everything that the game has to offer. For goal-seeking play, *Skyrim* offers numerous side-quests in addition to the main quest. In any city, the player is never far from an NPC in need of some assistance. For narrative play, *Skyrim* features a highly developed fantasy world full of myths, legends, and lore. Players can spend their time learning about these by reading books that can be found scattered throughout the game, and the library at the College of Winterhold is particularly useful. Moreover, as an open-world game, *Skyrim* offers players the opportunity to explore, customize their avatar, build a collection, or experiment with blacksmithing, alchemy, and enchantment. Is *Skyrim* primarily a goal-seeking game, a narrative game, or a dollhouse game? That likely depends on who you ask.

4 Summing Up

The idea that there are specific mental attitudes associated with playing games is nothing new. We saw in the first section of this chapter that attitudinal accounts of gaming are quite popular among philosophers and game theorists. What I have sought to do here is argue that there are in fact three different kinds of attitudes that gamers take when they play a video game, and I have identified the key features of each. In the next three chapters, we can go into more detail about each attitude, consider further some of the subtle nuances in how these attitudes work, and think about how the aesthetic value of video games is dependent on the player's attitude.

3

Goal-Seeking Aesthetics

When we bought our Nintendo Switch, it came preloaded with *Mario Kart 8*. It had been years since I last owned a Nintendo console, which was when I was in graduate school. It was an N64. I had that console's version of *Mario Kart* then, and all my dormmates got delightfully competitive about it. I have deeply nostalgic memories about the *Mario Kart* tournaments that my dormmates and I used to hold. I can only imagine how much more intense our competitions would have been if we had had *Mario Kart 8*.

With *Mario Kart 8*, I sometimes get into "the zone," that feeling of being "one with the game." Getting into the zone with a video game is strange. I can feel certain things that I shouldn't be able to feel, like the weight of my car when I am sliding into corners. This is such a strange feeling to have because the car obviously doesn't have any weight. It is an imaginary car.

The only trouble with getting into the zone in *Mario Kart* is that I never stay there for long. It is difficult for me to stay in the zone when I am thwarted by seemingly arbitrary obstacles. I finally get into the zone and then I am zapped by a lightning strike. Or I lose my focus when I hear the blue shell coming for me. The zone is an enticing state to be in while playing, and I know that I'm playing well when I feel myself get there. But the absurdity of getting knocked out of the zone because I slipped on a banana peel can be really galling sometimes.

This chapter focuses on the aesthetic value that players get from the *game* aspects of video games. The question I aim to address is, which elements of games are properly objects of aesthetic attention when we take a goal-seeking attitude? Players can find aesthetic value by paying attention to numerous elements of video games. Some of the things that players derive aesthetic value from are not unique to video games, while others are. This chapter focuses specifically on the elements of video games that relate to their status as *games*—or what many theorists call the "ludic" elements of games.

Goal-seeking play is an attitude that the player can adopt, which is distinctive in three respects: the goals and challenges are set by the game itself, the player employs means–ends reasoning to figure out how to achieve the in-game goals, and the end result is quantifiable. But what is the aesthetic value of goal-seeking play? In the early days of game studies, it was common for theorists to draw on theories from other artforms to explain the appeal of video games. Games studies was populated largely by academics who were trained in literature, film studies, psychology, and sociology. They brought with them theories that were developed to explain fiction, film, and television; and they sought to show that many of the values we find in those artforms also appear in video games. This approach to studying video games is understandable. After all, the quickest way to demonstrate that video games are academically interesting is to show how they already fit into existing academic debates. However, this approach is also obviously quite limited. If we restrict the aesthetic value of video games to just the qualities of games that also appear in older artforms—narrative and cinematic qualities—then we would miss out on any potentially valuable qualities that are unique to video games, like gameplay. As Jesper Juul says, "if we think of video games as *games*, they are not successors of cinema, print literature, or new media, but continuations of a history of games that predate these [artforms] by millennia" (2005: 3–4). Of course, it would have been impossible for early game theorists to account for the aesthetic value of gameplay because the conceptual frameworks needed to explain gameplay weren't fully developed yet. The study of literature and film isn't going to help us to think about the value of good gameplay.

Part of the aesthetic value of video games—a big part—comes from many of the same features that make games appealing generally. We can examine the aesthetic value of video games in part by drawing on some of the foundational works in game studies and play studies from the past century. In what follows, we will consider how earlier theorists have thought about the aesthetics of gameplay and how their ideas can be applied to video games. First, we will briefly situate the aesthetics of games in the work of two early game theorists, Johan Huizinga and Roger Caillois. Of course, neither Huizinga nor Caillois, who were writing in the 1930s and 1960s, respectively, could have anticipated what video games might become. However, I will argue that many of the same sources of aesthetic enjoyment that Caillois describes generally can be found in video games.

Caillois is a helpful guide to the aesthetics of gameplay. My point, however, is not that we should all be devotees of Caillois. It can be helpful to draw on work about earlier cultural objects—whether that is fiction, film, or traditional games—but video games have unique features that are not shared by any of these. Primarily what interests me about Caillois' account is the way that it helpfully maps onto many of the features that theorists have recently identified as relevant to the aesthetics of video games. I don't mean to suggest that Caillois' account is the definitive theory of games. Instead, my thinking is that the value of video games is continuous with the value of games generally, as Juul suggests. So, it would be unsurprising if a general account of the value of games mapped onto the value of video games. And Caillois offers the most general account available.

1 The Aesthetics of Games and Play before Video Games

Huizinga primarily sought to understand play and the motivation that animates our desire to play. Philosophers have long sought to understand human actions and motivations, but the motivation to play was never central to those philosophical debates. Survival is a basic motivation. Humans will do lots of unpleasant things in order to merely survive. However, if we take survival to be the basis for our actions, then play seems inexplicable. Play needn't contribute to survival. Why expend so much energy unproductively? Alternatively, ethical concerns are one clear case where human actions and motivations can suspend, or at least alter, our concern for survival. Indeed, individuals will sometimes act in ways that put their survival at risk because they believe that it is morally good or morally required of them. But play doesn't seem to fit this explanation either. We do not play because we believe that it is morally good or one of our moral duties. So, what motivates us to play?

Huizinga argued that the play-instinct cannot be grounded in reason because this would limit play to rational creatures like us. We would then have a difficult time explaining the play of animals (1970: 21).[1] The foundations of play also cannot be discovered in some biological need because this would fail to explain why we become so absorbed in play (ibid.: 20). So, perhaps the play-instinct has its source in aesthetics. Huizinga acknowledges the possibility, saying,

> although the attribute of beauty does not attach to play as such, play nevertheless tends to assume marked elements of beauty. Mirth and grace adhere at the outset to the more primitive forms of play. In play the beauty of the human body in motion reaches its zenith. In its more developed forms it is saturated with rhythm and harmony, the noblest gifts of aesthetic perception known to man. Many and close are the links that connect play with beauty. (Ibid.: 25)

However, despite these "many and close" links, Huizinga ultimately declares that beauty is not an inherent part of play as such. Some play can achieve beauty, or at least mirth and grace. But mere correlation is not enough. If we are seeking the foundations of play, we cannot look to any rational, biological, or aesthetic analysis.

To philosophers of aesthetics today, this argument from Huizinga is much too quick. The problem simply is that Huizinga equates "aesthetics" too strongly with "beauty." Aestheticians today widely accept that there is more to aesthetics than the concern for beauty. Horror movies aim for fear and disgust, murder mysteries aim for a satisfying resolution to a puzzle, and punk music aims for chaotic exuberance. If we insist that "aesthetics" has to do solely with beauty, we would fail to recognize the aesthetic pleasure that people take in fear, disgust, satisfaction, chaos, and joy. Beauty is merely one aesthetic quality among many, even if it is a particularly valuable one. To Huizinga's credit, he does recognize the values of mirth and grace in play. Why not build from there? Perhaps play and the play-instinct *are* founded in aesthetics when understood broadly. To echo a point previously made by C. Thi Nguyen, if people use aesthetic terms to describe what they enjoy about play, then perhaps we should take them seriously (2021: 475).

Caillois is remembered today by philosophers of games and sports primarily for his claim that there are different forms of "play" that cannot be reduced to a single essential kind. Instead, Caillois argues that play can be classified into four kinds "depending upon whether ... the role of competition, chance, simulation, or vertigo is dominant" (2001: 12). These four forms of play he calls *agôn*, *alea*, *mimicry*, and *ilinx*, respectively. Competitive games (*agôn*) require the player to exhibit some specialized skill, as in *soccer* or *pole vaulting*. Games of chance (*alea*) are decided entirely by the role of the dice, like *craps*, or the drop of a marble, like *roulette*. Simulation games (*mimicry*) are characterized by make-believe, where "the subject makes believe or makes others believe that he is someone other than himself" (ibid.: 19; cf. Huizinga 1970: 32). Simulation games would include formal games—like *Dungeons & Dragons*—as well as informal games—like children playing *house*. Finally, games of vertigo (*ilinx*) are playful activities where one seeks unique bodily or sensory experiences. Two children holding hands while whirling in a circle are playing a game of vertigo where the pleasure comes from the unique sensation. Other examples of vertigo games that Caillois offers are downhill racing, tobogganing, and playing on swings (2001: 24).

Caillois' four types of play are not exclusive categories. Most games will exhibit some combination of the characteristics that Caillois identifies. For instance, *poker* is a game where players must develop skills for betting and bluffing (*agôn*) while players are also at the mercy of the turn of a card (*alea*). Nonetheless, it is possible to find games that are nearly exhausted by one characteristic or another—for instance, *chess* is purely a game of skill.

Two brief comments from Caillois are particularly helpful here. Both *agôn* and *alea* are goal-seeking and rule-bound forms of play; however, both forms of play correspond to very different psychological attitudes and are valued for different reasons. The distinctive feature of *agôn* (competition) is that players seek to minimize the effects of chance in order to compare their possession of some skill between themselves. By competing from a genuinely equal starting point, we then have some assurance that the resulting difference in outcome between the competitors is a result of a difference in their abilities as players. As Caillois states, *agôn* describes a group of games identified by "an equality of chances artificially created, in order that the adversaries should confront each other in ideal conditions, susceptible of giving precise and incontestable value to the winner's triumph" (ibid.: 14). By contrast, games of *alea* (chance) negate the player's possession of skill. Instead, games of *alea* invite the player to surrender entirely to chance. So, for Caillois, the pleasure of competitive play comes not just from victory but also from the careful and deliberate development of specialized skills; while the pleasure of chance play comes from chance itself: "It is the very capriciousness of chance that constitutes the unique appeal of the game" (ibid.: 17).

The second comment helpful to us is found in Caillois' discussion of *paidia* and *ludus* (ibid.: 27–8). Caillois describes these as two broad attitudes toward play, which are distinguished by their stance toward rules and formalization. *Paidia* is play that is improvisatory and free from rules, while *ludus* is play that is formalized by rules. *Paidia* and *ludus* form a spectrum, which combine with Caillois' four basic forms of play (*agôn, alea, mimicry,* and *ilnix*) to give rise to all the various games that we play. Within each of the four basic forms are games that lean more toward *paidia* and others more toward *ludus*. Consider two competitive games: a game of chess and a spontaneous running race ("the first one to the tree wins") are both instances of *agôn*; however, the running race can be comparatively loose with its rules (e.g., maybe there is no starting countdown) while the game of chess must follow the rules of chess, otherwise it is not chess that the players are playing.

In seeking to identify the source of pleasure that we find in play, Caillois suggests that *paidia* is a pleasure associated with causation. He says, "For the child it is a question of expressing himself, of feeling he is the *cause*, of forcing others to pay attention to him" (ibid.: 28, italics in original). Such play tends to be "a primary power of improvisation and joy" (ibid.: 27). Caillois takes as his cue the childish instinct to take pleasure in destruction: "The pleasure in endlessly cutting up paper with a pair of scissors, pulling cloth into thread, breaking up a gathering" (ibid.: 28). Very young children take great pleasure in simply throwing things or dropping things (e.g., food, or a fork from the table). Caillois' point is that *paidia* is a form of play that takes pleasure in *being the cause of something*. Children discover their own power and wonder at their ability to have an effect on the world. It seems likely that this never leaves us as a source of wonder.

While the pleasures of *paidia* are associated with spontaneity, freedom from rules, and agency, the pleasures of *ludus*—characterized by Caillois as the institutionalization of play through the adoption of rules—is related to "the taste for gratuitous difficulty" (ibid.: 27). This comment from Caillois is very brief, and yet there are still a few things worth noticing. First, the pleasure found in rule-following has to do with the difficulty of the task and noticeably not with successfully completing the task. It is a taste for *difficulty* that Caillois notes, not a taste for *victory*. The second point is that it is not mere difficulty that players value, but "gratuitous difficulty." For instance, consider the satisfaction that many players take from really difficult video games, like *Super Meat Boy* or *Dark Souls*. Many players often describe these as "unforgiving" games, and that is typically offered as a positive evaluation. It is unclear when we should say that the difficulty of some task becomes gratuitous; however, as a suggestion, "gratuitous difficulty" may indicate a level of difficulty that is not matched or justified by the value of the outcome. If we are pursuing a goal that is intrinsically worthwhile—for instance, the eradication of a terrible disease—then we are likely willing to justify high levels of difficulty with little complaint. But when playing a game, we are not pursuing a goal that is intrinsically worthwhile. Putting a golf ball in a tiny hole that is hundreds of yards away using only clubs makes an intrinsically uninteresting goal into a gratuitous challenge.

Finally, the difference between *paidia* and *ludus* has little to do with the actual activity that one engages in. Rather, the difference has more to do with the attitude that one takes toward that activity. Imagine that you find a ball and you spontaneously begin throwing it high in the air, taking great pleasure in this. Unbounded by rules and simply enjoying the novelty of it, your enjoyment is likely one of *paidia*. Now, imagine doing exactly the same thing, but this time you are thinking to yourself, "Throw the ball as high as possible and catch it without letting it hit the ground." This addition of a rule shifts the activity toward *ludus*. The shift here is something internal (it is the player's attitude toward the action) and not something external (the nature of the action itself). Indeed, an outside observer watching you throw the ball would be unable from their perspective to know whether you are engaging in the play of *paidia* or *ludus*. From an outside perspective, the action is the same.

These comments from Caillois on the value and pleasures of play are tantalizing, even if they are quite brief. The lessons that I want to take from Caillois are these: competition (*agôn*), chance (*alea*), freedom (*paidia*), and rules (*ludus*) are four basic elements of the aesthetics of play that we can look for in video games.[2] However, Caillois doesn't provide much of an explanation of why any of these elements are aesthetically enjoyable. There is a big difference between identifying a phenomenon and explaining it. Why exactly are rules a source of pleasure? Why would gratuitous difficulty lead to enjoyment? And how can the uncertainty of chance provide fun? Caillois offers us a number of good questions, but now we need answers. In the following sections, we will discuss some theories that aim to identify what is enjoyable about three of these basic elements that Caillois identifies—competition, chance, and rules. I will reserve a discussion of freedom in games until Chapter 5.

2 Competition and Goal-Seeking

The purpose of games of competition, according to Caillois, is "for each player to have his superiority in a given area recognized" (2001: 15). That seems right. But still, what aesthetic value could players take from competitive gameplay?

It would be natural to think that the pleasure of competition comes from winning. Obviously, winning is fun, while losing sucks. My ability to achieve some arbitrary goal while following restrictive rules perhaps becomes meaningful only because I can do it better than you can. Maybe *achieving the goal excellently* has something to do with the value of competition. However, the satisfaction of winning cannot explain everything about the enjoyment of competition. Winning is great, but losing happens often. And importantly, games are fun to play even when we lose. I love to play poker, but I don't win every hand. In fact, an exciting and enjoyable game might be one that I lose dramatically. Even in single-player video games with long campaigns, it is not as if the enjoyment of playing comes only from finishing the game. Beating the final boss is rewarding, but players don't spend 100+ hours on a campaign without finding some enjoyment in all those hours of play. Players who are obsessed only with winning are often insufferable poor-sports, and poor-sports seem to miss something important about the appreciation of games. So, what kind of aesthetic enjoyment can players get even when they are not winning?

I want to suggest that competition—with its emphasis on dividing players into winners and losers—doesn't explain the *aesthetic* enjoyment of games as well as goal-seeking does. I can still enjoy myself even when I am losing at poker because my experience is structured by an attitude of goal-seeking. Even in hopeless cases, where I have come to realize that I cannot possibly dig myself out of the hole I am in, I can still focus on the next hand and exercise what skill I have—and enjoy doing so.

Goal-seeking is ubiquitous in video games and it comes in many forms—like fighting, scoring goals, and solving puzzles. Goal-seeking lends itself easily to competitive play. However, goal-seeking is the more fundamental concept. Competitive play is a form of goal-seeking play. To see this point, consider that many players engage in goal-seeking play without any real interest or worry about competing. One can develop the skills needed to be an expert rock climber without taking much interest in whether others do it better. Or, I might set myself the goal to achieve every trophy that I can without trying to compare my gameplay to any other player. All one has to do to turn their goal-seeking play into a competition is stipulate some further condition on achieving the goal: that players must achieve the goal faster than other players (e.g., racing games), or more often within a specified timeframe than other players (e.g., point-scoring games), or more elegantly than other players (e.g., aesthetic games, like gymnastics or ice skating). Competition is goal-seeking with a highly effective, built-in motivation system: to achieve some goal better than someone else can.

We will consider two accounts that aim to identify the aesthetic value of games through goal-seeking play: Mihaly Csikszentmihalyi's account of "flow states" (1975, 1990, 1997)[3] and C. Thi Nguyen's account of "striving play" (2020). These theories identify different kinds of aesthetically pleasing experiences that players derive from games. But these theories are not mutually exclusive. We don't have to choose one over the other. Instead, both theories aim to address something real and distinctive about the value of gameplay. Additionally, it is notable that each of these theories puts very little stock in competition. A game does not need to be competitive in order to induce flow states or to produce instances of striving play. Instead, goal-seeking is all that is needed. Neither flow nor striving is possible without goal-seeking, but both are possible—indeed, entirely common—even in noncompetitive activities.

2.1 Flow States

Csikszentmihalyi's notion of "flow" is an influential and highly regarded account of the aesthetic enjoyment of gameplay. According to Csikszentmihalyi, flow is a psychological state characterized by the feeling of being totally absorbed in some activity. One of the earliest characterizations of flow that Csikszentmihalyi offers is this: "Flow denotes the wholistic sensation present when we act with total involvement. ... We experience it as a unified flowing from one moment to the next, in which we feel in control of our actions, and in which there is little distinction between self and environment" (1975: 43). We can see from this early definition three ideas that have remained central to Csikszentmihalyi's thinking about flow: that flow states are present when we act, that they have a distinctive phenomenal character, and that they absorb our attention. The link between the phenomenology of flow and its demands of total attention is an intrinsic one: "Because of the total demand on psychic energy, a person in flow is completely focused. There is no space in consciousness for distracting thoughts" (1997: 31). While the phrase "psychic energy" sounds worryingly esoteric and mystical, Csikszentmihalyi has in mind the Jungian idea that mental energy must be expended when players focus their attention, awareness, and action on one task (Jung 1969). Players find moments of flow when their skills are matched by the challenges of a game that is neither too easy nor too hard. When the challenges are too easy, players become bored; and when the challenges are too hard, players become anxious. A flow state is that enjoyable middle ground where the challenges are hard enough to push the player to their limit, thus requiring the player to focus their attention strictly on the task at hand, but staying within a range where the player is able to respond to the demands of the game with perfect precision.

While much more could be said about flow and the psychological evidence supporting it, three simple but important points stand out. First, flow states are extended and sustained in time. They are moments of total absorption, and, while most are fairly short, the hope among many game designers is that a very well-designed game can allow the player to experience extended flow states. Still, they cannot be sustained indefinitely. Second, flow states are not experienced only by experts or elite athletes. They are states that are open to anyone at any level of skill. All that matters in achieving a flow state is that the challenge is well tuned to the player's level of skill (Csikszentmihalyi 1975: 56–60). The more skilled a player is, the more they will need to be challenged to achieve flow. So, while highly skilled players might need games as difficult as *Dark Souls* to achieve flow, less skilled players may experience flow by playing early levels of *Dr. Mario*. Finally, Csikszentmihalyi identifies games as particularly notable cases of flow:

> Flow tends to occur when a person faces a clear set of goals that require appropriate responses. It is easy to enter flow in games such as chess, tennis, or poker, because they have goals and rules for action that make it possible for the player to act without questioning what should be done, and how. For the duration of the game the player lives in a self-contained universe where everything is black and white. (1997: 29)

Competitive games are likely to be particularly apt at producing flow states. An individual must be highly motivated to push themselves to the limits of their abilities. Competition offers an excellent motivation. In competitive games, players seek to "actualize [their] potential, and this task is made easier when others force us to do our best" (1990: 73). However, competitive games are not the only things that are capable of causing experiences of flow. Csikszentmihalyi thought that individuals could find flow states in any skillful, goal-seeking activity—"[t]he same clarity of goals [that we find in games] is present if you perform a religious ritual, play a musical piece, weave a rug, write a computer program, climb a mountain, or perform surgery" (1997: 30). In fact, Csikszentmihalyi hoped that his theory of flow would revolutionize our working lives so that the tasks that we face in our jobs would be both less alienating and more efficiently performed (1990: Ch. 7).

Flow theory has been taken up by game designers as the "gold standard" of good game design. In fact, Thatgamecompany even released a game titled *Flow* in 2006 that offers a fairly literal illustration of the idea of navigating between what is relatively easy or relatively hard for a player. Game scholars also widely acknowledge the applicability of flow theory to video games. Surprisingly few theorists object to the plausibility of the theory.[4] Still, some theorists have pointed out the limitations of flow theory. Specifically, there are many aspects of games that have nothing to do with flow.

Consider first that some enjoyable game mechanics do not lend themselves to flow. Some games are simply too slow to induce flow—like *The Banner Saga*—while other games focus on mechanics that don't require quick reflexive skills—deck-building games like *Hearthstone*. Moreover, flow requires a certain kind of challenge. Juul makes the point that many games are not challenging enough to produce flow states; yet, this is not a shortcoming (2005: 112–15). Unchallenging games are still enjoyable, just not for reasons having to do with flow. In *A Short Hike*, the player takes control of a young bird named Claire who is spending some time at her Aunt May's cabin during a summer vacation on a small mountainous island. To complete the game, the player must climb to the top of the island's mountain. Doing so requires the player to collect a number of "golden feathers," which allows Claire to climb higher. *A Short Hike* is ostensibly a puzzle game. However, collecting the feathers is not difficult, and climbing the mountain is not challenging. The game takes roughly one hour to complete if the player focuses on collecting all the feathers quickly. But completing the game quickly is not the point. Instead, *A Short Hike* is best enjoyed as a sandbox. After exploring the island and talking to the other visitors, the player can go fishing, play stickball, or ride a speedboat. One of the more enjoyable affordances offered in the game is the ability to gracefully glide through the air. Soaring through the sky after finding a good updraft is immensely pleasurable, but it is certainly not challenging or pushing my abilities to their limits. Indeed, if flow theory were the only way to explain the aesthetics of video games, then *A Short Hike* ought to be a dismal failure. But it isn't. Flow theory is able to account for some rewarding gameplay, but it is not the all-encompassing gold standard that it was long held up to be. To account for games like *The Banner Sage*, *Hearthstone*, and *A Short Hike*, we need to look somewhere else.

2.2 Striving Play

Bernard Suits' (2014) account of game-playing is foundational to the philosophy of games and sports. However, Suits' theory does not aim specifically to account for the *aesthetic* value of games. Instead, Suits aimed to offer an account of what games are and why playing games is a valuable activity. The account of value that Suits had in mind was particularly broad. Games are not a waste of time. Rather, they are able to provide meaning and value to our lives. That's true, but it doesn't address the aesthetic value of games. Fortunately, other philosophers have demonstrated how Suits' account can support a theory of the aesthetic value of games. Specifically, Nguyen (2020) has recently developed a strong and convincing account that is a direct extension out of Suits' general theory.

Nguyen broadly accepts the Suitsian account of games as the attempt to achieve a prelusory goal using only the means permitted by the rules, where less efficient means are preferred over more efficient means, and players accept such limitations just because doing so makes the activity possible—or, more succinctly, games are "the voluntary attempt to overcome unnecessary obstacles" (Suits 2014: 43). The value of games is found not just in winning but also in the value of *striving*, according to Nguyen. We temporarily adopt the desire to win because doing so offers us the motivation to engage in the struggle. Nguyen describes the motivational structure of game-playing as "backward-looking" (2020: 27 and 62). We don't struggle to win the game because we care so much about winning. Instead, it is the other way around: we play games and try to win because doing so enables us to enjoy the struggle of the game.

Nguyen offers a number of pieces of evidence in support of this backward-looking motivational structure. First, the desire to win is often easily set aside. When I realize that my friends aren't having as much fun as I had hoped, I abandon my desire to win. Instead, I might start handicapping my play in order to draw out the challenge (ibid.: 11) or I might suggest that we try a different game (ibid.: 65). Additionally, Nguyen notes that winning is just not the point of some games. Consider drinking games. The point is not to win but rather to get horribly drunk! Or consider "stupid games," which is a kind of party game where failure is more enjoyable than winning (ibid.: 41–2). What makes pin-the-tail-on-the-donkey a fun party game is watching dizzy kids stumble around blindly. The player who obsesses about winning at party games would be a terrible, boorish player. The kid who gets grumpy about losing pin-the-tail-on-the-donkey is the kid who doesn't get invited to many more parties.

Striving play is a central part of the enjoyment of playing games. The obstacles that we face in a game are "unnecessary" if we are solely concerned with achieving the prelusory goal. But the overcoming of those obstacles is part of the joy of game-playing. What makes hurdling a game is the hurdles, and not just the part where the runner crosses the finish line. In playing a game, players have already come to accept the struggle in overcoming the obstacles of a game. As Nguyen says, "the very fact that we are willing to impose inefficiencies on our path to the pre-lusory goals shows that we value these pre-lusory goals less than we value the activity of struggling for them under certain inefficiencies" (ibid.: 30).

Crucially, striving gives rise to its own form of aesthetic enjoyment. In some games, players take aesthetic pleasure in their own deliberation, planning, and decision-making. There is a distinct pleasure in forming a plan, modifying it in response to unexpected challenges, and seeing it through to its completion. In other games, players take aesthetic pleasure in the way that their body moves. Nguyen offers the example of rock climbing, where some climbing routes are "often set to induce climbers into some particular subtle, refined motion—for the sake of their experience of their own beauty and grace in motion" (ibid.: 102). Oftentimes, players take pleasure in recognizing a certain harmony between the challenges that they face and their own ability to meet those challenges, something that Nguyen calls the "harmony of capacity" (ibid.: 109).[5] In each of these cases, it is striving and the kind of sporting attitude it requires that makes these aesthetic experiences possible. Game designers create opportunities for players to engage in aesthetically rewarding forms of play by enabling unique forms of struggle.

Striving to overcome an obstacle, even when not in competition with others, can produce numerous kinds of aesthetics effects, where the harmony of capacity is one. Consider again Nguyen's claim that there is an aesthetic pleasure in the movement of one's own body in rock climbing, which would be a kind of proprioceptive aesthetic pleasure. Similar kinds of experiences occur for gamers. Many video games have a kind of physics to them, where the player's character experiences the weight of gravity. In coming to master a game, the player needs to learn how the physics engine of the game works, how their character moves within that space, and to master their movements. When this is successful, there are moments in video games where the player has come to feel the "weight" of their character, to feel how it moves and jumps, and to feel the effects of gravity on their character. *Unravel Two* is a puzzle-platform game where two yarn creatures—called "Yarnys"—are connected by a single length of yarn. They must cooperate to solve spatial puzzles by using the yarn that connects them to traverse their environment. In some puzzles, one Yarny must anchor itself on the edge of a platform and use momentum to swing the other Yarny onto another platform. To master the move, the player has to feel the momentum of the swing and time their jumps well.

The kind of learning and skill mastery that it takes to play a game well in this respect is not something that can be put into words or taught to someone else by merely offering a linguistic description of how to move. I can explain in words how to complete a puzzle in a game—"you have to find the key, which is hidden on the upper floor behind some rubble"—but I cannot explain to another player how to move gracefully and time their jumps well. It is a felt quality. Aderemi Artis (2021) offers a compelling account of this phenomenon. "Twitch" video games are those that require fast reflexes and subtle manipulation of the controller. Artis describes them as games that "call for and afford more or less continual, complex, varying, brisk paced, and difficult bodily movements from the player during gameplay sequences, with prominent traditional input methods being a joystick, a joystick and buttons, or a gamepad" (2021: 66). The pleasure of playing twitch games, even difficult and demanding games, is enjoying the feeling of one's body responding to the game's challenges. Twitch gameplay can produce a sense of harmony between the game's challenges and one's abilities or an awareness of the elegance of one's own movement (ibid.: 70).

The account that Nguyen defends offers an important piece to the puzzle of the aesthetics of video games. Many theorists who write about the "aesthetics of video games" often focus on the features of video games that align with more traditional facets of aesthetic attention—things like the visual appeal of the game's environments and character designs, the narrative elements of the story, or the sound design. Indeed, many theorists often talk about "the game" and "gameplay" as something separate and distinct from "the aesthetics" of video games.[6] What often gets ignored, however, is the aesthetic experience of the gameplay itself. Nguyen's account is enormously helpful as it rightly brings gameplay into the realm of the aesthetics of video games.

3 Chance—or Rather, Uncertainty

When Caillois identifies chance as one of the sources of value in games, what he seems to have in mind are games of pure chance. The examples he offers are "games of dice, roulette, heads or tails, baccara, [and] lotteries" (2001: 17). They offer the thrill of winning big against the mathematical likelihood of losing it all. For Caillois, the player in a game of chance is passive. Having given in completely to fate, the player merely waits for the outcome to be revealed. "Here, not only does one refrain from trying to eliminate the injustice of chance, but rather it is the very capriciousness of chance that constitutes the unique appeal of the game" (ibid.). The joy of playing games of chance for Caillois is apparently a kind of fatalistic ecstasy.

Games of pure chance like the sort that Caillois had in mind are uncommon in video games. Of course, there are plenty of real-world online casinos; but these are "video games" only in a loose sense. Online casinos are *real* casinos that happen to be played online. To avoid an ontological debate about what counts as a video game, perhaps it would be better to simply say that casino games are "video games" to the same extent that *chess* played on a computer is a "video game." I will let the reader decide whether these should count. Alternatively, there are a small number of video game versions of casino games, like *Casino, Casino Deluxe*, and *Golden Nugget Casino DS*. These are typically single-player games, they are not tied to a real-world casino, and the player isn't gambling with real money. Finally, games of chance often appear as minigames in a larger game. For instance, *Red Dead Redemption 2* offers minigames of poker and blackjack, while *Grand Theft Auto Online* additionally allows players to gamble on horse races and roulette.

Alternatively, all video games contain *uncertainty*. Uncertainty can be introduced into games in many ways. In tabletop games, it is typically introduced by shuffling a deck of cards or rolling dice. However, video games are incapable of genuine randomness because they must follow the deterministic logic of an algorithm. This isn't a problem though. Katie Salen and Eric Zimmerman argue that the player's perception of "a feeling of randomness" is more important to one's experience of the game than the actual appearance of an element of chance in the game's mechanics (2004: 176). A feeling of randomness can arise even when a game does not have true elements of chance. For instance, tactical shooters like *Tom Clancy's Rainbow Six Siege* can feel chaotic at times, though there is no game mechanic that introduces pure chance like that of a roulette wheel or a dice throw. Uncertainty can be introduced in ways that functionally appear like pure chance. For instance, Greg Costikyan points out that the amount of damage that a weapon inflicts is typically varied within a predetermined range, and the purpose of this is just so that players cannot be 100 percent certain of the success of each shot (2013: 27–8). Similarly, in the *Civilization* games by Sid Meier, the player has a good idea about the strength of their own forces and sometimes also a fairly clear idea about the strength of enemy forces; and yet, differences in strength are no guarantee of success in battle. The outcomes are varied relative to the difference in strength of the opposing forces. This seems about as close as video games get to the randomness of dice rolls in *Dungeons & Dragons*, where damaging an opponent is relativized to the difference between the attacker's strength and the defender's armor.

Costikyan (ibid.: Ch. 5) identifies eleven potential sources of uncertainty in games:

Performative uncertainty	the player's uncertainty that they will perform well
Solver's uncertainty	the uncertainty associated with puzzle-solving
Player unpredictability	multiplayer games introduce the uncertainty of the behavior of other players
Randomness	while genuinely impossible in computer games, apparent randomness is common (e.g. attack success, weapon damage, randomly generated encounters, procedurally generated environments, which tetromino will appear next in *Tetris*)
Analytic complexity	the uncertainty introduced where the outcomes of multiple strategic decisions build upon each other, or where emergent play increases in complexity
Hidden information	uncertainty arising from the player's awareness that information is missing (e.g. inaccessible areas of a map, quest objects hidden in a visual scene, the effects of combining spells or weapon combos)
Narrative anticipation	the uncertainty of how a story will unfold
Development anticipation	games can be continually patched and updated, allowing for the uncertainty of new challenges, enemies, and weapons

Schedule uncertainty	the uncertainty introduced by social and causal games that rely on a mechanic that requires the player to wait for (e.g.) a lootbox to open or to power up their energy again
Uncertainty of perception	the uncertainty produced by the inability to clearly and unambiguously perceive the figures represented in a game
Malaby's semiotic contingency	the uncertainty surrounding the ways in which cultural meanings may be applied to or arise from games

Costikyan admits that these are merely forms of uncertainty that he is able to identify currently, not the exhaustive list of all possible forms. Nonetheless, the number and variety that he offers is impressive, even if some of these seem less productive of aesthetic interest than others. Some of Costikyan's forms of uncertainty seem immediately capable of producing aesthetic interest—like performative uncertainty, player uncertainty, analytic complexity, and narrative anticipation—while others seem less relevant as sources of aesthetic interest—indeed, Costikyan specifically notes that schedule uncertainty is a "crude and fairly unaesthetic form of uncertainty" (ibid.: 100). Costikyan doesn't intend for each form of uncertainty to identify a potential aesthetic interest. Some can, but not all.

What aesthetic value does the player get from chance and uncertainty? Considering that real life is full of uncertainties, and these are often a source of anxiety, it may at first seem almost paradoxical that uncertainty could be a source of value in games. Yet, as Costikyan notes, games "thrive on uncertainty" (ibid.: 15), and their randomness provides "a sense of drama" (ibid.: 85). For Salen and Zimmerman, meaningful game play is facilitated by uncertainty. As they note, if the outcome of a game was certain in advance, then it likely wouldn't be very fun to play (2004: 174). We *want* uncertainty in games. Without it, they wouldn't be games.

Thinking of the various sources of uncertainty that Costikyan identifies—or at least those that are relevant to the player's aesthetic experience—they seem to share one common trait: they are uncertainties that are resolved through some action taken by the player. This might seem unimportant or obvious, but compare it to other forms of uncertainty that we encounter in other, passive art forms, like literature and film. Uncertainties in works of fiction abound. Who is the killer? How will the hero escape the castle? How does the story end? Yet, these uncertainties are either resolved by the author of the work or they remain unresolved. By contrast, the interactivity of video games allows for uncertainties that the player can resolve through their own action. But it isn't just the resolution that matters aesthetically. It is the way in which the uncertainties are resolved by the player.

The aesthetic import of uncertainty, I suggest, stems from its capacity to maintain tension in the player dynamically over time. Think about the experience where some uncertainty in a game is resolved: we can distinguish between the *object of resolution* and the *act of resolution*. The object of resolution refers to whatever is achieved by the resolution. This could be the solution of a puzzle, the discovery of a hidden object, or the death of an enemy boss. In many of these cases, the object of resolution likely has no aesthetic value in itself. Completing a set of collectable items ("collect all eight types of bird feathers!") usually does not produce an aesthetically valuable object, most hidden objects are not themselves worthwhile to look at, and seeing an enemy dead on the ground is not typically something that one aesthetically dwells on. Perhaps in some cases, the solution to a puzzle creates a pleasing aesthetic object. Part of the aesthetic value of solving puzzles in *Gris* is the way that color is introduced to the gameworld creating richer scenes. Or, building a complex and time-consuming structure in *Minecraft* likely derives much of its aesthetic value from the architectural properties of the completed structure and not the uncertainty of the unfinished structure.[7] However, this is certainly not true of all objects of resolution.

By contrast, the act of resolution is not an object but is instead an event. It is the complex event itself—the movement from tension to release—that is aesthetically pleasing. We do not derive aesthetic pleasure only at the moment where the object of resolution is revealed.

Instead, our aesthetic enjoyment is sustained during the uncertain moments themselves. Think about playing a game with a long, single-player campaign. Throughout the game, there will be many moments of uncertainty, some large and some small. Salen and Zimmerman distinguish between "macro-level uncertainty" and "micro-level uncertainty," where the former is the uncertainty about the ultimate outcome of a game while the latter is the uncertainty of "specific operations of chance within the designed system" (2004: 174). All games exhibit macro-level uncertainty—the player doesn't know from the outset whether or not they will win—while micro-level uncertainty likely arises within the context of specific game elements. In a long, single-player campaign, we can think of the final boss battle as the resolution of the game's macro-level uncertainty—the resolution to how the story ultimately ends. But it would be impossible for the player to sustain interest in just that one, large uncertainty throughout the 100+ hours it takes to complete the game. So, long campaigns are designed to provide numerous smaller uncertainties to resolve along the way. The player slowly makes progress through the game by resolving the small uncertainties while working their way up to resolve the final uncertainty. This structure provides the player with nice stopping points. When I am playing a campaign, I will sit down for two to three hours at a time to play. I cannot stop playing until I feel like I have resolved *something*. It would be maddening to just arbitrarily stop at some random point in the game. Instead, I have to pursue a few missions and feel some satisfaction that I have completed those before I can put the game down for the night.

Uncertainty in video games is both dynamic and temporal—that is, it is a process constituted by moments of tension and release that are extended in time. In a way, the aesthetic function of uncertainty in video games is very similar to the aesthetic function of dissonance in music, where listeners take pleasure in the way that the music moves from dissonance to consonance. It is not the fatalistic and passive value of throwing your life to chance that Caillois envisioned. It is instead a value that induces curiosity, creates tension and drama, and sustains the player's motivation throughout the long and arduous task of completing a game.

4 Rules and Mechanics

While there is still considerable disagreement among theorists about the definition of "games," it is widely agreed upon that games are intimately tied up with rules. The rule-bounded nature of games is somewhat perplexing (Juul 2005: 18; Suits 2014). Why do we enjoy following rules in our free time? Game-playing is not a necessary part of life. Indeed, game-playing is for most people a pastime, except for those few people who are able to make a career out of competitive gaming. Games are optional. If they were not optional, then they would be an odd form of work, to echo Caillois. Moreover, games are arbitrary. None of the goals that we pursue in games are worthwhile intrinsically. If they were, then we would find more efficient means to achieve those goals, to echo Suits. So, one perplexing thing about games is that many people seem to take pleasure in following optional rules to achieve arbitrary goals in their free time. When seen in this way, we can make some sense of the (wrongheaded) accusation that games are "a waste of time." In this section, we will focus on the contribution that rules make to the aesthetics of games.

Some theorists argue that the value and interest that we take in games comes largely from their rules. These theorists are broadly called *formalists*. Formalism comes in different forms, some of which are stronger than others. A formalist might argue that games ultimately *are* sets of rules, or that rules are the building materials of games, or that rules are the primary force that shapes the aesthetic possibilities of a game.

One of the more prominent formalists in video game studies is Jesper Juul (2005). Juul's formalism has both an ontological and an evaluative component. Ontologically, games are sets of rules. On Juul's account, video games are "half-real." He says, "Video games are two different things at the same time: video games are *real* in that they consist of real rules with which players actually interact. ... However, when winning a game by slaying a dragon, the dragon is not a real dragon but a fictional one. To play a video game is therefore to interact with real rules while imagining a fictional world" (2005: 1). And evaluatively, the rules provide context and meaning for the player's actions—"rules are the most consistent source of player enjoyment in games" (ibid.: 55). Rules do not merely limit the player's actions; they also afford the player opportunities to act in unique and effective ways (ibid.: 58). The rules of *Tomb Raider* give Lara Croft certain abilities (e.g., to move through the environment effectively, to fight back against her enemies). By mastering the game's affordances, the player is able to strategize, solve puzzles, and overcome the challenges set by the game.

Similarly, Salen and Zimmerman offer another formalist account. The aim of game design is to produce "meaningful play" (2004: 33), and the rules of the game are one of the primary tools that game designers have to work with. The rules of a game offer players choices, which have discernible outcomes that can be measured against the goal that the player seeks (ibid.: 34). Additionally, players become invested in gameplay when their choices are "integrated"—that is, when the player's choices have a meaningful impact on the outcome (ibid.: 34–5). They say, "From somewhere in the gap between action and outcome, in the friction between frustrated desire and the seductive goal of the game, bubbles up the unique enjoyment of game play" (ibid.: 98).

Formalism is an attractive theory for a few reasons. First, the rules of a game are fairly objective. They do not depend on the player's experience or interpretation. Juul describes the rules of a game as "above discussion" (2005: 61), while Salen and Zimmerman describe them as explicit, unambiguous, and binding (among other things; 2004: 122–3). Second, it seems rather undeniable that the success of a game is partly a matter of crafting a well-designed set of rules. The difference between an enjoyable game and terrible game can be as simple as one small rule. My daughter once insisted that it was fair game in *thumb war* to use the index finger to help capture an opponent's thumb, which she called the "snake" move. Fortunately, she quickly realized that if all opponents could use the snake, then thumb war isn't fun. Third, rules have the interesting quality of being transferable across different media (Juul 2005: 48–52; see also Salen and Zimmerman on the "repeatability" of rules, 2004: 123). Chess is a game that can be played using a tabletop board and pieces, or it can be played on a computer. Either way, the rules are the same. A game that can be played in different media is called a *transmedial* game, which is only possible because of the generalizable quality of rules.[8] Formalism is able to explain why some games are transmedial—because, if the rules are the same, then the game is the same.

But what *are* rules, and do video games really have *rules*? This might sound like an absurd question, but I'm not the first to worry about it. Salen and Zimmerman draw attention to the difficulty of figuring out exactly what counts as a rule for video games (2004: 141–9). Identifying the rules of a video game is not always straightforward. The basic rules of *Tetris* seem simple enough, but what about more complex games? We might initially think that the rules for a video game just *is* its program code. But that would offer too broad of an account of the game's rules. For instance, consider the way that many games allow the player to rotate the camera in a 360-degree arch around the visual field. This function is certainly part of the program code; is it therefore also a rule of the game? That seems odd. Or when players make an either-or choice that impacts the story of the game—like whether to ally with one NPC rather than another—this certainly is part of the game's code, but it seems strange to think that it is also a part of the rules. It would be better to say that video games have "formal structures" that affect the player's experience (ibid.: 144). Sometimes these formal structures are part of the rules of the game and sometimes they are not. Ultimately for Salen and Zimmerman, it may not be terribly important to identify when something is a rule and when it is not; however, it is very important for game designers to be able to think clearly about what sort of experience players are supposed to take from playing their game, which requires some thoughtfulness about the game's rules (ibid.: 148).

To capture the difficulty that Salen and Zimmerman point to, we should recognize the subtle distinction between *rules* and *game mechanics*. When many gamers talk about the "rules of a video game," what they often have in mind are the game's mechanics. It may be more accurate for us to distinguish between these two. What exactly counts as a "rule" is, of course, open to philosophical debate, and philosophers have identified many different functions and roles that "rules" can play. However, when comparing video games to traditional games, three distinctive qualities of rules in traditional games become apparent. First, a rule of a game is a guiding principle that governs human actions that require group cooperation; second, rules typically require some degree of judgment on the part of those who employ the rule; and, finally, rules prescribe what sort of actions participants should value.

On the first point, games are a species of social phenomena that requires groups of people to coordinate their actions to produce some collective good. They are loose and voluntary actions. Each individual player has their own will, their own motivations, and their own aims. Yet, to play a game, these individuals must come together and coordinate their efforts; they take on the collective will of the group. For instance, when a group of friends engages in a game of pick-up basketball, it comes down to the collective will of the group to uphold the rules and play a fair game. Games could not exist if players did not voluntarily coordinate their individual actions into one group effort. And games are not the only social phenomenon like this. There are rules for driving a car, rules for good etiquette at a dinner party, and even rules of engagement in war. In each of these cases, there is some collective good that can only be achieved by the coordinated actions of many individuals—respectively, the avoidance of traffic accidents, the mutual enjoyment of a social gathering, and the avoidance of civilian casualties in war. These are all collective goods that require some governance of all the individuals involved.

Second, to ensure that these collective good are achieved, often some people are put into positions of authority to enforce the rules. In sports, there are referees and umpires. In casual and informal games, the role of enforcer often falls to the players collectively. Interestingly, one of the key functions of these authorities is to know when to enforce the rules and when to exercise their discretion and allow the players to play on. A game where all the rules are strictly enforced along with all their minutiae can wind up as a joyless event.[9]

Third, rules are prescriptive in a way that mechanics are not. The rules of a game tell us not only what we are able to do but also what we should value or prefer (Nguyen 2020). Rules are value-laden. Think about hurdling: a runner is penalized if they knock a hurdle over. This rule tells us that we should prefer not to knock over the hurdles.

Tabletop games and sports all have rules in the sense identified above. The rules are voluntarily adopted, they are sustained by the collective will of all players, their enforcement often requires discretion, and they are value-laden. By contrast, natural laws—like the laws of physics, biology, or mathematics—are not *rules* in this sense (or, perhaps, in any sense). They are not voluntary or value-laden, they do not require collective will, nor do they require referees or judges to exercise their discretion. By comparison, video game mechanics are not voluntary, willful, or discretionary, though they may be value-laden.[10] A game's mechanics work more like natural laws than they do like the rules of a tabletop game. A game's mechanics are enforced exactly, automatically, and without any need to exercise human judgment (Juul 2005: 37–9, 60; also Salen and Zimmerman 2004: 88).

Rules and mechanics are two different things. Some games have rules *and* mechanics, while other games only have mechanics. To simplify this distinction, I suggest that the mechanics of a game are what you *can* do while the rules of a game are what you *must* do. For instance, some games allow for the casual killing of NPCs while other games do not. In *Horizon Zero Dawn*, the player cannot kill NPC villagers; in *Red Dead Redemption*, villagers are killable, but doing so comes at the cost of being hunted by the authorities. The difference here is subtle, but important. It is part of the *mechanics* of *Horizon Zero Dawn* that villagers cannot be killed. The player simply can't do that. Alternatively, it is part of the *rules* of *Red Dead Redemption* that killing a villager is costly. The game suggests that you ought not to prefer harming the villagers.

To try to better capture the distinction between *rules* and *mechanics*, especially as it applies to video games, we should lean into the terminology that is implied by the term "mechanics"—it implies something *mechanical*, or *machine-like*. The interesting thing about a machine is that it functions following simple cause-and-effect processes. The engine of a car is a machine that transfers energy into motion, and it does so through a complex chain of causes and effects. Video games are machines too, but ones that take the player's input to change some state within the game. Juul argues that games are, in a literal sense, "state machines," which is "a machine that has an initial state, accepts a specific amount of input events, changes state in response to inputs using a state transition function (i.e., rules), and produces specific outputs using an output function" (2005: 60). For any game, there are numerous possibilities for how a game could progress given both the current state of the game and the number of possible inputs. But, importantly for us, the transition from one game state to another is a mechanical process where the player's input has a direct impact on the state of the game. There is a distinctive aesthetic pleasure to well-crafted game mechanics, just as there is a distinctive pleasure to using a well-crafted machine. The efficiency and responsiveness of a high-end car feels almost like an extension of the driver's body. A video game's mechanics can offer this feeling of extended control too.

Some games aim for a degree of realism in their mechanics. The combat in *Ghost of Tsushima* is surprisingly beautiful, not simply for the way that it looks, but rather in the way that the experienced player is able to move fluidly through a battle. The player controls a thirteenth-century samurai named Jin Sakai. As the player progresses through the game, different sword stances are unlocked. Each stance is more effective against different types of enemies. When battling against a mixed group of enemies, the player must switch between stances frequently, sometimes switching stances after each swing of the sword. Battles become fluid, dance-like sequences where the player threads their way through the various attacks by responding quickly and shifting their stance appropriately.[11] The combat mechanics in *Ghost of Tsushima* does something remarkable: it attempts to represent what it means for fighters to anticipate their opponent's moves.

However, well-crafted game mechanics are not necessarily realistic or even easy to use. In *The Legend of Zelda: Breath of the Wild*, there is a shrine that must be completed by guiding a large ball through a maze (the Myahm Agana Shrine, near Hateno Village). The player must use the gyroscope in the Switch controller to guide the ball through the maze, in the style of old wooden maze puzzles. It takes a number of tries to get the hang of manipulating the puzzle using a gyroscope, but it is immensely satisfying when the player is successful. There is nothing realistic about it, but it is a fun demonstration of what the Switch gyroscope can do.

In other games, the mechanics are distinctly unrealistic or difficult to master. Yet, such games can still turn their difficult mechanics to an advantage as when the particular nature of the game mechanics themselves provide the challenge that must be overcome. For instance, in *Hellblade: Senua's Sacrifice*,[12] there are few combat controls available to the player (heavy attack, light attack, parry, block, and dodge). Additionally, the controls are somewhat sticky—if my opponent attacks just at the moment when I have triggered an attack, there is no going back or changing course mid-attack. It is easy to get Senua injured in combat by committing to an attack too early or failing to anticipate an opponent's attack. When compared to *Ghost of Tsushima*, the combat in *Hellblade* feels very stiff and confining. On the face of it, this should make the combat disappointing. But it doesn't. The challenge of combat in *Hellblade* is dealing with its limitations. Moreover, the stiffness of *Hellblade*'s combat reinforces the fact that Senua is not supposed to be a highly skilled warrior. The stickiness of the combat controls represents to the player that Senua is herself an inexpert fighter—she is untested and uncertain—thus increasing the tension and anxiety of combat.

Artis (2021: 71–2) offers some helpful terminology to describe particular characteristics of game mechanics. Good twitch-like gameplay has the characteristics of being *fair, transparent,* and *fine-tuned.* Fairness is "a matter of clear, consistent, and reliable mapping of player input with in-game character behavior" (ibid.: 71). Transparency refers to the feeling of immediacy of the controls—controls achieve high transparency by responding quickly, with little lag between pressing a button on the controller and the response of the player-character. Finally, a finely tuned game is one where the gameworld is designed to reward and facilitate the fairness and transparency of the controls. By contrast, a poorly tuned game may still contain fair and transparent controls, but the tasks the player is given are too simple or repetitive for the player to take much pleasure in them. One limitation of Artis' account, however, is that the terms he offers are fairly restricted to twitch-like gameplay. So, Artis' account cannot be straightforwardly applied to turn-based gameplay or puzzle-solving gameplay. Nonetheless, his account is a highly apt description of the qualities of good twitch games, and, given the centrality of twitch games to gaming culture, the qualities Artis describes set the tone for what other types of games are judged against.

Before leaving this discussion of rules, one quick note about difficulty. Recall that Caillois identifies the pleasure of rule-following as a pleasure grounded in "gratuitous difficulty." Why would this be? If we enjoy following rules, then why not make life easier on ourselves and play games with easy-to-master rules. Success would be guaranteed. Yet, easy games are immensely disappointing.

When thinking of the place of difficulty, there are a few points we should keep in mind. First, the quality of being "difficult" is ultimately a three-part relationship between the goal that one seeks, the affordances one has to achieve the goal, and the limitations that stand in the way. We can quibble about what "gratuitous difficulty" means or whether it really is as valuable as Caillois suggests. But we shouldn't lose sight of the more important point: the limitations of a game are not there to make the game easier. The limitations are there to make success into an achievement.

Second, not all difficulty in games is the same, or is experienced similarly. Juul offers the helpful distinction between *failure* in games and *punishment* (2013: 70). Players constantly face the possibility of failure in a game, but some games are also punishing. A punishing game is one where the cost of failure is particularly high. In "old-school" arcade games, players typically had a limited number of lives. Once those were lost, the game was over and the player had to start again. There was nothing more frustrating as a child than losing my last life on the final level of *Super Mario Bros.*, which meant that I had to start the game over from World 1–1. Many modern games that have a strong focus on storytelling are not punishing in this respect. *Ghost of Tsushima* effectively offers the player an infinite number of lives. After a failure, the player simply starts a mission over from a nearby location. All that the player loses is a little time (ibid.: 72). Many critics decry this development in games, arguing that modern games have become "too easy," while holding up punishing games as the ideal. Whether punishing games are desirable or not clearly seems to be a matter of taste. The development of modern games with infinite lives coincides with the development of greater storytelling in games. It would be stunningly frustrating to tell the story of *Ghost of Tsushima* if the player only had three lives. By contrast, punishingly difficult old-school games weren't particularly known for their storytelling capabilities.

Finally, difficulty in a game can be frustrating, but it can also be rewarding. Specifically, difficulty is often a good measure of skill development. The reward of a challenging game is (typically) the improvement of one's skills. When a player fails, they receive feedback on how their skills are not yet up to the task. Part of the joy of replaying a game is the realization that I now have the skills to sail through the early levels with ease, even when I've increased the difficulty level of the game.

5 Summing Up

Good gameplay is essential to the aesthetic appreciation of video games. But what makes gameplay "good" must be dependent on a number of factors. We can at least say this: good gameplay is constructed by working with three variables—goal-seeking, uncertainty, and mechanics. It is not necessary for good gameplay to find some sort of balance between each of these. Some games exhibit good gameplay when they focus on only one or two variables. But the more general point is that we can analyze what makes gameplay good by looking at how these variables are addressed and accommodated in different ways by different games.

4

Narrative Aesthetics

Red Dead Redemption (*RDR*) was the first game that made me feel an emotional reaction toward its characters. I didn't *cry*. But I definitely got a bit misty.

Spoiler alert! *Red Dead Redemption* is set in 1911, in the final days of the Wild West. While much of the West is still unruly, newly built railroads and telegraph lines are beginning to connect the West to the rest of the country. With modernization comes increased oversight and law enforcement. The West is still a dangerous place, but the old outlaw gangs are being broken up, arrested, or killed, if necessary. The days of freewheeling outlaws having their way are coming to an end.

The game focuses on the story of John Marston, a seemingly reformed outlaw who has been contracted by US federal agents to track down his on-the-run former gang members. In particular, the agents want to find the gang's leader, Dutch van der Linde. Marston is in a difficult situation. While he has ostensibly given up his former life, he also clearly doesn't want to turn on his ex-gang members. However, the agents who have contracted him have kidnapped his wife, Abigail, and young son, Jack, and are holding them in custody. They will languish in their incarceration and Marston will never see them again unless he tracks down and captures Dutch and the rest of the gang.

After a long and difficult search, Marston finally locates Dutch high up in a mountainous hideout. With the help of federal agents and the US Army, Marston leads an assault on Dutch's camp. In the lengthy battle, many soldiers die along with the members of Dutch's new gang.

Marston continues to pursue Dutch until he is cornered. Realizing that he has reached his end, Dutch jumps to his death.

Marston is finally free, both of his criminal past and his obligation to the federal agents who coerced him into tracking down Dutch. Marston is then informed that his wife and son are waiting for him at the humble farm that he built after leaving Dutch's gang. Marston then mounts his horse for the long ride back to the farm.

At this point, the sound in the game changes. Previously, the player could hear incidental noises in the background everywhere they went. There would be the sound of birds, horses, and occasionally of fighting in the distance. When Marston begins riding back to the farm, all the incidental sounds fade away to be replaced with a song, Jamie Lidell's "Compass." The chorus is wistful and somewhat ethereal, but edged with pain. With Marston riding back to Abigail, the player hears Lidell sing, "Now I know/the only compass that I need/is the one/that leads back to you." Unexpectedly, I found myself getting choked up and misty-eyed at this point—*John was going home, to Abigail!*

Video games had always been mere entertainment for me—a fun diversion where I could enjoy frivolous stories about zombies and dragons and alien invasions. Now, with *RDR*, they became, for me, a form of storytelling that could move me to feel the longing of missing someone that I never expected to see again.

Narrative play is a kind of attitude that the player takes when they are focused on the story of the game. It differs from the goal-seeking attitude in that the interest in enjoying a complex, meaningful, or satisfying story takes precedence over mastering a skill or efficiently completing a task. While the goal-seeking player wants to maximize their efficiency and mastery of the game, the narrative player wants to see the story play out in a satisfying way. Sometimes enjoying a narrative means making choices in the game that result in less efficient goal-seeking. Players might drag out a mission or pursue an unnecessary quest because the story is better that way.

Let us contrast these two kinds of play. In goal-seeking play, the player adopts the underlying formal logic of the rules and mechanics of the game. This sort of thinking treats the game as a system for achieving certain ends through particular means. By contrast, means–ends reasoning often does not help in narrative play. I cannot always strategize my way through a story. For instance, *The Banner Saga* is a tactical role-playing game that follows a band of villagers who are fleeing their homes due to the return of an ancient enemy, the Dredge. There are two main forms of gameplay: most of the game is presented in the form of a narrative where the leaders of the village must make difficult choices about where to go and how to manage the supplies, and then there are turn-based set battles. When playing a set battle, the player must economize the movements and attacks of their group to maximize effectiveness on the battlefield. However, when making a narrative decision, there is no underlying formal rule that can aid players in making the "right" decision. There is no strategy one can follow to decide whether to ford a river or find another crossing. The results of the narrative choices are fixed in advance. In some cases, making a bold choice might lead to better results than making the compassionate choice, while in other cases this is reversed. There is no way for the player to predict the expected outcome. Thus, the player does not engage with these narrative choices like they are a skill that can be mastered, but rather as an interactive novel, one where the best-laid plans sometimes go awry.

Insofar as games have narratives and stories, we can understand their aesthetic value by drawing on the time-tested theories of narratives in other media. There has been much discussion about the narrative power and potential of games among theorists who come from a variety of different academic disciplines. Some theorists have demonstrated successfully that work on literature (Ryan 2006), film (Gaut 2010, Wolf 2001), and theater (Murray 1997) can offer helpful ways to understand narratives in video games.

The interactivity of games leads to what I think makes narratives distinctively valuable in video games: the appreciation of how one's decisions are related to consequences. When we make decisions in real life, we never really know if our choices have led to the best outcome as we can never experience the results of the decisions that we do not make. But in video games, we can. Games can be replayed, allowing the player to see which of their choices leads to the best—or most preferred—results. Novels and films are more like real life—events move inexorably to one conclusion, and neither the characters in the story nor the viewing audience ever get to see how things could have been differently.[1] Video games allow us to peek behind the curtain, to choose differently, and thus see how things might have been. This gives the player some creative control over the narrative, allowing the player to define what a "good" or satisfying outcome to the narrative would be. For instance, *The Walking Dead*—a point-and-click game where the player directs the choices of a group of zombie-apocalypse survivors—is ultimately a game about choice and consequence. It warrants replay just to see if one could possibly get a better outcome by making different choices.

Some video games focus heavily on their stories. *Dear Esther* is often referred to derisively as a "walking simulator" because the only thing that the player can do is walk around. But that description is unfair, and the reason why is precisely because it assumes that we should describe video games by referring to *what the player is able to do* instead of *what the story is about*. *Dear Esther* tells the story of a man searching for meaning after losing his wife. Set on a seemingly desolate island in the Hebrides, the player searches for clues about what happened to Esther. Perhaps we should describe *Dear Esther* as a kind of digital novel rather than as a game, but doing so minimizes the importance of the player's agency as information is presented disjointedly and depends (somewhat) on which parts of the island the player explores.

More commonly, stories provide a setting and context for the action. In some case, the story is woven through the action. In *Batman: Arkham Asylum*, the story unfolds as Batman gains new abilities and travels to new areas on the map. The story is told through the changing scenery as the player gets a sense of the increasing chaos in the asylum and as Batman upgrades his abilities to confront the new challenges that he faces. In other games, the action and story somewhat come apart. The story is what happens in between stretches of action. *Super Mario Odyssey* follows the traditional storyline of a Mario game, where Mario saves the Princess from Bowser. Each kingdom has its puzzles and challenges, but these are disconnected from the story other than being thematically related.

How important or central are stories to the appreciation and understanding of video games? There is some reason to think that stories are highly important. First, video games are often marketed and advertised by focusing on their stories. Games are not just venues for scoring points but instead are opportunities to fight dragons, save princesses, and explore new worlds (Ryan 2006: 182). Second, in reviews of video games on websites like *Kotaku* or publications like *Game Informer*, descriptions of a game's story often take up a considerable percentage of the article, and sometimes the majority of it. However, there are also good reasons to think that stories are not that important or central to video games. Many highly successful video games have no story at all. And even when games do have a story, it is not always the driving force of the fanbase. Competitive players of *Rainbow Six Siege* aren't there for the story.

In the early days when Video Game Studies was just getting started as an independent academic field, there was a brief worry about whether video games should primarily be understood as narratives or as games. Some call this the "narratology versus ludology debate" (Frasca 2003a: 1; see also Aarseth 2014; Frasca 2003b; Ryan 2006: Ch. 8). The "ludologist's" position was that video games are primarily *games*, things that are in the same realm as sports, board games, and pinball machines. What all these things have in common is that they are systems of rules, which are best appreciated by playing them (Aarseth 1997 is often credited as the starting point of this view). To a ludologist, video games are distinctive because they are a technology that allows for new kinds of games. Additionally, the stories that video games tell are often superficial or incoherent, and competitive players learn to ignore them. Against this, the "narratologist's" position was that video games are primarily a new kind of fiction, things that are in the same realm as films, cartoons, and theatrical performances (some identify Murray 1997 as the first narratologist, but this is disputed; see Frasca 2003a). What these things have in common is that they engage the consumer in a fiction, one that the consumer becomes emotionally invested in. To a narratologist, video games are distinctive because they are a technology that allows for new kinds of stories and interactive storytelling. The audience of a film, novel, or theatrical performance is (typically) passive, while the player of a video game is actively involved in shaping the contours of the story.

From the outside, this looks like a tidy little academic debate, one where two positions are clearly marked out and where agreeing with one position means that you must disagree with the other. Interestingly, however, the debate didn't work out that way. It turned out that no one really held the strong position that these two views are mutually exclusive. Instead, scholars of video games quickly realized that we can have it both ways. Video games are games *and* they can tell stories. As Gonzalo Frasca simply put it, "ludologists love stories too" (2003a).

If there never really was a debate between narratologists and ludologists, then why should we bother to think about it now? Frasca quotes Susana Pajares-Tosca, who complained that the need for theorists to address the ludology–narratology debate is something that she "personally consider[s] terribly boring at this stage" (2003a: 96). If it was boring to mention the debate in 2003, then it would be really insufferable for us to talk about it now over twenty years later! And yet, it also seems wrong to *not* mention the debate in a chapter about the aesthetic value of narratives. Under the guise of the ludology–narratology debate, many theorists produced some excellent work—examining the scope of game studies, mapping out the theoretical territory, and developing some important ideas about the relationships between games and narratives. To understand and appreciate that scholarship today, it is worth knowing where it came from.

Additionally, it is worth mentioning the debate-that-never-happened because it demonstrates an important lesson: that not all distinctions are a source of conflict. A key point of the book you are reading now is that video games can be enjoyed in a number of different ways and they give rise to a wide range of aesthetic values. The aesthetic values we find in video games are dependent on what sort of attitude we take toward playing them: a goal-seeking attitude, a narrative attitude, or a dollhouse attitude. By taking one attitude or another, players will pay attention to different aspects of games and will find a variety of things aesthetically valuable in them. But there is no conflict between these attitudes. You don't have to pick one. There is no reason why taking a goal-seeking attitude toward a game at one time means that I cannot take a narrative attitude toward it at another time. Instead, we change our attitude toward a game as our interests change. When I am in the middle of a shootout in *RDR*, I am taking a goal-seeking attitude. I want to eliminate all of my enemies as efficiently as possible. When the battle is over and a cut-scene begins, then my attitude changes—I begin taking a narrative attitude toward the game because I am also interested in where the story is going. To rephrase Frasca's point, ludologists can love stories just as much as narratologists can love winning.

The purpose of this chapter is not to reopen old ludology–narratology wounds. I am not interested in whether *all* games are narratives (some are not). Nor am I interested in whether *all* games should be understood and evaluated through a narrative lens (some should not). This chapter aims to examine what contributes to the aesthetic value of video games when the player takes an interest in their narrative. However, some players simply don't take an interest in narratives. That's okay. These players might be leaving some aesthetic value on the table, as it were; but if narratives don't appeal to you, then they don't appeal to you. We don't have to try to make those players fall in love with narratives. Furthermore, this also means that there is no need for us to worry about video games that lack any narrative. *Gwent* doesn't have a narrative. It would be fruitless to try to pull a narrative out of *Gwent*. But that doesn't mean that *Gwent* is a "bad game." Of course it isn't! It just means that *Gwent* doesn't do something that *RDR* does. We should look for what value we can find in games and not worry about the values that we cannot find.

My questions in this chapter are the following: When a player takes a narrative attitude toward a game, what should they pay attention to? What is it about video games that can be rewarding to the narrative player?[2] There is a very large body of literature that examines different kinds of narrative values in video games. It is not my aim to review all of that scholarship here. Instead, I will draw on the sources that stand out for me and briefly highlight three sources of aesthetic value in narrative games that I believe are distinctive.

First, video games allow storytellers to use new kinds of narrative devices. In literature, storytelling primarily comes in the form of dialogue and description (which is an admitted oversimplification). In film, storytellers have additional resources available to them, like the lighting, movement, soundtrack, and the actors' performances. Video games are able to draw on all of these elements, but they can also leverage their interactivity to move the storytelling to the action, worldbuilding, lore, and the narrative structure. Both action and narrative structure enable the player to construct their own "emergent narratives," while both worldbuilding and lore allow the storyteller to offload some of the burden of describing features of the fictional world to these less obtrusive elements.

Second, it is well known that interactivity is a source of value in narrative games, but a full explanation needs to identify what it is about interactivity that is valuable. I will argue that the missing ingredient that explains the pleasure of interactive narratives must include a sense of *consequence*. What interactivity really provides the player with is consequential choices. The value of choice in a narrative has to do with appreciating how things could have been and seeing that my choice was the deciding factor that altered the state of things. This value is not diminished by my limited range of choices. Instead, it is diminished when I discover that my choices don't matter.

Third, video games allow players to engage in "narrative role-playing." Narrative role-playing is a way of answering questions about what the character does next. When the player makes a choice in the narrative, it is as if the game designer has asked the question, "What does the protagonist do here?" The player's job is to answer the question. Answering this question does not necessarily require that the player is immersed in the role-playing, or that they identify with the character, or that they are even particularly interested in the narrative. After all, one can make narrative choices in a video game inattentively. However, the results are aesthetically rewarding when the player engages in narrative role-playing sincerely. The player who takes a narrative attitude to role-playing is able to appreciate the protagonist in a distinctively empathetic way.

Before we can adequately address these ideas, however, we will first need to define "narrative." This will be the main task of Section 1. I will argue that there are three interrelated concepts—representation, fiction, and narrative. I will also argue that, while *representation* and *fiction* are two concepts that can be applied to all games, *narrative* is a concept that cannot. The remaining sections of this chapter will look at what is distinctively valuable about video game narratives. Section 2 will examine storytelling techniques, Section 3 will address the aesthetics of consequence, and Section 4 will examine the nature of narrative role-playing.

1 What Is a Narrative?

The concept of a *narrative* gets a lot of use in a lot of disparate fields—literature, film, and theater, but also in psychology and philosophy of mind. In each of these areas, "narrative" is defined in lots of different ways. Making matters worse, individual theorists often develop their own idiosyncratic definitions of "narrative." Unfortunately, I am going to contribute to this problem by offering my own definition. Definitions are good only insofar as they are explanatory and useful. I hope my definition is not only usefully explanatory but also intuitive.

Representation, fiction, and *narrative* are three interrelated concepts. In my usage, these concepts describe three different levels of description, where each higher level builds on the lower one(s). To summarize, *representation* is the most basic level of description that picks out simply what digital objects in a video game are supposed to be, *fiction* is a higher level of description that identifies the relationships between the individual representations, and *narrative* is an even higher level of description where stories emerge. By separating out these concepts, I hope we can more clearly identify what is contributing to a player's aesthetic experience.

A *representation* is something that symbolically stands for something else or signifies something else. With representations, things are no longer literal, but figurative. Representations are extremely common. We are surrounded by them every day. Paintings are often representational, where blobs of paint are arranged on a canvas to signify something—a portrait, a landscape, a historical event—unless a painting is abstract, in which case it is non-representational. Signs are often representational—a round yellow street sign with a black X and the letters "R R" means that there is a railroad crossing ahead, or a coffee shop that has a sign in the window with a drawing of a steaming mug of coffee means there is coffee inside.[3]

Video games too are representational. In a very abstract sense, we play a video game by rearranging lines of code in a save file; but that is not how we experience them. Instead, our experience of a game centers on our interaction with digital pictures, ones that represent characters, environments, and objects. Some video games are representationally rich and some are not. *BioShock* is very representationally rich. Every square inch of the screen represents something. Players see representations of a crumbling underwater city, they see representations of useful objects (like bandages, weapons, and ammunition), and they see representations of mutilated and crazed people who seek to harm the protagonist. Even the heads-up-display (HUD) is representational—it represents the status of my health and ADAM as two colored lines. By comparison, *Tetris* is not representationally rich. The falling blocks are *representations of blocks*—that is, the player is supposed to see the falling tetrominoes not merely as pixels on a screen but as bounded individual objects that can be manipulated and are being pulled by some force (e.g., gravity, magnetism, motion)—but the field that surrounds the play area and the boxes that display the level number and the player's score are not representations of anything.

Players use representations in video games to understand quickly what various digital objects do. We understand that cars can be driven, that guns are weapons, and that items of food might provide some healing to an injured player. The expectation that objects in a video game function in the same way as their real-world counterparts is so strong that it can be jarring or comedic when objects in games do not function in ways that correspond to what they represent. In *Horizon Zero Dawn*, Aloy is an excellent rock climber; so why can't she climb trees? Are trees not things-that-can-be-climbed?

Fiction is the next level of description.[4] In my usage, the fiction of the game is the explanation we give of how the representations we see on the screen are related to each other in a (presumably) unified fictional world. A video game with a coherent fiction will reasonably unify all the various representations under one explanation. Players typically expect the fiction of the game to be coherent, or at least to follow some predictable theme. Consider a game like *Dr. Mario*. It is a puzzle game that functions somewhat like *Tetris*. In this game, Mario tosses pills into a medicine bottle, which contains numerous viruses. The player's job is to kill the viruses by matching up the color of the pill to the color of the virus. The pills fall vertically and the player can flip the pills around and move them left or right to guide each one to the best position. If the player stacks the pills poorly, then the bottle fills up, stopping Mario from throwing in new pills. The fiction of the game is quite thin. Mario is a doctor. Viruses are bad. Pills kill viruses. Nonetheless, the fiction is coherent. The explanation of what each thing represents and what is happening in the game relies on an easily understood relationship between viruses, pills, and doctors. The fiction of a game is not a story. The description of *Dr. Mario* that I offered above doesn't amount to a story. It implies no plot, no dramatic arch, no movement from one moment to the next. A game's fiction is at best a description or a scenario, one that contextualizes what the player is seeing.

Some fictions are incoherent. Jesper Juul points out that, when a player tries to explain what is happening in a game, they might either refer to the fiction of the game or they might refer to the rules of the game (2005: 123–30). According to Juul, the fiction of a game breaks down—it becomes "incoherent"—when the player has to explain what is happening by referring to the rules of the game (ibid.: 130). Juul gives the example of *Donkey Kong*. There are some aspects of the game that we explain by referring to the game's fiction. Donkey Kong has kidnapped the Princess. Mario is trying to rescue her. But there are other parts of the game that we have to explain by referring to the fact that it is a *game*, one with rules. Why is it that Mario has three lives? When Mario gets hit by a falling barrel or a ball of fire, he dies. However, he doesn't stay dead for long. Rather, the player can start the level over again with Mario in (apparently) perfect health. As Juul notes, the player doesn't interpret Mario's reappearance as some magical ability to resurrect himself, or some odd form of reincarnation. Rather, the player understands Mario's three lives as a fact of the game's rules. Juul says,

> When we find it too hard to imagine a video game fiction, we can resort to explaining the events in the game by appealing to the rules. Mario is not reincarnated (fiction); the player just has three Marios (rules). If the effort required to fill in a blank in the game world becomes too big, we have to resort to a rule-oriented explanation. (ibid.: 130)

Whether we explain an event in a game by referring to the fiction or the rules on Juul's account seems to come down to whether the player is capable of reconciling the event in the fiction or not. It is a matter of finding the event "hard to imagine" or filling a "blank" that is "too big." These are obviously psychological factors about the player and their ability to imagine. This is a helpful way to think about the coherence of a fiction.

Using my terminology, here are a few other points that we can draw out. Coherence is something that comes in degrees. A coherent fiction is one that unifies the representations under one description. When it becomes difficult to unify the representations under one description, then the fiction becomes (by degrees) incoherent. The Atari 2600 game *Journey Escape* (1982), for those players old enough to remember it, was perplexing. The player takes control of the members of the 1980s rock band Journey, who just finished playing a concert. The player must navigate each band member through a field of "love-crazed groupies, sneaky photographers, and shifty-eyed promoters" to find the band's spaceship, shaped like a scarab, which will take them to the next concert.[5] The groupies are depicted as hearts with lips and legs. Photographers are depicted as just round flashing lights. There is also a helpful manager, who, if you can reach him, will take the player immediately to the scarab. Inexplicably, the manager is depicted as the Kool-Aid Man. *Why*? What does the Kool-Aid Man have to do with Journey? Or with rock concerts? In the late 1970s to early 1980s, there was a popular ad campaign for Kool-Aid where bored kids would be sitting around with nothing to drink when suddenly the Kool-Aid Man would burst through the wall, and then everyone was drinking Kool-Aid and having fun. Is that why the manager looks like the Kool-Aid Man? Because Kool-Aid Man can knock things down? Is that how the player is supposed to interpret what is happening in the game? That is a bit tenuous.

Fiction has been a hot topic in philosophical aesthetics for quite a long time. Arguably, the most influential philosophical account of fiction is Kendall Walton's (1990) theory of *mimesis*. On Walton's view, when we engage with a work of fiction—whether it is a film, a novel, or a video game—we make-believe that the things that we see on the screen or read on the page are a truthful report of what is happening in a fictional world. This fictional world is an imaginative construction. It is the player (or viewer, or reader) who imaginatively constructs the fictional world of the game (or film, or novel). Finally, the game itself (or the film, or the novel) functions as a prop in a game of make-believe. As a prop, the game prompts the player to imagine something and the player works the content of that imagining into their understanding of the fictional world.[6]

Without endorsing Walton's account of fiction, I will simply note that my claim that fiction functions as a level of description is consistent with this theory. On my view, players imaginatively construct a (Waltonian) fictional world out of the representations that they are presented with. Some fictions are coherent and some are incoherent, but the point is that we try to understand video games by fitting the representations that we encounter into some kind of unified description. Representations can stand alone as symbols or signifiers without being incorporated into a coherent fictional world; however, when we look for some unifying theme that ties representations together, we are engaged in the project of imaginatively constructing a fiction and its fictional world.

A *narrative* is more complex and is the highest level of description of our three concepts. While a fiction is merely a unifying description, a narrative will have a dramatic structure where action develops from one moment to the next. A narrative describes the movement of characters and events through time. A game has a narrative when players must explain what is happening at one moment in the game by referring to its relationship to earlier or later moments in the game. A narrative is a relationship between moments in a game, a relationship that entails the development of some action that occurs between the fictional characters, events, or spaces.

We typically explain the narrative of a game in the form of a story. *Horizon Zero Dawn* has a rich narrative, one where the events of the game form a complete story, one that could be told in some other form—like a film, a novel, or a comic book. The narratives of some games are rich enough to sustain transmedial stories (Blom 2023). Other games lack a narrative. These are cases where there is no story that the game tells. *Dr. Mario* doesn't have a narrative. Instead, all that *Dr. Mario* presents is a fictional scenario—kill the germs by piling on more pills. Similarly, games like *Hearthstone*, *MarioKart*, and *Clash of Clans* all have a fiction—they employ representations that can be unified under a single account; however, none of them have a narrative. The general lesson here is that all video games have a fiction, but not all video games have a narrative.[7]

Narratives are typically idealized. When I first played *Horizon Zero Dawn*, I died many times. Each time I died, Aloy respawned at a place nearby and at a time slightly before the encounter that killed me. Yet, when I tell the story of *Horizon Zero Dawn*, I leave out all of the times that I died. I tell an idealized version of the story, as if each of my deaths never happened. They are not part of the game's narrative, but they are part of my playthrough. What this means is that the narrative is imaginatively constructed by the player, and the player needs to keep track of which parts of their play become part of the narrative and which parts do not. The narrative of the game is something that is constructed out of the player's actions and choices. It is the complete account of events that happen to the fictional characters of the game. The parts of the game that are not part of the narrative are those things that the player has to describe either by referring to something in the real world (e.g., "I dropped out of the game because I lost my internet connection") or by referring to some formal part of the game's design (e.g., "My character respawned on the hillside").

Notice, however, that we can distinguish between whether *the game itself has a story* and whether *the player can explain what they are doing in a story*. The difference between these two is important. Salen and Zimmerman adopt a distinction that they take from Marc LeBlanc, between *embedded* and *emergent* narratives (2004: 383). An embedded narrative is the "pre-generated narrative content that exists prior to a player's interaction with the game," while an emergent narrative is the story that the player can tell about their own playthrough, which will "arise during play from the complex system of the game" (ibid.). When a player finally defeats a powerful boss after carefully preparing for the fight, they would likely describe the battle in the form of a narrative. After all, it is a sequence of events with a beginning, middle, and end. In this sense, narratives can arise in lots of forms of play. Even individual matches in sport games like *FIFA 20* and *Madden NFL* can be told in the form of an emergent narrative.

The distinction between embedded and emergent narratives is important partly because it tells us where to look for the aesthetic value of a narrative. With emergent narratives, whatever value the player finds in the narrative has to come from their own play. But with embedded narratives, whatever is valuable can be attributed to the author or game designer. This in turn is best understood by reflecting on the familiar distinction between *the game* and *a playthrough*. This distinction is intuitive to any experienced gamer. The game itself is an artifact, something made by a game designer, that is full of possible scenarios and pathways, while my playthrough is an event, something that I produce in the act of playing the game. This distinction becomes important when we make evaluative comments about *games* separately from *playthroughs*. When I say, "*Candy Crush Saga* is just another match-three game," I am making a (critical) comment about the game itself, not any particular playthrough; and when I say, "I crushed the competition in *MarioKart*," I am making a (boastful) comment about one particular playthrough, not the game itself. In any playthrough, only some possibilities are realized and only some pathways are explored. Every playthrough offers only a partial glimpse of all the content that is available in a game; and this is necessarily so, as many decisions that I make foreclose on some possibilities. If I choose to play *Dragon Age: Origins (DA:O)* as a male human, then certain storylines are open to me, but storylines for dwarves, elves, and female characters are closed to me. It is impossible for any playthrough to present every possibility that a game is capable of.

Marissa Willis (2019) applies the concept of a playthrough to account for the different kinds of truths that players will encounter in a video game. Some propositions are true *of the game itself* while other propositions are true *only of some particular playthrough*. The first kind are called "game-truths," which are "those which are fictionally true in every possible playthrough of the video game" (2019: 46). In every playthrough of *DA:O*, certain things are always true: that the player-character becomes a warden, their company is joined by Alistair, and they later meet both Morrigan and Leliana. These are game-truths that are indelibly part of the game's content. By contrast, "playthrough-truths" are things that are true of a particular playthrough, they are not necessarily true of every playthrough, and they are dependent on the actions of the player.[1] In some playthroughs, the warden is male, while in others they are female. On Willis' account, it is a game-truth that the player-character is a warden, but the gender of the warden is a playthrough-truth.

This distinction between a game and a playthrough maps onto the distinction between embedded narratives and emergent narratives: we attribute to the game designer what is built into the game (embedded), not what is the result of the players' actions (emergent). Some video games have an embedded narrative and some do not, while any particular playthrough can be described as an emergent narrative, though some of these narratives might not be particularly interesting or aesthetically rewarding. Throughout the remainder of this chapter, I will mostly focus on embedded narratives, though I will briefly discuss emergent narratives in Section 2.

An embedded narrative is not just any possible story that one could tell to make sense of a game. Rather, a narrative is a story (or a space of possible stories) that we attribute to the game designer. If I wanted to seem clever, I could perhaps tell a story about how *Dr. Mario* is a critique of the pharmaceutical industry: they incentivize doctors to over-prescribe pills and then keep feeding us more pills to take care of the problems caused by all the pills they give us. That is a fanciful interpretation and likely not a story that the game developers intended. Willful players can certainly find clever ways to force all kinds of interpretations onto games, but that is clearly different from the story that the game designer wishes to tell. *Dr. Mario* ostensibly has no embedded narrative, while *RDR* clearly does.

When we understand "fiction" in the sense described above, then all video games are "interactive fictions": the player attempts to make sense of the game by positing a fiction and they interact with the game through its gameplay (Tavinor 2009: 23–4). Additionally, some video games have an embedded narrative developed by the game designer. So, some video games are also "interactive narratives."[9] Interactive narratives offer new possibilities for storytelling and for engaging the audience in meaningful ways. The remaining sections of this chapter will explore those.

2 Elements of Storytelling

Video game designers have a number of tools available to them to tell a compelling story. Three tools that I will highlight here are the action, worldbuilding, and lore. Additionally, stories all have narrative structures, and video games offer the opportunity to create unique kinds of narrative structures. Finally, cut-scenes are a common form of storytelling in video games but often not the most loved. This section will briefly examine each of these and suggest some aesthetic contributions they make to the player's experience.

Action. By creating an interactive scenario, one where the player's input is tied directly to quantifiable outcomes, the action itself has the right temporal structure to create a story. This is because any event must have a beginning, middle, and end. The cause-and-effect relationship between one moment and the next provides the basis for creating a narrative. Indeed, emergent narratives depend wholly on the player's ability to act. Game designers provide a template for the construction of emergent narratives by offering the player specific kinds of affordances and limitations. For instance, *Stardew Valley* is built around farming, exploring the mines, and social interactions. Out of these elements, a distinct narrative emerges out of the activities and relationships that are favored by the player.

While action is one way in which game designers can tell a story, it is not one that is easily employed. In the early days, most action-oriented video games lacked embedded narratives.[10] Nearly all games had a fiction, but these were typically very thin. For instance, *Combat* was a video game for the Atari 2600 from 1977. The game depicts a birds-eye view of a battlefield with some geometrical obstacles. Two players each control a tank and can fire rockets at the other player. The game is a fiction—there are tanks on a battlefield—but there is no story or even an explanation of why the tanks are shooting at each other. While the gameplay allows players to develop an emergent narrative (as in, "I rounded the corner and fired the rocket that destroyed the enemy's tank!"), the game lacks any embedded narrative.

Action on its own can mean whatever the player takes it to mean. But when action is contextualized by an embedded narrative, it becomes a meaningful object of the player's narrative attitude and can take on different aesthetic qualities. An example of action contextualized into a narrative is the 2-D puzzle game *Thomas Was Alone*. The story of the game (its embedded narrative) is that computer engineers have been experimenting with artificial intelligence when individual programs become self-aware. Realizing that they are trapped somewhere, the self-aware programs learn about their surroundings and attempt to escape. The game is visually abstract. The playable characters are all differently sized and colored squares and rectangles. Each one has a different ability as well as certain limitations. One is tall and can jump high. Another is very small, allowing it to fit into small spaces. The player must employ each characters' abilities correctly to work their way through the maze. The game's soundtrack has a voiceover, which is a first-person narration of the inner thoughts of each personified program. The narration humanizes the mere squares and rectangles, attributing to them personalities with specific hopes, anxieties, and goals. The narrative voiceover is very effective at contextualizing the characters' perspectives, which lends an interesting quality to the player's own actions. Learning that the tall rectangle takes great pride in its ability to jump far, my own jumping in the game seems to take on a joyous quality. Without the voiceover, *Thomas Was Alone* would function as a perfectly good puzzle game, but one where the player's actions would likely feel meaningless and unmotivating. What is a simple abstract puzzle becomes a story of exploration, discovery, and rivalries through its contextualizing voiceover.

Worldbuilding. The writer's adage "show, don't tell" is good advice. For novelists, it means that some ideas can be conveyed indirectly to the reader through a character's behavior, instead of directly telling the reader something through description. Worldbuilding is a silent form of storytelling that *shows* rather than *tells*. All narratives have a setting—the backdrop in which the story unfolds—but worldbuilding is more than a backdrop. Rather, it can be a subtle way of filling out minor details of the story without explicitly relying on (potentially boring) exposition—details of how people live, their motivations, their history, or what social and political forces shape their worldview. It is also a risky form of storytelling. The game designer puts the nuance of the story in the game's setting with the hope that a perceptive player will notice it.

Horizon Zero Dawn wields its worldbuilding well. The clearest example comes from its presentation of the main tribes. The game and its downloadable content focus on four tribes: the Nora, the Carja, the Oseram, and the Banuk.[11] Each tribe is clearly distinct, which can be seen in their dress, their political structures, and their religions. Moreover, each tribe seems to reflect the distinctive environments in which they reside, which interestingly suggests the ways in which the culture of a people is linked to their environment. The Nora are a hunter-gatherer society who live in the Sacred Lands, a lush, mountainous landscape with tall pines. The Nora's style of dress is primarily made from animal hides and decorated with machine parts, clearly materials gained from their hunts. The Carja are a wealthy city-state of merchants and artisans. Their capital city—Meridian—is located in a lush plateau surrounded by an arid desert landscape. The Carja's style of dress features fine silks, polished metals, and delicate symmetrical face painting, suggesting greater worldly refinement. The Oseram are a rowdy tribe with an affinity for machine work, building, and drinking. They often appear dressed in greasy leathers and goggles. Finally, the Banuk are a nomadic tribe that lives further north in the Frozen Wilds. Like the Nora, they are also hunter-gatherers; however, their clothing features more machine parts, reflecting perhaps their greater dependence on the machines and the lack of larger animals in their snowy environment. These distinctive styles of dress express a shared experience of the peoples of each tribe.

Why is worldbuilding a particularly effective form of storytelling in video games? After all, it is not distinctive of video games. Novels and films rely on worldbuilding too. I suggest that what is distinctive about worldbuilding in video games is the way in which the world is presented to the player. In literature and film, the storyteller controls exactly what aspects of the world are revealed to the reader or viewer, and at exactly what moment in the story. In video games, the worldbuilding is revealed to the player at their own pace. Moreover, exactly what information is revealed depends strongly on the player's own adventurous spirit. The player is partly responsible for discovering the worldbuilding.

Lore. What I am calling "lore" is a form of storytelling that is embedded in the worldbuilding, one that requires greater effort from the player to actively seek out. Just as with worldbuilding, it is a form of storytelling that places the onus on the player to discover it. In many games, items are distributed throughout the game space that contain information about the world. Oftentimes players are incentivized to collect these items in order to unlock an achievement or a special reward. If players are motivated to search for the lore solely for the sake of these extrinsic gains, then their motivation is a goal-seeking one. By contrast, some players will seek out the lore because they enjoy discovering more about the game world. These sorts of players are taking a narrative attitude.

Lore can come in lots of different forms, appropriate to the theme of the game. As discussed previously in Chapter 2, *Elder Scrolls V: Skyrim* is a game with rich and detailed lore. The player can read books in the College of Winterhold to learn more about the history, politics, and mythology of the game. But there are additionally more scrolls and books scattered throughout the province of Skyrim for the narrative player to seek out. In *Middle-earth: Shadow of Mordor*, the player has the opportunity to dig deeper into the expanded legendarium of Tolkien's

Lord of the Rings universe. However, there is no helpfully placed college stocked full of books for the player to read in the game. The game is set in the land of Mordor sometime before the events of *The Lord of the Rings* where the player controls the reanimated body of a deceased ranger who is living as a shadow among the orcs seeking to sabotage and delay the coming return of Sauron. Scattered throughout Mordor are artifacts that have been imbued with the remnants of a memory. Some are human artifacts that were left either by warriors fighting in Mordor or those unfortunate enough to have been abducted by orcs and taken to Mordor. Other artifacts come from the orcs themselves. These shed some light on the nature of orc society. The artifacts might be a broken sword, the blade of a hoe, or a simple bowl.

While "lore" is a term that is most likely associated with the fantasy genre, I intend for it to cover all genres of games that employ this form of storytelling. *Ghost of Tsushima* is not a fantasy game, and yet it uses lore in the form of Mongol artifacts. These provide information about Mongolian culture, history, and war tactics. What is unclear, however, is whether this information is available to the main character, Jin Sakai, or only to the player. Compare this to the previous two examples. In *Skyrim*, the player accesses the lore of the game by directing their avatar to read books and scrolls. The player is reading the books of lore at the same time as the avatar in the game. So, the avatar presumably has all the same information as the player. *Shadow of Mordor* handles this issue differently, where the main character and the player have the same information because they access an artifact's memories through some (unexplained) magical connection. Perhaps the memories embedded in the artifacts have an aura that the main character can sense? Either way, in *Skyrim* and *Shadow of Mordor*, the main character has all the same information as the player. But, in *Ghost of Tsushima*, this is uncertain. When Jin Sakai finds a Mongolian artifact, how exactly does he access the information about it? Perhaps we are supposed to presume that Jin already knows what these artifacts are because he is a highly educated member of the samurai class? This issue aside, it is to *Ghost of Tsushima*'s credit that the player learns about Mongolian history through the game's lore. Indeed, it is a humanizing feature of the game, presenting the Mongols not just as a brutal, faceless invading force but as a society with their own customs, religion, and history.

Narrative Structure. Finally, the interactivity of video games allows the embedded narrative to depart from the strict linear structure of passive media, thus allowing for different kinds of sequence structures. A "sequence structure"—or what Ryan calls "textual architecture" (2006: 100)—is the order in which events that make up a narrative are presented to the audience or the user. Films and novels are (typically) *linear* in their sequence structure—because of the fixed nature of the medium, the filmmaker or novelist decides in advance what sequences the events are presented and the audience members passively follow along until the end.

Some video games have a *linear narrative* also, which allows the game designer to tell a very detailed story, confident in their knowledge that the story will be followed in the order that the designer has determined with no interruptions. *Max Payne 3* tells the story of a former police detective who has become a private security agent investigating the kidnapping of his boss's wife. The story progresses from one plot point to the next. Additionally, *Max Payne 3* could be described as an *exclusive linear narrative*, meaning that the plot exclusively follows the game designer's plan, with no opportunity to pursue any side-quests. Other linear narrative games have an *inclusive* structure, meaning that the main story follows the game designer's plan, but the player has the option to include side-quests into the story. For instance, most open-world games give the player the ability to choose what order to complete the missions, to choose whether to pursue or avoid some missions, and to freely explore the game world. In these games, the main storyline is effectively linear—there is a deterministic movement from one mission to the next in the main campaign—but there are optional side-quests that can complement the main narrative of the game.

Another kind of sequence structure could be described as *branching*. These are games where the player's choices open some storylines up while closing down other storylines. In these games, choices that the player makes will impact the final outcome of the story. An example is *The Witcher 3: Wild Hunt*, which follows the adventures of Geralt of Rivia as he searches for his missing adopted daughter, Ciri. Choices that the player makes along the way will have repercussions toward the end. The player's choices at earlier points in the game—the allies that one selects, the romances that one pursues, and the rivals whom one chooses to punish—have a rippling effect at later points.

Finally, other games offer a freer, *expanding structure*. These are cases where the gameworld has many individual narratives, but there is no overarching narrative that players must follow. Think of persistent massively multiplayer online role-playing games (MMORPGs) like *World of Warcraft*. Set in the fantasy world of Azeroth, the world has its own history, mythology, and lore. There are many missions and events in the game, each with their own contained narrative. But there is no overarching, final story of *World of Warcraft*. Whatever embedded narrative the player finds, it is one that continuously expands as the game is updated.

Cut-scenes. Before leaving this section, we would be remiss if we did not say something about cut-scenes and their use in storytelling. Cut-scenes are the obvious way to tell a story as they rely quite heavily on storytelling norms developed in the medium of film; however, they are also one of the least satisfying. Many gamers complain that cut-scenes force the player to pause their game just to passively watch what is effectively a movie. Some cut-scenes can be quite long. I have had a PS4 controller go dormant because a cut-scene was so long. To mitigate this, games often allow the player to effectively fast-forward through a long cut-scene by "clicking through." However, some games don't allow the player to click through the cut-scene—as is the case with *Ghost of Tsushima*.

However, cut-scenes are not all bad. They can be employed quite effectively. First, they can provide the necessary context for the player to make sense of their action (Klevjer 2016). This can be especially helpful when there is a distinctive change in the gameplay, as when players are given a new ability or a unique task. Second, cut-scenes can incorporate some interactivity by turning them into consequential and meaningful conversations. Some dialogues can be consequential, as when the right dialogue option opens up a new quest, impacts the player's relationship to some NPC, or reveals useful information; while other dialogues can be meaningful, as when the player's choice lends to the aesthetic character of a conversation. Games like those in the *Dragon Age* series or the *Mass Effect* series are highly effective at creating consequential and meaningful dialogues. The right sequence of choices can lead to new quests, some can lead the player to develop an alliance or rivalry with an NPC, and some can lead to romance options with the NPCs. Other games allow for meaningful but inconsequential dialogues. These are moments where the dialogue has no impact on the game—that is, the player's choice does not open up new quests or changes the NPC's relationship to the player-character—but where the choices available can still be meaningful for the player. In *Horizon Zero Dawn*, there are many cut-scenes where the player has the option to choose whether Aloy responds to an NPC with kindness, toughness, or insight. Most of these have no impact on the game, apart from how the NPC responds to Aloy. However, they can still have a meaningful impact for the player. Effectively, the player decides how Aloy emotionally responds to events in her world, both giving the player some emotional stake in Aloy's quests as well as the opportunity to empathetically enter into Aloy's perspective.

3 Narrative and the Aesthetics of Consequence

In a very basic sense, there is a raw and likely irreducible pleasure to be had in interactivity. As Daniel Hardcastle playfully writes, video games are "magic. *Actual magic.* Plug a machine into your TV and suddenly, *you control what happens on the TV*. That's not science, that's spellcraft" (2019: 1, italics in original). Many researchers point to the interactivity of video games to explain their appeal, which is by now an obvious point. Yet, interactivity in itself isn't really what is so exciting. After all, a calculator responds to my inputs too. So, the pleasure of interactivity must require something more. What is needed is an explanation: what is it about interactivity that leads to this appeal?

One plausible answer is offered by Torben Grodal (2000, 2003). Both active and passive media are capable of evoking emotions—and sometimes strong emotional responses—but Grodal argues that emotional responses are strengthened in active media through the activation of motor neurons. Interactivity feels a certain way. One feels the interactivity of a game when perceptual representations are coupled with motor responses. Moreover, this coupling of perceptual representations with motor actions intensifies the emotional resonance of the represented content. This is a fascinating explanation because it both answers an interesting philosophical question about the nature of our emotional responses to fiction and it identifies why video games would be particularly effective instruments of fiction. That being said, Grodal's reliance on the function of motor neurons for his explanation raises some questions. It is certainly plausible that motor neurons function in the way Grodal describes, but the empirical evidence supporting this position is also incomplete.

Another answer locates the pleasure of interactivity in the player's sense of agency. We examined C. Thi Nguyen's (2020) account in the previous chapter. Nguyen situates his account within the framework of Bernard Suits' theory of games, which is limited to competitive games. Yet, agency certainly has a role to play in noncompetitive contexts as well. According to Nguyen, games offer players the opportunity to try on different kinds of agency. In the case of narrative play, it is the agency to try on different roles, scenarios, and character types. *Red Dead Redemption* offers me the opportunity to experience what it would be like to make decisions from the point of view of a barely reformed outlaw. I believe that Nguyen's account, once it is liberated from its restriction to Suitsian games, can be applied to narrative play too. In fact, much of my argument in the remainder of this section can be seen either as an attempt to extend Nguyen's account to narrative play or at least as a complimentary view alongside his.

While *agency* and *interactivity* are related concepts, I suggest that we see them as two distinct things: agency is the internal feeling of one's own ability, following Nguyen, while interactivity is a property of an artifact that is designed to facilitate experiences of agency. Put another way, agency is an aesthetic effect while interactivity is an artifactual property. It is interactivity that enables agency and choice. When video game developers design a game, they craft specific kinds of interactivity.[12] They decide what affordances to give to the player, when those affordances can be used, and what their effects and limits are. Choice is built into the structure of the artifact itself. In competitive video games, that choice is typically about what the player can do to affect the game state, while for a video game's embedded narrative, it is additionally a choice about how the story progresses and develops.

In the case of narrative play, interactivity becomes a source of aesthetic value when the player feels the weight of their choices. The missing ingredient to make interactivity a source of aesthetic interest is *consequence*. Interactive narratives give players choices, some of which are weighty and can have a significant impact on the eventual outcome of the game. The player is fully aware that their choices matter. Some choices are laid bare to the player (e.g., dialogue options) while other choices are implicit (e.g., the player's exploration). Part of the phenomenology of playing video games is the uncertainty of what to choose and the sense of meaningful deliberation. Moments of choice are often points in the game where the player must make a "forced choice"—that is, a choice that commits the player to some state of affairs that necessarily excludes certain other possibilities. Perhaps there are two (or more) potential allies that the player can choose from, but selecting one ally will turn the other into a rival. Or, perhaps there are two (or more) potential strategies that one could adopt to solve some problem, but selecting one strategy necessarily means abandoning the other. We could think of these as forks or branches in the storyline. Once the player makes the decision to choose one option over another, there is no going back. Branches might differ over their style of play—some branches might favor a direct, confrontational approach, while other branches might require a more subtle, strategic approach. Some branches might be consequential enough to lead to different endings of the game. Games that employ many different decision points might be structured such that decisions become compounded leading to unique possibilities later on in the game.

Despite however many choices we are asked to make in a game, we should not overestimate the degree of control and choice that the player actually has. Players can choose what happens in the narrative, but they can only choose from the options that are given to them by the game designer. Certain choices have been *sanctioned* by the game designer in advance—the player has effectively been given permission to have some control over this specific aspect of the game. Early in *The Walking Dead* (Season One), there is a scene where the player has the choice to save one person from a zombie attack. The player can only choose to save either Carley or Doug. That is a meaningful choice, but think about all the things that the player cannot choose: they cannot sacrifice themselves to save both, call someone else for help, or sadistically stand there and watch as both die. The limitations in narrative video games are no different than those of a choose-your-own-adventure book—while the reader has the choice to decide which branch of the story to follow, the author fully determines how the events play out in each branch.

The player's narrative choices are ultimately quite limited, but this does not diminish their value. Having more choices is less important than having meaningful choices. What diminishes the value of my choices is when I discover that my choices don't actually matter. In games like *Horizon Zero Dawn* and *Ghost of Tsushima*, my narrative choices are inconsequential.[13] It doesn't matter how Aloy responds to an NPC in a dialogue and it doesn't matter in what order Jin Sakai completes his missions. No matter what I choose, these stories go on just as they were written. Alternatively, games like *The Witcher 3* and *Dragon Age* offer the player choices with consequences. It matters to the story how Geralt responds to the NPCs and who the Grey Warden chooses to ally with.

There are two pieces of evidence that demonstrate the weightiness of narrative choices. First, walkthroughs of these games will often provide recommendations for dialogue options or strategy guides for choices. For instance, Geralt has a few romance options in *The Witcher 3*, but you have to play your cards right. There is no shortage of videos on YouTube made by players demonstrating how to achieve the "best" outcome. Players will look up decision trees for dialogues for the simple reason that it matters to them how the dialogue turns out. Second, and more importantly, games that offer consequential narrative choices are very satisfying to replay. Often, players will try to make choices that match what they really think is best during their first playthrough but will make different choices on subsequent playthroughs just to see what else the game offers (Lange 2014).

The aesthetic value of consequence in narrative games is grounded in the feeling that the narrative is contingent on the player—that the player feels that their actions and choices have *gravitas*. Choices become consequential and meaningful when some choices are perceived by the player to be "better" or "worse" and it is genuinely within the player's power to make a valuable choice. It is through replaying a game that the player can see for themselves what impact their choices have on the narrative. If it weren't for the player's actions, the world of the game would have been significantly different.

4 Narrative Role-Playing

Role-playing in video games is ubiquitous. It is hard to overstate how common or important it is. Roger Caillois identifies role-playing (or *mimicry*) as one of the four primary forms of play (2001: 19–23). Given the narrative potential of video games, it is not surprising that role-playing would figure so strongly. The aesthetic value of role-playing in video games can come in different forms, depending on whether the player takes a narrative attitude toward their play or a dollhouse attitude. Here, I will first talk about some general characteristics of role-playing in video games before considering its aesthetic value in narrative play. The main point that I will defend here is that there is a distinctively empathetic appreciation of video game characters and their plight that players can access by taking a narrative attitude to role-playing. We will return to the topic of role-playing in Chapter 5, where it again arises in dollhouse play.[14]

First, what is "role-playing"? This is an interesting question, but it is not my aim to offer a definition. José Zagal and Sebastian Deterding (2018) observe that role-playing happens in many different contexts and in different media—like tabletop games, single-player video games, multiplayer video games, and live-action games. In each context, different features of each game seem to have greater importance than other features in other contexts. This makes it difficult to offer a once-and-for-all definition of "role-playing." Fortunately, we don't need to worry about the different ways that role-playing arises in other contexts. Our aim is just to think about role-playing in video games. So, instead of trying to define "role-playing," we can take the easier route of simply stipulating the kind of phenomenon we are interested in. For our purposes, I am interested in a kind of relationship that players take to their avatars where players make both strategic and narrative decisions by imaginatively taking on roles that are different and distinct from the players themselves. Role-playing in a video game happens when the player's in-game decisions are not dominated by means–ends reasoning, nor is the player simply using the avatar as a digital proxy for themselves, but where the player's in-game decisions are influenced by factors having to do with the narrative or the perceived identity of the avatar.

In some video games, the main player-character has a distinct perspective or identity. When I play *Ghost of Tsushima*, I imagine that I am role-playing as Jin Sakai. I make decisions from Jin's point of view, which are informed by his values and circumstances. I don't make decisions based on what I imagine that *I* would do in his circumstances. Instead, I base my decisions on what I think would be authentic for *him*, which requires some judgment or interpretation on my part. On my playing of the game, I perceive Jin as noble, sincere, conscientious, and very anxious to minimize the suffering of the people of Tsushima. These are the values that inform my decision-making in that game—at least, when I am role-playing it. When I am role-playing a different game—for instance, *Red Dead Redemption 2*—I again try to make decisions that are authentic for my player-character. In this case, the main character is Arthur Morgan, a bandit and member of a criminal gang in the Wild West. To role-play as Arthur, I need to make decisions that are informed by his values, which often run contrary to my own. I perceive Arthur as overconfident, uncurious, and highly opportunistic, but also somewhat sentimental. When I am faced with a decision in *RDR2*, I try to imagine what an overconfident, uncurious, opportunistic, yet sentimental person would do.

Both of these examples are cases where the game offers the player a well-defined character. Jin and Arthur are richly designed characters complete with their own personalities, backstories, and values. In other role-playing games, the player gets to design the character themselves. When I play *Skyrim*, I might play as a female Breton mage who has traveled to Skyrim to study at the College of Winterhold. Everything about the character was designed by my choosing, from her appearance to her backstory. Nonetheless, I am still role-playing, though it is a role that I have designed myself. When I am faced with a decision in *Skyrim*, I try to imagine what would be an authentic decision for her. For instance, the story of *Skyrim* includes one subplot where dissatisfied Nords across the province have organized a rebellion against Imperial rule. The player has the option to either join the rebels or the Imperials, or they can try to stay neutral in the conflict. If I am playing as a Breton mage, I imagine that her motivation would be to keep the province of Skyrim in the Empire. After all, she is an outsider to Skyrim who benefits from the open borders within the Empire. I imagine that she fears breaking off the province from the Empire as it might mean that she would no longer be welcome to study at the College. However, I also imagine that she is sympathetic to the people of Skyrim and interested in their culture. So, perhaps she admires their desire to worship Talos, a religious practice that has been outlawed by the Empire.

Role-playing is about decision-making. It is about making decisions from the perspective of some role. Whenever we play a video game, we are making strategic decisions from *some* perspective, even if it is an abstract one. *Sid Meier's Civilization VI* is a turn-based strategy game where the player takes on the role of a godlike ruler in their quest to create the greatest nation on Earth. The player follows their civilization over millennia, guiding them to evolve, establish new cities, and wage war against their rivals. At every turn, the player will have certain affordances and limitations, given what technologies and resources their civilization has to hand. To play the game well, the player must consider those affordances and limitations, and thus make decisions from that point of view. This is interesting, but it isn't yet a case of role-playing. The *Civilization* player can choose what to do moment-to-moment purely strategically, like one would in a game of chess. However, when they are role-playing, strategic considerations are just one part of how players make decisions. In addition to strategic considerations, the player also considers narrative elements—the character's backstory, values, and beliefs. If I decide to attack a neighboring city out of revenge for some slight that I suffered from them earlier in the game, then I'm starting to role-play.

Of course, decisions and motivations can be complex. One of the (enjoyable) struggles of video games is balancing my narrative interests against my goal-seeking interests. This struggle can lead to indecision, as when my desire for an interesting story conflicts with what I think is in my goal-seeking interests. Returning to the example of *Skyrim*, I might think that my Breton mage would want to remain loyal to the Empire, but she might also worry that siding with the Imperials would put her at odds with the Nords, thus making her time at the College of Winterhold difficult. Still, these kinds of motivational conflicts are part of what makes gameplay meaningful.

What kind of play doesn't count as role-playing? Players can take different kinds of relationships to their avatars.[15] Role-playing is one kind, which is a form of decision-making that takes narrative elements into account. A second kind of relationship is when a player views their avatar as a proxy or a representative of themselves in a game world, which we could think of as *embodiment*. In virtual reality spaces like Meta's *Horizon Worlds*, I might design my avatar to be an idealized version of myself. I make decisions from my own point of view, where the values that inform my decision-making are my real-world values. I might have a meeting with my colleagues or teach a class where my students all meet with me in VR. In these cases, I am not acting out a role that is distinct from myself—I am not role-playing. Instead, I am acting in the gameworld as myself but doing so *through* my avatar. In these cases, whatever decision-making I engage in is informed by my real-world values. After all, my colleagues and students are interacting with *me*, albeit through a digital proxy.

A third kind of relationship between a player and their avatar is when players disregard the avatar's identity entirely, which we could call *instrumentalism*. In these cases, I don't care what the avatar's backstory is, or whether they even have a backstory. Additionally, I don't construct a backstory for them, nor do I imagine that they have values or identities. Instead, I merely regard the avatar as a digital object—a tool or an instrument—through which I interact with the game. For instance, a *Hearthstone* player might not know Jaina Proudmoore's backstory, care about it, or imaginatively refer to her identity as a factor in their decision-making. Similarly, the *Clash Royale* player likely doesn't think about the Valkyrie's identity, her values, or her motivations when playing her on the field. In these cases, decision-making is dominated by means–ends reasoning for the sake of goal-seeking. Instances of instrumental play are not cases of role-playing—that is, the player doesn't role-play as Jaina or as a Valkyrie. Instead, these characters are merely digital objects that have a specific function within the game. This sort of instrumental relationship is likely very common in highly competitive games where players choose to employ some avatar for purely strategic reasons.

Reiterating a point from earlier, decisions and motivations can be complex, and these three different player–avatar relationships are often comingled. It is unlikely that any player forms just one relationship to their avatar unflinchingly. Whenever human psychology is involved, we shouldn't expect neat and tidy. Instead, the player's relationship to their avatar is messy and changeable. In one moment, I might be role-playing as a character in the narrative, making decisions that I think are authentic for that character. In the next moment, I make decisions from my own perspective, imagining what *I* would do if I were in *that* situation. And in other moments, I might regard the avatar as nothing more than an instrument that has distinctive affordances and limitations. This changeability isn't really a problem, not for players at least. It may be difficult for philosophers and game theorists to describe these rapidly changing motivations, but players themselves seem to have no trouble with the fluidity of their player–avatar relationships.

What aesthetic contribution can role-playing make to the player's narrative appreciation of video games? Let's think about how narrative role-playing answers questions about what the character does. Partly, the player must consider their affordances and limitations—what they are capable of doing given the resources and skills that they currently possess. But crucially, the narrative role-player also considers the character's perspective when making decisions. What would the character want? What do they value? What would be an authentic choice for them? This last question is interesting because an authentic choice for the character might be an inauthentic choice for the player. This happens often. I neither share Jin Sakai's rigid notion of duty nor Arthur Morgan's criminal tendencies, yet I can still play these characters with some conviction. To make a choice that would be authentic for these characters, I need to enter into their perspectives. Basically, I need to empathize with them.

Despite the fact that video game characters are not real people and don't really have feelings, video games can still be an effective vehicle for empathy.[16] There has been considerable debate about what "empathy" is (see Matravers 2017 for an overview). Briefly, I understand empathy to be a form of imaginative perspective shifting that results in some shared mental state with another. Empathy involves imaginatively taking the perspective of another, and, having done so, one comes to understand what another person thinks (Spaulding 2017; Stueber

2006; Waldow 2019) or feels (Matravers 2017). Video games are an excellent medium for empathetic fiction. The reason for this is because video games are well-suited to foregrounding what is distinctive of another's perspective—their abilities, limitations, and circumstances.[17] As we discussed above, players always have to make in-game decisions from some perspective. I decide what strategies to pursue by thinking about my character's abilities and limitations. Moreover, I come to *see* challenges in the game from the character's perspective. I perceive certain enemies as being particularly fearsome in the early stages of a game when my character is fairly weak. After enough levelling-up, my view of them changes. And that change in my perception is one instance of a mental state that I (fictionally) share with the protagonist. In the early stages of *Horizon Zero Dawn*, I see the prospect of harvesting resources from a herd of grazers as a challenge that requires some strategy, stealth, and all my attention. But after a certain point, a herd of grazers is no challenge for me anymore. Importantly, I imagine that Aloy feels the same way too (Cf. Tavinor 2005). At Level-1, when Aloy is hiding in the grass from the grazers, I feel the tension and anxiety that she (fictionally) feels; while at Level-20, when Aloy is running headlong into a herd of grazers, I feel the exhilaration and confidence that she (fictionally) feels. This is possible because I have come to share her perspective and to view the world through her eyes.

Now, to see the role of empathetic play in narratives, we just have to add one more thought: when I am engaged in narrative role-playing, I come to see the world not just through the lens of Aloy's abilities and limitations but also through the lens of her values, history, and identity. I perceive some NPCs as mean and petty, like High Matriarch Lansra, because I remember Aloy's time as an outcast. I make decisions about how to respond to Lansra through the background of that history. And I respond to confrontations with Lansra with disgust and disappointment because I have come to see her as Aloy sees her. The aesthetic value of this form of narrative play is (in part) due to the way that empathetic play in video games provides a deeper understanding of the character. It enables a kind of emotional engagement that rivals the aesthetic potential of some of the best fiction. To return to the example of *RDR*, I am choked-up by feelings of hope and longing to see Abigail again because I've come to see the world through John Marston's eyes.

Narrative role-playing is a special kind of player–avatar relationship because it can act as a vehicle to provoke empathy in players. The other avatar–player relationships that were discussed earlier—embodiment and instrumentalism—cannot provoke empathy. In the case of embodiment, the reason for this is obvious: the player does not engage in any form of perspective shifting when the avatar acts as their digital proxy. I cannot empathize with the avatar that I use in my VR classroom because it is just a tool I use to act through it. And, in the case of instrumentalism, the player does not consider the avatar's identity at all. The kind of empathetic play that I have described here only works when the player engages in narrative role-playing.

5 Summing Up

Narrative play is a rich and distinctive form of video game play. It might not be for everyone. But it doesn't have to be for everyone to still be valuable. I have argued here that there are numerous places where players who take a narrative attitude can look to find aesthetically valuable experiences in video games. Players construct emergent narratives through their own action and the choices they make regarding the narrative structure of a game. Embedded narratives are richly filled out by careful worldbuilding and lore. Meaningful and consequential choices can spark delicious moments of indecision for the player who is looking for the "best" conclusion of the story. Finally, narrative role-playing offers a powerful tool to better understand video game characters through empathetic play. Narrative play might not be for everyone, but those who neglect it might just be missing out.

5

Dollhouse Aesthetics

Ghost of Tsushima is a video game exclusive to the PlayStation that was released in 2020. Set in the thirteenth century, it is an open-world game where the player takes control of Jin Sakai, a samurai who survived the initial invasion of Mongol forces on the Japanese island of Tsushima. Gamers drawn to goal-seeking play would have much to appreciate about the game. The gameplay primarily revolves around melee combat, though players can also develop skills using ranged weapons and stealth attacks. *Ghost of Tsushima* also offers an online, multiplayer mode where players compete in teams to complete various challenges.

Those looking for narrative play will find a game with a rich and detailed story. Jin was trained to value honor above all else. An honorable warrior is one who faces down an enemy, looking them in the eye with respect and without resorting to tricks and deceit. However, Jin's commitment to the samurai honor code is tested when Mongol invaders brutally kill, torture, and terrorize the people of Tsushima. Faced with an overwhelming force, one that is too large to take on directly, Jin turns to guerilla tactics to spread terror among the invaders and to inspire those survivors that he can find to organize a resistance. The story is a fascinating meditation on the limits of honor.

When I first played through *Ghost of Tsushima*, there was one aspect of it that perplexed me. Scattered across the island of Tsushima are many different kinds of collectable items that allow the player to customize their avatar. There are many different suits of armor that the player can collect, each one offering the player different abilities and bonuses that become useful in different scenarios. If I need to be stealthy, I put on the *ronin* armor, while a big fight calls for the clan Sakai armor. The player can collect many items of headwear, like hats, headbands, and masks. There are also decorative saddles, sword kits, bow wraps, and armor dyes. It takes considerable time and effort to collect all the items that one can in the game. But it can be worth it. In many games, different kinds of armor provide various strategic advantages. So, I threw myself into collecting every hat, headband, and sword kit that I could find; but I was surprised that these items in particular had no impact on the gameplay or the narrative.

Here are two questions to ask. First, why would players spend time collecting items that neither offer any gameplay benefits nor open any new story content? One reason to collect them all is for the sake of completionism. Many players take pride in "platinuming" a game— finding every bit of content that the game designers included and achieving a 100 percent completion rate. This is the familiar kind of play that we expect from video games—they offer contests, puzzles, and challenges that require players to hone their skills, and platinuming the game is just one more challenge to overcome. Many games award these players with a special trophy for achieving completion. Players who are motivated to platinum *Ghost of Tsushima* are taking a goal-seeking attitude to the collection of all the wearable items in the game.

The second question is where it gets interesting: why bother to *change* Jin Sakai's hat? If your aim is either to complete the game or enjoy the story, then once you have discovered that the hats and headbands do nothing, there is no reason for the player to ever change their headwear. You might *collect* every piece of headwear in order to platinum the game, but you don't have to *wear* every piece. By contrast, the various kinds of armor offer different advantages, so the goal-seeking player has a good reason to change their armor in response to the challenges that they face. But this is not the case for headwear. There is no reason for the player to change their hat if their aims are goal-seeking play or narrative play.[1] The player can just put on the first hat that they find and leave it on for the rest of the game.

However, if I always have the same hat on, then my character *looks* dumb. I can't let Jin Sakai run around wearing a hat that doesn't match his armor. What would the other samurai think?! I can just imagine Sensei Ishikawa's disapproval, charging in with my hakama half-tied. I often find myself picking through my collection of headwear to find just the right piece. I have some favorite pieces as well as some that I never use. And some hats look better with different kinds of armor. If I dye my armor, then I have to try on different headbands to see which color combinations look best. But, at that point, what am I doing? Am I not just playing dress-up? I am making aesthetic choices for my avatar, not strategic goal-seeking choices or narrative choices. Jin Sakai is effectively a digital doll and I'm changing his outfits.

Dollhouse play is one of the three main attitudes that video game players take. It is distinctive for its lack of means–ends reasoning, its de-emphasis on goals and quantifiable outcomes, and for the way that players project their own stories onto a game's world and characters. In this chapter, we will examine the main forms of dollhouse play in video games and consider what makes those aesthetically valuable. Here is my plan. First, I will consider some other related terms that are often used in game criticism—specifically, open-world games, sandboxes, and cozy games—in an attempt to refine the concept of dollhouse play further in Section 1. Then, I will talk about the three main forms of dollhouse play for video games in Section 2: dress-up, collecting, and role-playing. Dollhouse play is subtly distinct from both goal-seeking play and narrative play, but it still involves its own special kinds of goals and narratives. In Section 3, we will examine how goals and narratives can figure in dollhouse play. Section 4 will examine the transformative value of the dollhouse attitude using an extended discussion of *American Truck Simulator*. Finally, in Section 5, I'll make some speculative comments about why video games are particularly good at enabling dollhouse play.

Before getting started, I want to make an admission: researching the topic for this chapter was the most difficult. The aspect of video game play that I'm trying to get at here—which is something like toy-play—has been noticed by other theorists, but it hasn't been the focus of much scholarly attention. The kind of play that I'm interested in has been around for a while and game developers have long been aware of its "different" status. Satoru Iwata, president and CEO of Nintendo until his death in 2015, was quoted as using the term "non-game game" to describe a video game that "doesn't have a winner, or even a real conclusion" (Casamassina 2005). Will Wright is the game designer behind *SimCity* and *The Sims*, who is noted for describing his games as "software toys" and particularly for describing *The Sims* as an "interactive doll house" (Seabrook 2006).

Some video game theorists have hinted at the possibility of dollhouse play, but thinking deeply about it hasn't been a major concern. Still, some theorists have developed ideas that intersect with my notion of dollhouse play in helpful ways. In Chapter 2, we briefly talked about Ian Bogost's (2010) criticism of casual games and Jesper Juul's (2013) point about games of labor.[2] Both of those theorists have noticed that there is something more to video games that isn't captured by goal-seeking play and narrative play. Mia Consalvo and Christopher Paul's (2019) work on why some games are considered "real games" while others are not is also related. Not surprisingly, video games that primarily focus on dollhouse play are typically dismissed as "not real games." Finally, some scholarly work on video games marketed to girls notes a de-emphasis on competitive play and a greater emphasis on social play. Rosa Martey and Jennifer Stromer-Galley (2007) analyze how players navigate social interactions following real-world social expectations in *The Sims Online*, which they describe as a "dollhouse-like environment." Elisabeth Hayes and Elizabeth King (2009) describe how *The Sims 2* is "more than a dollhouse" as it offers female players a chance to develop internet and computer skills.[3] Karen Wohlwend (2017) offers a fascinating analysis of play trends across *Monster High* games where she identifies "dress-up, toy collecting, and doll play" as the "familiar practices" associated with dollhouses, which is the nearest precursor to my notion of dollhouse play that I have found. These studies are helpful and highly instructive, but they do not directly address our main questions: what is distinctive of dollhouse play? And what is its aesthetic impact?

Turning finally to the few philosophers who have written about games and play, it is unfortunate that even fewer have had anything to say about toys. Both Johan Huizinga and Roger Caillois mention toys and toy-play, but their comments are very general. Walter Benjamin, who wrote two reviews in 1928—one about a book on the history of toys and one on an exhibition of toys at the Märkisches Museum in Berlin—is perhaps the most directly helpful here. Though his essays are very brief, Benjamin offers some speculative comments on the nature and value of toys. One particularly intriguing comment is where he notes that toys are often imposed on children by adults. Because toys are typically designed by adults, and given to children by adults, most toys are really an adult's idea of what a child would find interesting. According to Benjamin, it is through the child's imagination that the object really becomes a toy (1999a: 118). Interestingly, the same thing can be said about video games: it is through the player's imagination, through taking the right attitude, that digital objects in video games become objects of dollhouse play.

There hasn't been a lot written about toy-play in video games, and extremely little has been written from a philosophical perspective. So, I don't have the benefit of commenting on something that has been widely discussed. Therefore, much of what I am going to say in this chapter is going to be speculative. I'm sure that I am going to get some things wrong and also overlook some possibilities. Still, my aim in this chapter is to say something suggestive and worthwhile, even if it is not definitive.

1 Dollhouse Play Compared to Open-worlds, Sandboxes, and Cozy Games

"Dollhouse play" is closely related to some existing terms that people already use in gaming—specifically, open-world games, sandboxes, and cozy games. Each of these terms overlaps with what I am calling "dollhouse play," but either the overlap isn't perfect or it doesn't emphasize the right things, which is why I think the term "dollhouse" is more fitting.

There is a strong overlap between dollhouse play and open-world games. Because the player can move around the map freely and access the missions in the order of their choosing, the player is therefore also free to ignore the missions set by the game and go off on their own imaginative adventures. So, the open-world structure of the narrative lends itself to some key forms of dollhouse play. However, there are other forms of dollhouse play that have nothing to do with the open-world narrative structure, and some games that are not open-world still allow players to play dress-up or engage in collecting. So, the open-world structure isn't a necessary feature of dollhouse play.

The same is true of sandbox games. The term "sandbox" is often used to refer to play that is free and explorative. *Minecraft* is the quintessential example of a sandbox game. While players can play in "survival mode" and attempt to defeat the Ender Dragon, the vast majority of the time that players spend in *Minecraft* has nothing to do with the pursuit of these goals. Instead, *Minecraft* is a space where players can freely build and explore, which sounds a lot like dollhouse play. Certainly, dollhouse play requires a degree of freedom and a lack of obligations. The player needs the space to construct their own aims and goals, which is exactly what a sandbox game provides. But, just like with "open-world," there are forms of dollhouse play that happen even in games that are not sandboxes. A game doesn't have to be a sandbox to play dress-up with it.

Two other reasons to prefer using the term "dollhouse" over either "open-world" or "sandbox" are these. First, the term "dollhouse" is a nice tribute to Will Wright, creator of *The Sims*, given his explicit goal of creating an interactive dollhouse. Second, the term "dollhouse" nicely emphasizes the importance of dress-up play. Dress-up is a central part of what people do with dolls, and it is one of the most common and widespread forms of toy-play in video games. So, using the word "dollhouse" helps to highlight that.

The idea of "cozy games" has become popular recently. While the definition of the term is still being debated, it is typically used to talk about video games that focus on nonviolent play, cooperative actions, or gameplay that revolves around domestic life. A useful and constructive definition of cozy games comes from Daniel Cook (2018), who identifies cozy games as typified by their *safety* (a lack of danger and risk), *abundance* (the needs of survival are met), and *softness* (there is a general mood of comfort and low anxiety).[4] Cook relates the value of cozy games to their ability to satisfy some of the higher stages of A. H. Maslow's (1943) hierarchy of needs. According to the original formulation of the theory, Maslow posited that human motivations form a fairly stable hierarchy, which he identified as physiological needs, needs of safety, love, esteem, and self-actualization (1943: 372–83). Cook observes that most video games focus on the satisfaction of lower needs, like survival and safety; however, cozy games offer the player guaranteed survival and safety, which frees the player to pursue goals like love, esteem, and self-actualization (2018).[5]

However we define it, you know a cozy game when you see one. *Unpacking* is a game where the player follows the life of a woman from girlhood to college to marriage. We never see the woman on-screen, but we see her stuff in moving boxes at the start of each stage of her life. The player's job is to unpack her stuff and neatly arrange things in her new apartment. It is very cozy. But it is *not* a dollhouse game. *Unpacking* is a spatial puzzle game. The challenge is to unpack everything neatly and the player cannot move on to the next stage until everything is put in its proper place. It is a goal-seeking game, one that offers no opportunities for dress-up, collecting, or role-playing. What makes it "cozy" is the fact that there are no time limits and the player isn't punished harshly when they put something in the wrong place. Misplaced objects will flash red until the player moves it to somewhere more appropriate. The only punishment is that the player cannot yet move on to the next level. So, cozy games are not necessarily dollhouse games.

Instead, I suggest that "cozy" is a distinctive aesthetic quality that some games have, but the kinds of games that have this cozy aesthetic may come in any form of play—goal-seeking, narrative, or dollhouse. For example, the developer of *Stardew Valley*, Eric Barone, organized a tournament in 2021, called the *Stardew Valley Cup*, where players compete in teams to complete as many challenges as possible within three hours (Yu 2021). Clearly, tournament players are taking a goal-seeking attitude toward the game, but this doesn't change anything about the cozy qualities of *Stardew Valley*. A consequence of this view is that coziness is not a distinctive quality of dollhouse play. When I am looking for the right hat for Jin Sakai to wear in *Ghost of Tsushima*, I am engaging in the dollhouse play of dress-up, but there is nothing cozy about *Ghost of Tsushima*.

Dollhouse play is conceptually related to open-world games and sandbox games, but it is also distinct from them. Some dollhouse play is cozy, but the cozy aesthetic is not a distinctive feature of dollhouse play. Dollhouse play is distinct and unique in its own right. Still, I anticipate that some readers might be resistant to use the term "dollhouse" because of its feminine associations. Gaming has long been a site of gendered conflict, having been associated with masculinity from its earliest days despite the fact that women have been present in gaming and the gaming industry all along (Kocurek 2015). Many gamers today still hold this old-fashioned view and are hostile to anything feminine or female-associated in games. There are other related terms that have feminine associations, and for that reason, some readers might be resistant to them also. Gamers use "customization" instead of "dress-up" even though they effectively mean the same thing—making aesthetic choices that have no strategic or narrative impact. The same is true of the terms "doll" and "action figure"—there is no difference between a doll and an action figure, except for the expected gender of the user. "Action figure" is the male-appropriate term for dolls, just as "customization" is the male-appropriate term for playing dress-up. I am not interested in perpetuating the stereotype that gaming is a male activity, so I am going to use the words "dollhouse" and "dress-up."

2 The Main Forms of Dollhouse Play

In this section, I will briefly describe the main forms of dollhouse play—dress-up, collecting, and role-playing—and make some suggestions about why these forms of play are aesthetically valuable. The discussion of each will necessarily be very brief. There is far more that can be said, and, in the case of role-playing, far more has already been said by other scholars. My aim here is not to offer an exhaustive theory of each, but rather to describe why these kinds of play fall under the dollhouse attitude while paying attention to their potential for aesthetic value.

2.1 Dress-Up

When children play with dolls and action figures, changing their outfits, brushing their hair, and attaching accessories is often a large part of what they do. Oddly enough, gamers do the same things. While some video games are expressly dress-up and make-up games—like *DIY Paper Doll* or *Barbie Dreamhouse Adventures*—big "Triple-A" action video games will offer substantial customization options too. It is extremely common in role-playing games for the player to customize their avatar at the start of the game. In many games, the player customizes their avatar at the beginning and then they are stuck with that look throughout. Other games allow the player to update their look. In *Red Dead Redemption 2* (*RDR2*), the player can take Arthur to the barber shop to cut and style his hair and beard, which keeps growing throughout the game. In *Cyberpunk 2077*, the player can continue to update the avatar's look as they go. Games can receive praise for their customization options. For instance, *Baldur's Gate 3* has been noted as offering exceptionally good options (Shepard 2023). Games can also be highly criticized for offering poor, unworkable, or disappointingly narrow customization options. In particular, options for Black hair have been notably lacking, and for a long time (Winslow and Colbert 2023).

Customizing the avatar is the most obvious example of dress-up play, but avatars are not the only things that can be customized in video games. Inanimate objects and environments can be customized in some games too. Many games allow players to change the appearance of things like their weapons and vehicles. *Counter Strike: Global Offensive* is a multiplayer first-person shooter where players compete in teams. It is a highly competitive esports game. Players can get cosmetic finishes for their weapons—or "skins"—either by receiving them in a loot drop or by purchasing them. These cosmetic skins give the player no tactical advantage in the game. It is ultimately an aesthetic choice. In this case, players are playing dress-up with a gun. Another example is *Gran Turismo 7*, which is a highly realistic auto racing game. There are many cars that the player can choose from, and there are many options for changing the color, the rims, and adding racing decals. When gamers customize their cars, they are basically playing dress-up, but their doll is car-shaped. (As I write this, I can almost hear the angry bros screaming at the page, "That's not dress-up!" Okay, but if it is not dress-up, then what is it? When players make cosmetic choices in a game that offer no strategic advantage and have no impact on the narrative, then you are aestheticizing a toy. Call that whatever you want. I call it "dress-up.")

Environments in some games can also be customized. These are cases where the player is decorating a space, not just an avatar or an object. *LittleBigPlanet* is a puzzle platformer where the player collects stickers and uses them to decorate a navigation pod and parts of the gameworld. Other games offer players the opportunity to decorate a house. There are games that are essentially interior design simulators—*Kawaii Home Design*, *Design My Room*, and *Home Design 3D*. Other games offer decorating not as a primary activity but definitely as a strong secondary activity. For instance, social massively multiplayer online games like *Second Life*, *The Sims Online*, and *Habbo* allow players to purchase furniture and decorations for their rooms where players can hang out and interact with each other online. Decorating a room in a multiplayer social game makes some intuitive sense—socializing in a bare, empty room would just be sad. It is likely that the desire to decorate a space in these games can be explained partly as a social requirement. But there are also single-player games where decorating is an option.

There are houses that players can decorate in *Elder Scrolls: Skyrim* and *The Legend of Zelda: Breath of the Wild* (*BOTW*). In these games, there is no expectation that other players will see inside my house. The player is decorating for themselves only.

Why do players customize their avatars? Why spend your precious gaming time making what are essentially empty aesthetic choices? There are no single answers to these questions, and so there is likely no single explanation of the aesthetic value and pleasure of customization. But it would be interesting and helpful to think about some of the possible motivations. For some players, their avatar is an idealized projection of their real-world sense of self in the gameworld; but that doesn't always mean that the avatar looks just like the player. Some players try to recreate themselves in digital form, while other players try to create an avatar that expresses what the player wishes they looked like in real life.[6] For yet other players, the avatar is just a doll that they role-play with. And my attitude toward my avatar changes from one game to the next. When I play *World of Warcraft*, I might make an avatar who looks like me, and I might think of my avatar as my projected identity in the game; but when I play *Ghost of Tsushima*, I don't worry that Jin Sakai doesn't look like me, and I don't think that Jin is a projection of me.

Sometimes we dress-up our avatars because it is part of a role-playing game (see Section 2.3 below). Role-playing is not the same thing as identity projection. When I customize an avatar because I want it to project *my* identity into the gameworld, I am not role-playing. Instead, I am creating a digital representative for myself. Role-playing is when we imagine being someone else and acting *as if* we inhabited that role. I will never be a samurai, but I can imagine playing that role. Role-playing involves an interestingly complex imaginative state. By imagining what it is like to be Jin Sakai, I experience a little bit of his emotional state. I feel some shame and regret when I fail to live up to the samurai code, and I feel pride when I face my enemies head-on. Customizing my avatar to dress him in the proper clothes heightens the role-playing experience. When I dress Jin in the right armor and pair it with the right headwear, I am imaginatively putting myself in Jin's position, thinking about what would be authentic to him and finding the right way to visually express his ideals and values. In these cases, dress-up is an indispensable part of immersing myself in the fantasy of role-playing a samurai.

One final possibility is that, while dress-up with a toy is a form of aestheticizing the toy, it can also be a form of caring for it. This is likely more applicable to physical toys than video games, but it still deserves some brief mention. When a child changes a doll's clothes and brushes its hair, it is clearly doing so not just for the sake of how it looks. The child is paying attention to the toy in a caring way, just as one would do in real life with a pet. Think about video games where the player has a customizable animal companion, like *The Sims* or *Second Life*. Players might change the appearance of their animal companion partly out of purely aesthetic concerns, but the player is also showing some level of care for it. While this could be another instance of role-playing (specifically, role-playing the part of a pet owner), it is equally possible that the player treats the digital animal as if it was a pet—essentially, like a Tamagotchi.

2.2 Collecting

Collecting is a common practice in real life that nearly everyone participates in to some degree. Some people have a vinyl record collection, some people collect shoes, many people have book collections. These collections might be fairly small-scale. My personal book collection is not nearly as large as I would like it to be. There are other people who have more extensive collections—like, an entire wall of *Funko Pops!* figurines, or a room full of Lego sets, or a pair of Nike Air Jordans for every model produced. Considering how common collecting is in real life, it is not surprising that the desire to collect things arises in video games too.

One clarification: I am not talking about *collecting video games themselves*. While that is interesting, it is really no different from any other kind of real-world collection, like collecting comic books or movie posters. Instead, I am talking about *collecting digital objects in video games*. Think of the player who has a complete collection of the lore books in *Skyrim*. It would take considerable time and effort to amass this book collection, just like collecting books in the real world. Except that these are imaginary books. They only exist in the fictional world of *Elder Scrolls*. Or, think of all of the deck building games available, like *Clash Royale*, *Gwent*, *Hearthstone*, and the Pokémon video games. Some players might attempt to collect every type of card or every type of Pokémon but have no intention of playing them in their battle deck.

Why would someone bother to collect something that they have no intention to use? Not all collectors are alike. I can think of at least three reasons, which we could call *intrinsic*, *extrinsic*, and *indirect* reasons. *Intrinsic* collectors collect things simply because they like them. The player finds some *intrinsic* value in the object. In *Skyrim*, a player might collect a full suit of glass armor because they like the way that it looks. Perhaps it isn't the best armor that the player owns, so they don't wear it into battle. Rather than get rid of it, they might display the armor in one of their houses. *Extrinsic* collectors do not necessarily like the objects they collect or find them intrinsically valuable. Instead, extrinsic collectors hope that the objects they collect will be useful one day. The value comes from its anticipated use, not from the object itself. I might collect a full suit of glass armor because I believe that it might be useful in some upcoming mission. This form of collecting is really motivated by means–ends reasoning, so it is not actually an instance of dollhouse play. If my only reason to collect something is because I believe that it will get me something else that I really want, then I'm not really collecting. I'm just investing.[7] Finally, some collectors value the objects that they collect *indirectly*. Imagine a player who sets out to collect the rarest suits of armor in *Skyrim* because doing so is challenging. They have no intention of using the armor in battle, so their interest in the armor is not extrinsic. But their interest isn't intrinsic either. What this player really values *is the challenge*—acquiring the rarest suits of armor is a difficult task. Another way to think of it is that the indirect collector cares primarily about the provenance of the armor—where it came from, who was the previous owner, and how difficult it was to find.[8] These are not intrinsic properties of the armor; instead, they are contingent or relational properties.

Is collecting in video games an aesthetic practice? Is there an aesthetic pleasure to collecting? Both the intrinsic and indirect forms of collecting are likely to be aesthetically relevant to dollhouse play. Kevin Melchionne (1999) offers an interesting theory that I believe can be applied to both. According to Melchionne, a collection is a group of objects that the collector finds aesthetically interesting and displays them together. The objects selected for the display have some common link for the collector. Maybe the collector likes the way that they look together or maybe there is some common aesthetic quality that is shared by each object in the collection. In these cases, the collection itself reveals something about the collector's tastes. Collecting and displaying is a form of "taste-formation" (1999: 154). The collector is showing us a particular way of viewing the objects together and valuing them. What matters for the intrinsic collector is that the objects themselves are special and worthwhile in some way, and this is true not only for my real-life book collection, but even for my armor collection in *Skyrim*. The same point holds for the indirect collector too, but with the caveat that the quality that makes the object worthwhile is something contingent and relational. Some of the armor that I collect in *Skyrim* is intrinsically valuable to me because I like the way that it looks, but other pieces of armor are indirectly valuable to me because of their rareness or the difficulty that I endured to collect them.

Melchionne's theory hints at something that is easy to overlook—that there are really two aspects to collecting: there is the act of *acquiring* stuff and the act of *displaying* it. Collecting isn't just about acquisition. It is also about display. Think about literal dollhouses: some adults keep a dollhouse, but they don't play with it. They will instead use them as displays. Some will stage a scene in their dollhouse, setting up a tableau using dolls and their furniture, with no intention of touching them or playing with them further. Or think again about book collections: it is not just a pile of books, but also a display set up like trophies on a shelf—we keep books that we don't intend to read again because they represent ideas that we have conquered. One of the main distinctions between video games that involve some form of collecting is that some allow a collection to be displayed while others do not. *Minecraft* is a game that is not only about building but also about displaying impressive builds on the public servers. By contrast, I might take some pleasure in collecting and maxing out all the available cards in *Clash Royale*, but I can't easily display that to anyone. When I display my collection of armor in the single-player campaign of *Skyrim*, other people can see my collection only if I stream my game on Twitch or Discord, or if I record a video walk-through of my collection and post it to YouTube.

Melchionne's account is interesting, and I believe that it is a correct assessment of what happens when collectors make fairly formal displays of their collections. But the theory also has its limitations. Most people's collections tend to be a bit more haphazard than Melchionne's account acknowledges. For many collectors, I'm sure there is no singular thread running through their collection that explains why *these* objects are worthwhile to the collector, or why they are displayed together. But this point aside, Melchionne's theory is still helpful for us.

What about the extrinsic collector? The extrinsic collector doesn't care about any particular formal quality of the object at all. And they don't care about its indirect value either. Instead, the extrinsic collector really just hoards objects that might be useful someday. When I start playing a new game, I am often uncertain what will be useful to me later on. Should I pick up every stick, flower, and rock that I find? At the start of a game, I don't know. So, to be safe, I just start picking up everything until I figure out what I use most often. At this point, I am collecting objects for their potential extrinsic value. This kind of collecting doesn't seem to have much aesthetic value. If extrinsic collecting is aesthetically relevant at all, then it is likely a form of completionism, which would fall under the aesthetics of goal-seeking play.

2.3 Role-Playing

We previously discussed some aspects of the aesthetics of role-playing in video games in Chapter 4, where we considered how some role-playing is clearly motivated by the attitude of narrative play.[9] There, we examined how players relate to their avatar in a few distinct ways. I argued that role-playing occurs when players make decisions in the game that are influenced by the narrative or the perceived identity of the avatar. When players take a narrative attitude, they role-play by taking on the identity of the player-character as it has been defined by the game designer and attempt to make decisions from the perspective of that character. I referred to this simply as *narrative role-playing*. When I role-play as Jin Sakai, I make decisions from his point of view, which are informed by his values and circumstances. My decisions are informed by my understanding of the narrative and the character's identity. I try to imagine what *this character* would do in *this situation*. My aim is to construct a satisfying narrative, given what I know about the plot, by playing the character in a way that I perceive as authentic *for him*.

Dollhouse role-playing is subtly different. This occurs when the character's identity, backstory, and values are projected onto the game by the player. *I* am the one who decides who my character is and what they value. This counts as a form of role-playing because I am not playing *as myself*—it is not embodiment—but I am also not beholden to the game designer's vision of who the character is. The character and their identity are *my* inventions. Dollhouse role-playing can be imaginatively demanding—like when players invent whole backstories for their avatars—or it can be very casual—where players merely imagine a brief scenario. In many respects, dollhouse role-playing is just like narrative role-playing—they are both forms of role-play after all; however, there is an important difference between having a character defined *for* me (narrative) and defining my character *myself* (dollhouse). The distinction here is analogous to the distinction between an actor who plays a clearly defined character in a play and an actor who fully improvises their role.

The aesthetic value of dollhouse role-playing is complex and informed by a number of factors. Here, we will briefly consider three. First, dollhouse role-playing is aesthetically valued for the novelty of inhabiting a unique role. In my real life, I am (sadly) not an elf mage, but I get to play one in *Dragon Age: Origins*. This gives me the opportunity to make decisions from a perspective that is so different from my real-life perspective. As we discussed in Chapter 2, C. Thi Nguyen (2020) argues that there is a distinctive aesthetic value that players take from exercising unique forms of agency in games. While Nguyen's account largely examines goal-seeking play—and specifically play that satisfies a Suitsian account of games—the sort of agential decision-making that is valued in his account clearly also arises in dollhouse role-playing.

The value of dollhouse role-play also has something to do with self-directed, improvisational storytelling: the player improvises their own story through the act of playing and the player takes some pleasure in their own creativity.[10] Players take ownership of their characters, but they also take ownership of the stories that arise from their adventures. When playing a multiplayer role-playing game, there is an additional pleasure that comes from telling a story together.

Finally, the value of dollhouse role-play has something to do with the freedom of play—the freedom to pursue whatever actions interest the player without worrying about whether their efforts serve some instrumental need. One of my students once told me about how, when he plays *RDR2*, he completely ignores the story and missions. Instead, he likes to go fishing, camping, and riding his horse. Effectively, he plays *RDR2* as a camping-and-fishing simulator.[11] The pleasure he takes from the game has nothing to do with either competition or the story. It is the pleasure of free play.

3 Goals and Narratives in Dollhouse Play

Dollhouse play is distinct from both goal-seeking play and narrative play; however, this does not mean that dollhouse play is devoid of both goals and narratives. When players take a dollhouse attitude, they still pursue goals and engage with a story, but the goals and stories that feature in dollhouse play are subtly different.

Games are designed with specific goals built in—like rescuing the princess, getting the highest score, or killing the ancient dragon. Goals like these are imposed on the player. By taking a goal-seeking attitude, the player takes these goals at face value, accepting them as valid and worthwhile. The goals defined by the game are what it takes to *win* the game. As such, they have a kind of objectivity to them, at least in the sense that they are goals that are fixed in advance, independent from any players' agenda, and they offer a standard by which players can compare each other's efforts and skills.

But when players take a dollhouse attitude, their goals are more subjective. They are goals that are invented by the player themselves. Suppose that, while I am playing *BOTW*, I decide to set my own goal, to climb all the mountains of Hyrule. This goal is one that I am projecting onto the game. The mechanics of the game allow the player to climb most mountains. So, I have no trouble throwing myself into this imaginary role of intrepid Hyrulean mountain climber. But completing this goal isn't required to win the game, nor do I really care about comparing my achievement to anyone else. If you climbed all the mountains of Hyrule faster than I did, then I'm happy for you![12] What is interesting about the goals that players pursue in dollhouse play is that they are projected onto the game by the player and have their own purposes and constraints that are independent of the game's programming. This distinction between *the goals set by the game* and *the goals invented by the player* might seem rather thin, but from the player's perspective, the distinction is a substantial one.

To appreciate this point, it would be helpful to consider the kinds of goals that legitimately figure in dollhouse play. Some dollhouse players will pursue *self-defined goals*, which are goals that are entirely invented by the player and unacknowledged by the game. An example is giving myself the goal of walking the entire coastline of the Tsushima islands. *Ghost of Tsushima* does not prompt me to adopt this goal; it is one that

I invented. And the game does not acknowledge my completion of the goal—I don't get any loot, or experience points, or a special trophy when I finish. Another example would be recreating a perfect replica of my house in *Minecraft*. Again, this is a goal that is invented by the player and one that goes unacknowledged by the game.

Another kind of goal that is legitimately a form of dollhouse play are *self-selected goals*. These are interestingly either goals that are prompted by the game but not acknowledged, or they are goals that are acknowledged by the game but not prompted. An example of the first kind—a goal that is prompted but not acknowledged—is the ability to ride wild deer in *BOTW*. Deer can be ridden in *BOTW* just as horses can; however, the player cannot register a deer at a stable and thereby keep it. Catching a deer is just like catching a horse. The player must sneak up close enough until a prompt appears—*press A to mount*—then the player has to calm the deer until it allows the player to ride it. The prompt is built into the game to tell the player what they can do. Thus, the action is prompted by the game but not acknowledged—there is no trophy or achievement, and you can't keep the deer.

An example of the second kind—a goal that is acknowledged by the game but not prompted—comes from *Ghost of Tsushima*. (Spoiler alert!) At the end of Act II, Jin Sakai has fallen out with his powerful uncle, Lord Shimura, who has been ordered by the shogun to arrest Jin for breaking the samurai's honor code. Jin escapes from his imprisonment and flees north; however, in his flight from Lord Shimura's forces, archers shoot his horse and, though it carries Jin to safety, it eventually dies. Grateful for the sacrifice of his faithful horse, Jin buries it and marks the site of the grave. At this point, the player can simply walk away from the grave. However, if the player turns to the grave and bows or plays a mournful tune on Jin's flute, then embers will rise up from the grave to encircle Jin. This is unprompted—the game doesn't tell the player that they ought to mourn their horse—but the action is acknowledged by the game.

To generalize, players still pursue goals in dollhouse play, but the goals are ones that come from the player, not from the game.

The same is true of narratives. In narrative play, the player engages with a story that has been crafted by the game designer, while in dollhouse play, the player tells their own story. In games like *The Sims*, players construct their own stories. They devise their avatar's identity, occupation, and their relationships to other characters in the game. In fact, the player's constructed, imaginary story satisfies the definition of narrative that we offered previously: a game has a narrative when players must explain what is happening in the game by referring to fictional characters, events, and spaces. The kind of narratives that we offer in dollhouse play are emergent narratives—remember, an embedded narrative is one predetermined by the game, while an emergent narrative can be attributed to a playthrough rather than the game itself.[13] Speaking of *Ghost of Tsushima* as a game, we can say that it has an embedded narrative because the game designers have built certain fictional characters, relationships, and events into the game; but when we are speaking of *The Sims*, we must say that my playthrough has an emergent narrative when I imagine that the characters and events stand in certain fictional relationships to each other in my own dollhouse play.

The most crucial and defining aspect of dollhouse play is that the player projects their own will onto the game. We can see this in both the goals that players pursue and the stories that they tell—these are the player's own inventions.

4 The Transformative Value of Dollhouse Play

The dollhouse attitude frees the player to find valuable experiences in games, experiences that would be closed to the player who only takes either a goal-seeking attitude or a narrative attitude. Play can be transformed such that certain aesthetic values arise depending on what attitude players take. To see this, we will consider an extended example, one that hopefully offers some demonstration of what an attitudinal theory of play can do.

Think about realistic simulators, many of which seem perplexing when compared to the standard expectation of what a video game is supposed to be.[14] *American Truck Simulator* is an open-world game where players drive commercial trucks across the western United States. Players make deliveries, driving from city to city, and they are required to follow all traffic and shipping regulations. Players can drive digital versions of big rigs like the Kenworth T680 or the Peterbilt 579. The base game includes the states of California, Nevada, and Arizona, with ten other western states available as additional downloadable content. The in-game map is to 1/20 scale. Some players will purchase a steering wheel, foot pedals, and a stick shift for their gaming computer as well as multiple monitors to cover the 180-degree visual field of a cab. There is an active modding community. Some modders produce extended maps into regions that are not currently covered by the game. Some produce custom skins for their trucks. There is an online multiplayer mod, called TruckersMP, that allows players to drive together in a convoy and talk via a "CB radio" function. Additionally, members of the game's community have developed an online radio station that players can listen to while driving, called Truckers.FM.

What is the value of playing *American Truck Simulator*? Dedicated players who log hundreds of hours on its digital roads and spend time developing detailed mods aren't doing it ironically. A closely related question is, *who* plays *American Truck Simulator*? That question is difficult to answer. Accurate demographic data of the player base is not readily available. Reading through online discussion boards can offer some insights, even if they are nonrepresentative. It is noticeable that at least some players seem to have first-hand knowledge of trucking. Indeed, some players are retired truck drivers who find some peace in driving their old routes but without having to deal with the paperwork and responsibility of a real job (Moss 2016). If this is escapism, then it is a *very* nuanced form.

There are many kinds of realistic simulators. *American Truck Simulator* is made by the same company that produced the *Euro Truck Simulator* games. There are also games like *Farming Simulator*, where players operate heavy farming equipment to cultivate and harvest their crops. Of course, one of the oldest and most famous is *Microsoft Flight Simulator*, which offers players the opportunity to pilot numerous kinds of civilian aircraft. The sort of simulators that I am interested in exhibit three similarities to varying degrees. First, there is a strong emphasis on realism. Many games aim to faithfully represent the vehicle controls of their real-world counterparts, often as well as changing weather conditions and realistic physics engines. On discussion boards and chat forums dedicated to simulator games, it is striking how fans talk at great length about their realism implicitly. Fans discuss the pros and cons of different vehicles as if they were talking about the real thing. Reading through the *Farming Simulator* discussion boards, it is often difficult to tell whether people are talking about *the game* or *a real farm*.

Second, for many players, simulators are not simply an opportunity to master a skill and compete with others. The skills involved are usually fairly easy to master and do not require much practice. Most simulators offer in-game goals; however, the goals are typically optional and failing to achieve them is easily overcome (Leino 2018). Juul describes simulators as games that have goals and win conditions, but they lack "the element of games where players improve their skills, where they improvise creatively, where they *play*" (2018). With no opportunity to improve one's skills, there is little value in comparing one's accomplishments to others. Instead, simulators offer players the opportunity to enjoy an activity for its own sake without the constraints having to achieve anything, or—perhaps more accurately—without having to quantify one's achievements for comparison with others. Instead, the main concern for fans of simulators is something unquantifiable. Consider the game *Lawn Mowing Simulator*, which was released for the PC and Xbox in 2021 and for the PlayStation in 2022. In it, players mow lawns in a small English village using commercial ride-on mowers. A description from the game's website doesn't promise the player glorious competition but instead a job well done:

> Lay your eyes on a picture of perfection set in a beautiful British countryside town. Visit a variety of stunning locales from large

equestrian fields, vast castle grounds, quaint cottage greens and even the comfort of a private garden, all beautifully created using Unity Engine. Each area has been meticulously handcrafted to provide you the satisfaction of cutting every blade of grass to the perfect length.[15]

Lawn Mowing Simulator offers a "career mode" where the player builds a lawn care empire one mow at a time as well as a "free roam" mode where players can mow to their heart's content. At the start of the game, only a small number of spaces are available to explore in the free roam mode. Players need to unlock additional free roaming spaces by making progress in the career mode. Effectively, free roam mode is the reward for making progress in the career mode. If you do well at mowing digital lawns, you are rewarded with the opportunity to mow more digital lawns.

Finally, and importantly for this discussion, many simulators are unabashedly *boring*. Getting stuck in virtual traffic is just as much fun as getting stuck in real-world traffic. Whether driving, mowing a lawn, or flying a plane, simulators offer gameplay that requires continuous attention coupled with minimal skill. Yet, what is interesting is that players do not play simulators *despite* their boredom. Rather, it seems to be that players find distinctive and unique aesthetic experiences in the boredom of a simulator. Olli Leino (2018) offers a helpful distinction here between boredom *about* a game and boredom *within* a game. When players grow bored *about* a game, boredom is the "last feeling" they experience before quitting; but when players feel boredom *within* a game, it can be the "first feeling" they have before discovering a richer, nuanced appreciation of the game (2018: 2).

The appreciation of boring and mundane actions goes against the dominant trend in video games, which typically incentivizes the player to complete their goals quickly and efficiently. John Vanderhoef and Matthew Thomas Payne (2022) offer an interesting distinction here. Games that demand quick and efficient action employ "hegemonic game time," which is the standard expectation that games are supposed to be about maximizing our efforts and being productive. By contrast, some games employ "slow game time," the purpose of which is to slow down action in order to achieve other aesthetic effects. Writing about some of the player backlash against the slower aspects of *RDR2*, Vanderhoef and Payne say that slow game time "produces ludic moments that frustrate player expectations of speed and efficiency in the service of contemplation, stillness, unproductive wait time and emotional resonance" (2022; also cf. Juul 2018).

To understand the aesthetic appeal of simulators, I suggest we first return to the concern for realism. In fan discussions of simulators, the accuracy and realism of the games seem to be the most widely discussed factors. Generally, when gamers talk about "realism," what they mean is something like "life-likeness."[16] Games (or pictures, or literary descriptions) are considered realistic in common usage when they are "faithful" to something in life. However, exactly *what aspect of life it must be faithful to* will differ from one art form or genre to the next. For instance, *pictorial realism* refers to the rendering of an image, where an image possesses higher degrees of pictorial realism as it looks more lifelike. *Literary realism* aims for a truthful presentation of its subject matter, like hard science fiction, which aims for scientific accuracy. *Social realism* refers to the representation of social realities where we would describe a work as "social realism" if it, for example, is particularly candid about the nature of people's lives or included some degree of social critique.

What kind of realism do simulator games aim for? Certainly, pictorial realism is highly valued. Fans of simulators expect a high degree of lifelike imagery, and one would expect fans to be even more enthusiastic about future games as the images become even more realistic. However, it is doubtful that pictorial realism is the main concern for simulator fans. Pictorial realism is likely able to sustain a viewer's interest only for a short time. When viewing a realistic painting, most people are at first impressed by the lifelike depiction, they linger on the image for a time, and then they move on. It is unlikely that the players who invest hundreds of hours into *American Truck Simulator* are there just for the pictorial realism. Additionally, simulators typically do not aim for any degree of literary realism or social realism. I think it would be interesting if *American Truck Simulator* examined some of the social and economic barriers to getting a commercial driver's license, or the environmental impacts of trucking, or how difficult it is for truckers to make payments on their rigs and keep up with maintenance while wages continue to plummet But social realism isn't what *American Truck Simulator* is about.[17]

Instead, I suggest the primary interest in simulator games lies in what we could call *procedural realism*.[18] Video games offer players the opportunity to engage in an activity that unfolds over time through a system that is responsive to the player's input. There is a mechanistic give-and-take where the player responds to the game's ongoing challenges and the internal game state continually updates in response. A video game is realistic procedurally when the player's interaction with the game faithfully reflects what it would be like to interact with the real thing. To put it another way, the aim of procedural realism is to digitally represent a process faithfully. Players of simulators are typically interested in the mechanics of how something works. What is it like to fly a plane, or to drive a big rig, or to pilot a submarine? I cannot really learn any of these skills without radically changing my life, not to mention the investment in time and money that it would take. However, simulators give me the opportunity to experience something of what it is like, at least to see how it feels for the controls to respond to my inputs, within only a few minutes of starting up a game. Even better, simulators offer the parts of the experience that players want without the drudgery. I can drive a big rig without dealing with the paperwork, or mow a lawn without getting a sunburn.

Procedural realism might sound like it promises too much. After all, no video game can really act as a substitute for real-world action. Shooting a gun in real life is nothing like pushing a button on a video game controller. And no matter how good I am at playing *FIFA 22*, I'm still terrible at real-world soccer. The skills that I acquire in these games simply do not translate into their real-world counterparts, no matter how realistic the games might be (Bartel 2018). However, the problem here isn't that procedural realism promises too much; it is that this objection asks too much. There are aspects of an experience that video games can represent with some fidelity, and there are aspects that it cannot. Video games cannot represent the feel of sitting in the cab of a truck, bouncing along the road; or the smell of mowed grass; or the painful recoil of a shotgun. But video games are very good at representing mechanical processes. The subjective experience of a process in a game corresponds to the subjective experience of the process in real life. The tedium of driving in *American Truck Simulator* is a realistic representation of the challenges of long-distance driving. In *Lawn Mowing Simulator*, if the player cuts a corner too sharp, then it is easy to miss some blades of grass. The result is a little crescent shaped patch of grass left behind—mocking evidence of my sloppy turn—that I have to go back over again with the strimmer, *just like real-life lawn mowing!*

What could be the aesthetic appeal of realistic simulators? Clearly, many people find them insufferably boring. And they are not wrong. Simulators almost seem designed to be oppressively boring. I mean, a video game about *lawn mowing*?! It is almost perverse.

My suggestion is that there are two things going on here: realistic simulators have a particular formal quality to them, which I am calling "procedural realism," and fans of these games appreciate this quality by taking a dollhouse attitude toward them. First, locating the value of realistic simulators in procedural realism has an obvious explanatory advantage over pictorial realism, which can only hold a viewer's attention for a short time. By contrast, procedural realism can sustain the user's interest because it unfolds over time. Driving a truck is a process, and players can only appreciate the accuracy of the controls by going through the process. Additionally, the process is renewed with each new challenging variation. There are various road conditions to experience—traffic, narrow city streets, reversing into a loading bay—as well as changing weather patterns. However, this mere fidelity is unlikely to be the full story either. Simulators are able to represent a process with some fidelity, but fidelity cannot make a boring process somehow no longer boring.

The second part of the answer has to do with the player's attitude. Players of simulators don't take a goal-seeking attitude toward their play. *American Truck Simulator* is a deeply boring game to the goal-seeking player due to its lack of challenges and the simplicity of the skills involved. Instead, fans of these games take a dollhouse attitude. This attitude relieves the player of the need to *do* anything or to achieve anything. Dollhouse play allows one to enjoy the fantasy of role-playing as a trucker. The player who takes the right attitude to the game doesn't experience it as boring—or perhaps it is more accurate to say that there is a certain quality to the game that dollhouse players recognize would be boring to other players, but which they experience as a relaxing peacefulness.

Procedural realism is a specific quality of simulator games that players are sensitive to. That quality does different things for different players. For the goal-seeking player, procedural realism is a negative quality. It is the source of their boredom. Goal-seeking players might interpret the realism of a simulator as cringeworthy, worthless tedium, or a nerd's sad and fussy obsession with accuracy. For the dollhouse player, procedural realism is a positive quality. Players of *American Truck Simulator* are not merely interested in the mechanical accuracy of how the system works, but they are also interested in accurately feeling something of what it is like to be a long-haul trucker. In that case, the tedium of driving a truck is part of the game's appeal. Through faithfully representing the procedure of driving, the game offers a realistic, authentic view of what it is like.[19]

Some theorists have noted this phenomenon and sought to explain it. Others have noted how, once the player embraces boredom, they are able to work past the boredom and come to find other kinds of valuable experiences—like a state of reflection, meditative play, self-realization, or peace (Leino 2018; Möring 2014; Vanderhoef and Payne 2022). Boredom is a state that one experiences on the way to something else. The experience begins in boredom but transforms into, for example, meditative peacefulness. On this view, boredom is not itself something to be valued but is instead a first step toward an experience that is valuable. So, we shouldn't be afraid of boredom and seek to avoid it. It is an experience that we should embrace because something better is on the way.

In its broad outlines, this is correct—an experience can be initially boring but then (perhaps unexpectedly) transform into something else. However, what is needed is an explanation of how that transformation takes place. What has to happen for boredom to give way to peacefulness? My account of gaming attitudes offers an explanation. What happens is that the player initially approaches the game in the way that they have come to approach all video games—as goal-seeking players looking for competitive challenges to be conquered and won—and they experience the game as boring. But, once the player realizes that *American Truck Simulator* is not a game to be won, they can either put the game down in frustration or they can embrace the experience, accepting the game as a free space to enjoy role-playing. Leino's point that boredom is either the "last feeling" before giving up or the "first feeling" before discovering something new is an apt one that describes the difference between the goal-seeking player who rejects the experience and the dollhouse player who comes to realize that *American Truck Simulator* is a dollhouse, one where the dolls are truck-shaped.

5 What Makes Video Games Effective Dollhouses

Many objects can be transformed into a plaything if the user is imaginative and willful enough. The instinct to play is a powerful one. However, some objects are more inclined toward play than others. The same is true of video games. Some offer excellent opportunities for dollhouse play while others do not. *Animal Crossing: New Horizons* is an ideal dollhouse video game. The primary activities are dress-up, collecting, and role-playing. By contrast, *Tetris* doesn't offer any opportunity for dollhouse play. I could ignore the objective of the game and simply stack the tetrominoes in ways that I find aesthetically pleasing, but my game would then be over very quickly.

Video games function well as dollhouses when they possess four qualities: freedom from instrumental needs, evocativeness, responsiveness, and persistence. The first quality—freedom from instrumental needs—is essential. In order to function as a dollhouse game at all, a video game must offer the player the freedom to pursue their own whims independently from any demands that are built into the game. The reason why *Tetris* doesn't work well as a dollhouse game is because the only freedom that the player is given is the choice of how exactly to stack the tetrominoes, which serves only to pursue the goal of achieving a high score. If the player is given little freedom to pursue non-instrumental activities, they have no opportunity to set their own goals or tell their own stories.

The other three qualities—evocativeness, responsiveness, and persistence—are elements of good toy design, and they come in degrees. These are not essential qualities, but they are qualities that make some video games relatively better than others as opportunities for dollhouse play. Some video games are rich with opportunities for dollhouse play, while others are very limited. The richness of those opportunities corresponds to their possession and implementation of these three qualities.

Evocative. There is a fine balance between the chaos of imagination and the rigid constraints of a game. A well-designed toy finds the mean on the spectrum between these two extremes. On one end of the spectrum are single-function toys. Some toys are designed for one purpose—for instance, remote-controlled cars, snow cone machines, toy guns. These toys are prescriptive in the sense that their design suggests one particular function. Toys that are limited to a single function can only sustain the user's attention so long as that function remains interesting. Once the user loses interest in that function, then they lose interest in the toy as well. The extreme at the other end of the spectrum are toys that are highly abstract. Think about playing with a stick: as a natural object, it was not designed, and so it does not suggest any kind of function. Instead, one can use a stick for any function that one can imagine. This seems like it should be ideal—abstract toys offer the ultimate freedom as they prescribe nothing at all. Yet, abstract toys present a different problem: they require greater imaginative effort from the user. A stick can be anything, as long as you have the imagination for it. It can be done, but it can also be cognitively taxing for the user. Sometimes I'm too tired, I run out of ideas, and all I see is a stick.

Between the two extremes of prescriptive toys and abstract toys is what we could call *evocative toys*. Toys are evocative when they offer the user a function, where that function is versatile enough to allow the user to explore a range of activities, but it does not prescribe a single use. For example, Lego bricks make for excellent toys because they prescribe a function—sticking together bricks of various shapes and sizes—but then allow the user to employ their imagination to construct whatever they can. When video games are evocative, they suggest a function that is specific enough to prompt an activity from the player but then allow the player to fill out the details of the imagined world. *A Short Hike* is effectively a puzzle game, but the puzzle can be completed very quickly. The player controls a young bird, named Claire, who is staying at an island campground with her aunt. The campground offers many fun games and activities: stickball, fishing, climbing, and a speedboat. The player can also explore the island and help the other guests with their side-quests. *A Short Hike* is an excellent example of an evocative game. It offers a scenario—a puzzle to complete—but then allows the player the freedom to pursue the activities that they enjoy most—*just like a real campground!*

Responsive. Toys that are responsive to the user are more fun than toys that are not. Of course, in one bland sense, all toys are responsive to the user—when I throw a ball, it moves. But that isn't particularly interesting. Toys increase in their interest when the responses become more varied and nuanced. Think of a child playing with a doll: a doll that does nothing may be fine, but a doll that makes a "burp" noise when I pretend to feed it is a bit more fun. Video games of course excel at being responsive to players, which is admittedly an understatement. Yet, it is worth noticing that video games excel at this in two specific ways. First, video games can offer a wider range of varied responses than traditional toys. They can account for subtle differences in the actions of players, which can in turn produce responses from the game that feel more organic. Second, a video game's responses can be sensitive to previous choices and actions that the user made. Video games can save choices that I made early in the game and incorporate those into the scenarios and storylines that arise at later points. Those choices can be built up layer by layer such that the game's responses become increasingly complex, specific to my playthrough, and therefore more meaningful. This is one way in which video games can construct richly detailed imaginary worlds, ones where the player choices seem to have some consequence.

Persistent. Finally, whenever one plays with a toy, one also builds an imaginary world. I don't just imagine that a stick is a sword; I also have to imagine the world in which my stick-sword is a powerful weapon. This imagined world of toy-play depends necessarily on the capacity and creativity to imagine and must be sustained by the player. We could call the need to create and sustain a rich imaginary world the "Calvin and Hobbes problem": the more richness and detail the imaginary world has, the more cognitive effort is required from the player. It would require immense cognitive capacity for someone to play an imagination game with sticks that rivals the level of detail of a video game like *Ghost of Tsushima*. Yet, video games can sustain detailed imaginary worlds with ease. The world of the game persists with all its rich detail independently from the player's imaginative capacity.

For all these reasons, video games make excellent objects for dollhouse play. Of course, not all video games possess each of these qualities in equal measure. *Max Payne 3* doesn't function well as a dollhouse because of its lack of non-instrumental freedom. The game is very linear, forcing the player to move from one interaction—a battle, a cut-scene—to the next. There is little space to explore, nothing to collect, and no options for dress-up. *Hearthstone* does not allow players to engage in dress-up or role-playing. Its battles are responsive and its persistence allows the player to engage in card collecting, but what *Hearthstone* lacks is non-instrumental freedom and evocativeness.

The only actions that players can take are those that result in some instrumental gain, and the actions available to the player are all designed to serve the functions of deck-building and battling. The classic arcade version of *Donkey Kong* is highly responsive, but it lacks non-instrumental freedom, evocativeness, and persistence. Players can only take direct actions against Donkey Kong, it prescribes a single goal (rescue the princess), and it is not designed to save game states that would allow for rich imaginative play. Now, I'm not suggesting that these are *bad video games*. They are excellent for what they do, and no game can be expected to excel at everything. The point simply is that the reason why these games offer little opportunity for dollhouse play is due to the specific qualities that they lack.

6 Summing Up

Dollhouse play is a legitimate form of play that many find aesthetically valuable. Players find value in games that allow them to engage in dress-up, collecting, and role-playing by adopting a different attitudinal stance toward the game, one that isn't focused on scoring goals or enjoying someone else's story. When we set aside our concerns for goal-seeking and narrative, our play can be transformed into something both unexpected and yet deeply rewarding and personal.

Dollhouse play offers a brief escape from the drudgery of instrumental values. In our modern societies, we are incentivized to maximize our productivity, so much so that we eventually feel guilty about taking time off. Even our hobbies need to be productive. One of my favorite hobbies is baking. Often when I bake something for friends, they will pay me a compliment, saying, "You could start a bakery!" I appreciate the compliment, but taking the suggestion seriously would mean turning my hobby into another job. My wife likes to knit. People often tell her, "You could sell that on Etsy!" Again, the suggestion is that she should monetize her hobby. Social media is supposed to be a means of keeping in touch with others or finding people with similar interests, yet many have found numerous ways to monetize that too, turning our time to socialize into a business of influence. In all aspects of our lives, we are pressured to be productive in our every waking moment. This is true of gaming as well. When gamers are confronted with the accusation that playing video games is a waste of time, many gamers will defensively point out how much money professional esports players can make. Gaming can be monetized; therefore, it is a valuable hobby.

Dollhouse play offers a refreshing escape from the pressures of productivity. Whether I am playing dress-up, collecting, or role-playing, I value the activity non-instrumentally. I enjoy it for its own sake. For a brief moment, I step outside of the anxiety of productivity and just enjoy making aesthetic choices that bring me pleasure but have no value to anyone else. The choices we make when playing dress-up in a video game are *empty choices*—they are choices that have no productive outcome. But, if nothing else, *that* is the reason why you should enjoy customizing your avatar. These empty choices that lie beyond the scope of productivity may be meaningful and valuable only to the player, but they are still meaningful and valuable. Your own joy is worthwhile. So, don't let anyone tell you that playing video games is a waste of time— even dollhouse games. Enjoying your life is not a waste of time.

6

The Aesthetics of Moral Choice

BioShock Infinite is an ambitious and engaging entry in the *BioShock* series. Set in the city of Columbia, which is composed of numerous interchangeable floating city blocks, the game focuses on Booker DeWitt, a Pinkerton agent who has been set the task of finding Elizabeth, a mysterious young woman being held captive by the city's leaders. After rescuing Elizabeth, she becomes his constant companion and proves to be more powerful than Booker could have imagined.

As with the previous *BioShock* games, *Infinite* takes on an overtly satirical tone. Set in 1912, the game takes a critical view of American expansionism, the mythology of America's Founding Fathers, and political extremism. During the game, the player quickly learns that Columbia is a deeply racist city. The founders of Columbia are able to maintain their power partly by creating a quasi-religious mythology for themselves and partly by maintaining a strict racial boundary where the well-off White citizens of Columbia are able to thrive only through the crushing and degrading labor of its Black citizens. The player encounters a city on the edge of a civil war, one where the racist Founders battle against the rebellious Vox Populi, a leftist populist resistance group. The tone of the game is politically ambiguous. Neither side is shown to be clearly in the right. Instead, both sides are presented as extremists who, when given power, will inevitably abuse it to devastating ends.

The political ambiguity is pervasive throughout the game and not always successful. At the start of the game, Booker must keep his identity a secret while he infiltrates the city of Columbia. Upon exploring the city, Booker soon stumbles upon a bizarre spectacle: a carnivalesque raffle where people buy tickets to win the opportunity to be the first person to throw a baseball at a pair of captive criminals. They are a White man and a Black woman who are being publicly punished for carrying on a secret love affair. The couple are going to be stoned to death with baseballs. The man and woman are displayed on an outdoor proscenium stage, bound to a post, and accompanied by a cajoling announcer. Booker buys a raffle ticket from a pretty, flirtatious girl, not knowing what the ticket is for, until his ticket is called as the winning one. Booker is handed a baseball. It is at this point that Booker, and the player, learns about the deep racism and classism of the city.

It is also at this point that the player is presented with a quick-time decision. The player may either throw their ball at the couple or at the announcer. Alternatively, the player can do nothing and wait for the timer to run out. No matter what the player chooses, the scene quickly erupts in violence because, when the crowd's attention turns to Booker, his cover is blown.

One way in which *BioShock Infinite* differs from previous games in the series is that the player's moral decisions have no impact on the gameplay. In the earlier games, the player was given the choice to either save or "harvest" the Little Sisters—beings who look like little girls. Harvesting them would kill the Little Sister, but the player would then be able to withdraw a serum from their bodies that would allow the player to power up their abilities faster. Alternatively, the player could save the Little Sisters, which results in the girls offering the player only a small gift of the serum. This presents the player with an interesting moral conflict: collect as much serum as possible in order to make the gameplay easier, though this would require killing what appears like a little girl, or free the creatures and struggle along in the game at a lower degree of power. This sort of moral choice is one that has an impact on the gameplay. As such, one might wonder whether the player's choices are really motivated by concerns about morality or concerns about gameplay. One difficulty with tying moral choices to gameplay is that the player often makes their decisions based on pragmatic needs. I might choose one option just because it makes the game easier, or because it gives me some advantage, or because it makes the game deliciously harder. Actual moral considerations—about what kind of person one wants to be, what sort of values and principles matter, or what kind of world one wants to live in—are set aside in favor of gameplay choices.

The moral choices in *BioShock Infinite* do not raise this question because there is no impact on the gameplay—the choices may be meaningful to the player, but they are inconsequential to the gameplay. *BioShock Infinite*'s moral choices are ultimately personal choices, ones that perhaps color the emotional tone of the game but otherwise carry no lasting impact on the game. This raises a slightly different question. If moral choices have no impact, then what exactly are we choosing? Or, why should we bother to choose anything at all? If our moral choices are detached from consequences, then they are not really *moral* choices. Instead, it is like they are a kind of aesthetic choice: we merely choose what kind of person we want to *appear* to be. This is an interesting issue to think about, but it isn't the focus of my story. Instead, my story here is about legitimacy in moral choices.

When I first encountered the captive couple in *BioShock Infinite* and was faced with the choice of either throwing my ball at them or at the announcer, I was stunned. I couldn't believe that I was being given this choice. What monster would choose to side with racists? Why give the player the choice? Perhaps some players might be motivated to throw their ball at the couple, believing that doing so would avoid blowing Booker's cover. However, once one learns that moral choices in this game have no impact on gameplay, this motivation disappears. If the choice is really just an aesthetic choice, then this implies that either choice is a legitimate one. Additionally, remember that the game is politically ambiguous. Within that context where the competing political factions are equally bad, we are supposed to see our choices as equally bad. But for this choice in particular, the options are not equally bad. Throwing your baseball at the couple is just cruelty. When a game offers the player a choice, the choice takes on a sense of legitimacy. There is an implicit suggestion that one could legitimately choose either option because both have some value—that is what makes moral choices philosophically interesting and what makes moral deliberation hard in practice. I was stunned by this scene because I do not accept that both options are legitimate.

In interviews, the game's creative director, Ken Levine, has offered a few arguments in defense of the depiction of racism of *BioShock Infinite*. One reason that Levine offers is that, as the game is set in 1912, egregious scenes of racism would have been historically accurate (Lahti 2012). Superficially, Levine is right. Racism was rampant in the early twentieth century and many of the "great men" of America's past were imperfect people. But there are a number of questions we could ask. First, why is historical accuracy so important for this game? The game presents a fantastical, impossible world—I'm pretty sure that there were no flying cities in 1912—so it is not as if *BioShock Infinite* must be held to the highest standards of historical accuracy. Second, why did the game have to be set in 1912 in the first place? It is not as if there were no other time periods available. Presumably, the game is set in 1912 specifically because Levine wanted to tell a story about *that* time. If the time period is important to the story, then I understand the need to get the setting of the period right. However, even this defense doesn't offer a convincing counterpoint to my criticism. Crucially, the problem with the scene described above is not the *mere appearance of racism*; instead, the problem is that the game *gives the player the choice to join in*. In that case, it doesn't really matter what time period the game is set in or how accurately that period is portrayed. What matters is that the player is playing it today and making choices about what to do in the game today. So, I think the more important question is, what is the value of allowing the player the choice to join in? Why are we being given this choice today?

Moral concerns often find their way into aesthetic discussions of video games. In game reviews and online forums, one can find accusations that some video games are sexist, racist, or homophobic. There is no shortage of news reports about working conditions in game design studios, which reveal that some studios treat their workers abysmally or are hostile to minority employees. And some games require players to commit in-game acts that, despite the fact that they are merely fictional, still leave players feeling uncomfortable and sometimes even feeling guilty.

Gamers often fight back against claims like these. Sometimes the pushback is careful, thoughtful, and right on target. Other times, gamers anxious to defend their hobby in knee-jerk fashion can completely miss the point, appear stunningly tone-deaf, or exacerbate the problem. For instance, there is a loud and aggressive minority of gamers online who respond to the accusations above by arguing that, for example, sexism isn't a problem because video games are for boys anyway; that gaming studios can treat their employees however they wish to as long as they keep churning out good games; and that if your in-game actions make you feel uncomfortable or guilty, then maybe you're just not hard enough to play video games. Gaming is about dominance and conquest, and there is nothing wrong with winning—or so some gamers will say. These sorts of arguments are usually easy to reject as they are largely based on faulty assumptions and poor reasoning.

A more interesting and thoughtful defense that gamers sometimes employ is the claim that such *moral* criticisms are irrelevant to the *aesthetic* enjoyment of a game. On this view, whether a video game is "good" or "bad" is a question about the quality of the game itself—its storytelling, its gameplay, and its overall production values—and any moral or political criticism of games has nothing to do with whether or not the game is fun to play or tells an engaging story. Video games offer fictional worlds complete with their own histories and values. Real-world moral and political values are external to the game itself. Therefore, criticisms of games that rely on such judgments are wrongly imposing moral or political issues in a place where they do not belong. This is a view that we could call *aesthetic autonomism*, where the basic idea is that the aesthetic value of an object is independent from any moral or political value that it might have.

Aesthetic autonomism is a popular view among philosophers. There is no shortage of philosophers (and theorists in other disciplines) defending various version of it. Few philosophers argue generally that judgments of a work of art's aesthetic value should be separate from any judgment of its moral value (Anderson and Dean 1998; Dickie 2005). Those who defend autonomism today take a more nuanced view, one where their autonomism allows for exceptions or is limited to a particular set of cases (Harold 2011). Still, the more strident versions of autonomism tend to come from game critics and fans online—look at the online commentary over "keeping politics out of games"—rather than from philosophers. In this chapter, I will argue against aesthetic autonomism. We cannot keep morals (or politics) out of games.

The basic point of this chapter is that moral judgment and decision-making is a part of the aesthetic appreciation of video games. However, this comes in two broad forms: internal and external (Bartel 2023). Internal moral judgment is the idea that video games have their own in-game moral perspectives, that this moral perspective applies to both characters and players, and that part of the aesthetic value of a game is the moral decision-making that happens in the game. When video games ask us to make moral choices, it is not as if we stop aesthetically appreciating the game and begin the separate job of making moral judgments. Rather, there is an aesthetic component to moral choice games. External moral judgment is the idea that video games, as cultural objects, are themselves open to moral judgment and criticism. Some are sexist and racist. Others are inclusive. Some game companies are ruthless. Some of the practices of the gaming industry have harmful effects on the economy, the environment, and on gaming culture. Even these external moral judgments have a role to play in the aesthetics of video games.

The argument of this chapter goes like this. Section 1: Video games are internally value-laden. They not only fictionally represent moral actions and situations, but they also can engage players in moral reasoning and require players to make moral judgments. Section 2: The fact that video games engage players in moral reasoning is what makes moral choice video games so compelling. There really is nothing at stake in moral choice games because the choices we are making are fictional. Yet, moral choices in games can feel weighty and meaningful to players because, when we make moral choices in games, we actually employ our real-world sense of moral value. Section 3: Our aesthetic evaluation of video games is not morally neutral. Our (internal) moral judgments about video games play a role in our aesthetic experience and evaluation of those games. Section 4: Some external factors play a role in our aesthetic experience too. We cannot neatly partition off our aesthetic lives from our moral lives. The two are intertwined.

1 Games are Value-Laden

There is an ongoing debate within philosophy about whether objects are "value-laden," which is generally the idea that objects have certain moral or political values inherently. Actually, it is more accurate to say that there are multiple ongoing debates within different subfields of philosophy, debates that typically take place in isolation from one another. For instance: in the philosophy of technology, philosophers debate whether pieces of technology are mere tools that can be used for either good or bad ends or whether technology can be good or bad in itself (Klenk 2021; Peterson and Spahn 2011; van den Hoven 2005; Verbeek 2006). In aesthetics, philosophers debate whether works of art have moral values in addition to aesthetic values (Eaton 2012; Gaut 1998; Kieran 2002; Paris 2019), which extend into the more specific debate about whether works of art inherit immoral qualities when they are made by immoral artists (Bartel 2019; Harold 2020; Matthes 2022; Willard 2021). Feminist philosophers have long questioned whether pornography embodies a kind of harm (Eaton 2007; Langton 1993; MacKinnon 1987).

Within the philosophy of games, it has long been debated whether games have their own internal values. It is difficult to say where this debate originated. Plato and Aristotle certainly expressed views about the value of games. But saying that games are good *for* something is not the same as saying that games have values inherently. Of the philosophers we have discussed, Johan Huizinga is often interpreted as claiming that games are not value-laden, given that they are separate from real life. He says, "Play lies outside the antithesis of wisdom and folly, and equally outside those of truth and falsehood, good and evil" (1970: 25). Roger Caillois agrees with Huizinga that games are separate from real life, but he also claims that the moral character of a society can be seen in the games that the society esteems, and that different societies are drawn to different games because of the formal qualities those games possess (2001: 83). This is not directly the claim that games themselves have moral qualities, but it is also not far off. Among contemporary philosophers, Fred D'Agostino (1981) is often credited as making a major contribution to this debate for his claim that games have an "ethos." He argues that games have certain values and, when questions arise concerning the interpretation of the rules, our interpretation should be informed by those values. Following D'Agostino, there has been an ongoing debate about the "internal" values of sports (Dixon 2016; Morgan 2012; Russell 1999; Simon 2000). Finally, some game developers have sought to design games to encourage the development of positive values in players, which only makes sense if you believe that games in fact have values (Flanagan 2009; Flanagan and Nissenbaum 2014).

As these debates appear in many different fields and concern different kinds of objects, philosophers have developed different accounts of what it means for an object to be "value-laden." Roughly, we can put these different accounts into two camps: some theorists argue that cultural objects have moral values when they are reliably linked to certain causal effects—call this the *causal thesis*—while others argue that the values inherent to an object stem from social factors about its creation—call this the *contextual thesis*. Against both of these views stand the amoralist—or the "value-neutral" theorist (Klenk 2021: 2)— who believes that objects do not possess moral values inherently. Instead, objects can be used in good or bad ways, but the object cannot be good or bad in itself. This view is perfectly captured by the well-known gun rights slogan, "Guns don't kill people, people kill people."

The causal thesis is associated with the long-running debate about violence in video games.[1] In this context, the causal thesis holds that violent video games have some capacity to cause people either to commit acts of violence or to have a lowered sensitivity toward violence.[2] The thought is that something about the technology itself or the imagery used might have some psychological impact that causes users to adopt new attitudes or behaviors. While concerns about violence tend to dominate media effects studies, researchers have invoked the causal thesis to also ask whether there is something about video games or their imagery that can cause users to develop, for example, sexist attitudes (Gabbiadini et al. 2016; Stermer and Burkley 2015) or racist attitudes (Burgess et al. 2011). Additionally, it is important to remember that the causal thesis does not always have a negative outcome—that is, it doesn't always imply something bad about video games. Rather, the causal thesis has been invoked in research on video game users' increased visual attention (Green and Bavelier 2003), ability to manipulate objects in space (De Lisi and Wolford 2002), and increased hand-eye coordination (Griffith et al. 1983).

The contextualist thesis is broadly the idea that cultural objects inherit some values from the context of their creation. There may be two reasons for this. Either objects inherit certain values because they are linked to the creator's intentions in the right kind of way or because of some social-structural factors having to do with market forces. The version that focuses on authorial intentions is most commonly found in the works of analytic (or "Anglo-American") philosophers, while arguments that stem from social-structural factors are more commonly associated with philosophers influenced by critical theory. However, the line between these two "camps" has increasingly blurred in recent years such that intentional and social-structural accounts can be blended, as neither account necessarily excludes the other. What I am calling "contextualism" could be thought of as encompassing a family of views on a Venn diagram, where one circle of the diagram represents intentional factors and the other circle represents social-structural factors—some theorists argue that objects have inherent values on purely intentional grounds, some argue on purely social-structural grounds, and some will draw on both sorts of arguments.[3] In the remainder of this chapter, I will freely draw from both versions of contextualism, paying little regard to camp boundaries.

Video games can be described as value-laden in a few senses. Video games are value-laden in the sense that players must employ their own moral reasoning and sensibilities in order to understand the drama and conflicts that they fictionally represent. Noel Carroll (1996) points out that all works of fiction have values built into them insofar as consumers are supposed to be responsive to the moral aspects of the drama. When we watch movies or read novels, we are not morally detached. Instead, our reading or viewing is informed by numerous moral judgments. I am supposed to recognize the moral conflicts that the characters face, feel sympathy for characters who are treated unjustly, and feel indignation when the bad guy gets ahead. It would be nearly impossible to appreciate the drama of a work of fiction without engaging our moral sentiments. All video games have certain values built into them in Carroll's sense. It is built into the game that some characters are heroes and some are villains, that some actions are "good" while others are not, and that some scenarios call for violent resolutions while others do not.

Another sense in which games can be value-laden is that its outcomes can be tied, at least symbolically, to real-world values. Ian Bogost (2008) argues that video games can make arguments. Video games are procedural: they take the user's inputs, perform computations, and deliver outputs that track evolving changes within the game state. Most video games represent fictional scenarios, but they don't have to. Game designers can represent real-world processes through video games. Developers can create procedural systems that mimic real-world economies, weather patterns, or the process of driving a long-haul truck. By representing real-world processes, video game designers can also comment on those real-world processes and even make arguments about them. By representing how real-world processes work and allowing users to see for themselves the outcomes generated by making certain choices, game designers can implicitly suggest what kind of choices users ought to make. Bogost refers to this as "procedural rhetoric"—simulations can be used as tools of persuasion because of their ability to provide demonstrations of how a system works. In his own work as a game designer, Bogost describes how he designed a game for the Republican party of Illinois—called *Take Back Illinois*—to demonstrate how Republican policy initiatives would play out. Users were given control of a city and the opportunity to implement policies of their choosing. Users could then see how the implementation of their choices would affect certain metrics, like public health, education standards, and economic performance.[4] What is important for our purposes is how Bogost's procedural rhetoric must be premised on the value-laden nature of games. For users to make meaningful choices in a simulation and to care about their outcomes, the users must see the relationship between the outcomes of the simulation and real-world situations. Indeed, Bogost's political policy game would be a total failure if voters didn't see the game as commenting on real-world policies and thus influencing what sort of policies they would like to see in real life. The player who thought it was "just a game" would have failed to appreciate the game's procedural rhetoric.

Finally, video game can be value-laden in the sense that they require the player to engage in moral reasoning and to make moral judgments. Moral choice mechanics in games are fairly common, and some can be highly effective at sparking moral reflection for players. Marcus Schulzke (2013) argues that video games can function in a way like philosophical thought experiments, but games can be more effective than thought experiments. Academic discussion of a thought experiment—like the famous Runaway Trolley case[5]—tend to be highly abstract and detached. Philosophers sitting in their armchairs have the luxury to make bold pronouncements about how one ought to answer a thought experiment because they never have to live with the consequences of their decisions. By contrast, video games offer the player some taste of consequence—though certainly not substantial enough to be like real life. Still, in video games, the player must live with the consequence of their choices, which forces the player into the kind of cost–benefit analysis that often characterizes moral reasoning (Schulzke 2013: 260). Similarly, Miguel Sicart (2009) argues that games can induce moral reasoning by coupling together the fiction with their gameplay. A game's affordances and limitations condition what the player is able to do, while the fictional representation of the game shows they player what they are doing. Importantly, the rules and mechanics also condition what the player should value. In order to perform well in the game, we need to internalize its rules and come to see the challenges of the game through the lens of those rules. The rules of the game encode "values we *have* to play by" (2009: 22). An ethically designed game is one that enables the player to question what they should do, whether their actions are right, or whether the game should allow the player to do *this* (ibid.; see also Zagal 2009).

The sort of value-ladenness described by Bogost, Schulzke, and Sicart is substantial. It is not merely that games represent actions as having moral qualities, but that games impact players morally. Following in the Aristotelian tradition, morality is something that we must learn through practice.[6] By engaging our moral sensibilities and reasoning, we thereby strengthen them. Players practice making moral choices and having moral responses in the safe environment of a game. We engage in hypothetical thought experiments to exercise our moral reasoning. And through their ability to make rhetorical arguments, they can influence us to change our minds.

Taking these points together, the conclusion we should draw is this: players are not morally neutral when they play games. They are already morally engaged, employing their values and sensibilities to make judgments and to even comprehend the action that is taking place in the game. In games with a strong fiction, the player needs to recognize what is represented as things having moral weight. In moral choice games, the player needs to feel the moral conflict in order for the choice to be meaningful. The rules of a game tell the player what to do, what to value in order to succeed, and what goals are worthwhile to pursue. Some games even function as forms of rhetoric, using action and interactivity itself as a tool of persuasion. No one is imposing values onto video games from outside. Games have always possessed values intrinsically. Finally, it is worth noticing that each of these accounts are versions of a contextual view of the value-laden nature of games. These theorists do not argue that games are value-laden because of any causal consequences. Instead, their arguments tend to focus on the nature of fictional representations, the impact of interactivity, and the role of the player's moral reasoning skills.

2 Playing with Ethics

The value-laden nature of video games means that moral choices can form a part of gameplay. Some players might make moral choices in games that fall in line with their own real-world moral sensibilities, while other players treat video games as a safe opportunity to make different kinds of moral choices than they would in real life. Both of these cases are interesting, and for a number of reasons. Here, I want to examine the aesthetic value of moral choices in games. The main point of departure here is that, when we make moral choices in games, we are genuinely making moral judgments. We are not pretending to make them. The core of my argument is that the moral judgments that we make in reality are not fundamentally different from those that we make in fiction. The basic architecture of our moral psychology—how we make moral judgments and what matters to us—remains the same whether we are making real moral choices or fictional ones. Moral choices, whether real or fictional, are a source of affective response. This is a source of aesthetic value for players as we enjoy the deliberation, emotional tension, and the drama of moral choice. Finally, I take this to partially refute aesthetic autonomism because of the mechanism involved: one does not get to enjoy the aesthetic value of moral choices without actually employing one's moral judgment.

When players make moral choices in games, how closely do their choices match their real-world values? It would seem natural for players to make moral choices that align with their real-world values. Nothing could be easier than choosing to do what you really believe to be right. However, to some gamers, "playing good" in a video game often represents something of a missed opportunity. Given that the game is a work of fiction, there are no real consequences to choosing the "evil" option. So, why not? Amanda Lange says,

> I find myself frustrated in conversations with gamers with similar tastes to mine in their absence of moral imagination. I know I am not my avatar in the game, so I like to experiment. Sometimes it's entertaining to me to see the results of a choice I would never make in reality. Sometimes it's just plain fun to be the bad guy. But it seemed to me that many other gamers I have spoken with have no interest in transgressing moral boundaries in story-based gaming. Their aversion to this, though I find it boring, poses some interesting questions for game designers. (2014: 1–2)

Perhaps it is sometimes "boring" to choose the "good" option, but it is also understandable. It can be fun to make the evil choices that I would never make in reality, but it can also be very satisfying to see a good world for once, to imagine oneself as a hero, and to see justice being done by our own actions. The need to believe that good is possible in the world is not necessarily a lack of moral imagination. Instead, it may be a reflection that this need is not being served in our real lives. If narrative games allow us to tell the stories that we want to hear, then it should be unsurprising that players sometimes want to hear stories where good really does pay off in the end.

Taking her frustration as a starting point, Lange (2014) presents some empirical evidence to suggest that a clear majority of players typically make choices that are coded within the game as the "good" choice. Lange conducted a survey of over 1,000 players to examine what moral choices they tend to make, whether they make different moral choices on subsequent playthroughs, and whether there was any relationship between the players' gender and their moral choices. Lange divided the respondents into those who play a game only once and those who will replay a game. For the "one-timers," Lange reports that "59 percent of participants played the game as a good character. 39 percent of those who played the game only once did not expressly play good or evil. ... Five percent of participants played only evil" (ibid.: 5).[7] For the "double-dippers," Lange reports that "63 percent said that their first playthrough was the good one, 27 percent said they play on a choice-by-choice basis, and only 9 percent chose evil for their first playthrough" (ibid.: 6). Lange's study also suggests that players are more likely to choose the "evil" choices on subsequent playthroughs. "49 percent of those who played the game more than once said that the evil playthrough corresponded to their second playthrough. 35 percent reported that the second playthrough was the neutral one, leaving only 16 percent of respondents who considered good to be the second option" (ibid.). When taking gender into account, it turns out that there is little significant difference in the ways that men and women make moral choices in games (ibid.: 6–7). These results show, first, that players tend to make "good" choices, and they do so by a wide point spread. Second, it shows that players who replay a game are more willing to make different moral choices on their second playthrough. This result might be explained by observing how players often regard their first playthrough as the "canonical" one, while subsequent playthroughs offer the chance to explore the game further and see what other content it has.

It is not surprising that some players would identify their in-game moral choices with their real-world sense of values. This sort of identification would naturally come from the interactive nature of video games. Unlike passive media where readers or moviegoers merely watch the characters in a novel or a film making their own moral choices, video game players in some sense participate in making moral choices along with the player-character. One explanation of how this might happen comes from Jon Robson and Aaron Meskin (2016), who argue that video games are a special kind of fiction—they are "self-involving interactive fictions." Robson and Meskin's argument begins with an undeniable and uncontroversial premise: that video games are self-involving simply because the player must take control over what their avatar does. But this control also lends the player some sense of ownership over the avatar's actions (2016: 169). If I have Booker throw his baseball at the persecuted couple in *BioShock Infinite*, it is ultimately *my* choice, not Booker's. I am the author of everything that Booker does. Moreover, the identification between the player and their avatar's actions can be seen in the way that players easily employ first-person language to talk about their gameplay, referring to the player-character as "I." Players don't typically say, "And then Booker rescued Elizabeth from the Songbird." Instead, we would more naturally say, "And then *I* rescued Elizabeth from the Songbird." The interesting upshot of Robson and Meskin's view is that, by making choices in a game, the game becomes partly *about* the player themselves. The player's choices not only make things fictionally true in the game, but they also make certain things true of the player. If it is true of my playthrough that *Booker throws his baseball at the couple*, then it is also true of me that *I threw the baseball at the couple*. The player is a co-participant in the actions of the avatar such that they may even feel some guilt about their in-game actions (ibid.: 171).

Even when we don't identify particularly strongly with our avatar, games that require players to make moral choices engage the player's *moral psychology*, at least when the player is taking their moral choices seriously. An individual's "moral psychology" is the complex web of values, concepts, experiences, and strategies that inform their moral decision-making. A complete account of how moral psychology works in video games would require a very long explanation, which would take us far from our topic (see Bartel 2020 for my account). For us, it would be more beneficial to focus on the role of both emotion and imagination in moral decision-making.

Moral decision-making is not a purely rational enterprise. It is also partly an emotional one. Reason undoubtedly plays an important and multifaceted role in moral decision-making. We reflect on our values, gather and weigh evidence, and draw inferences about the effects of our actions and their possible consequences. But emotion plays a role too. We feel disgusted and outraged by injustice, we feel conflicted about competing loyalties, and we feel that some outcomes are unbearable. Emotion plays an important role in telling us what we can live with and what we cannot. Moral decision-making without emotion would be robotic and inhuman.[8]

Whenever we consider counterfactual possibilities or imagine what our futures might be like, we are employing imagination. We do so in order to simulate how we might feel about certain scenarios, to see how we would feel if they were to become real. We do the same thing with works of fiction—we know that they are not real and yet we still have emotional reactions to them. I take this to mean that our moral psychology is responsive to fictional scenarios just as it is responsive to real-world facts. And if that is correct, then this practice suggests that, when we imaginatively run through possible scenarios, we employ our actual moral values, concepts, and sensibilities. Our emotional responses to moral choices in video games is due to the typical workings of our moral psychology.

When playing a moral choice video game, of course we sometimes make moral judgments that we normally would not make in reality. The reasons for this are many. First, the stakes are higher in reality. Getting something wrong can cause irreparable damage. Morality is the kind of thing that you typically have to get right the first time. So, it is unsurprising that moral decisions in reality tend to be slow. The potential consequences of our actions can be so overwhelming that we often fail to act at all. We become crippled by anxiety, preferring to let fate decide what happens rather than take responsibility for a bad choice. In video games, the stakes are far lower. We can take risks, make hasty decisions, and take a more cavalier attitude toward the consequences. After all, I can always return to an earlier save-point if the outcome of my actions is too upsetting.

Second, I can take on a role that is alien to me in fiction and make moral judgments from a different point of view. When I am role-playing,

I might construct an imaginary morality for myself. I imagine that my values are quite different from how they really are. We still make moral judgments when role-playing, but they are informed by different values and experiences than our real-life moral judgments. Interestingly, this isn't all that different from how we typically use our moral imaginations. Instead, it is more like considering a hypothetical. When playing as Arthur Morgan in *Red Dead Redemption 2* (*RDR2*), I imagine that loyalty to Dutch and the gang matters more to me than anything else. From that hypothetical standpoint, I can then make moral choices that I believe to be authentic for him. We take on hypotheticals every time we imagine counterfactual scenarios, whether those hypotheticals are part of our engagement with a work of fiction or are part of the typical mode of imagining my real-world future possibilities. Crucially, when we are role-playing, my real-world moral values still tell me that certain choices are good or bad. The difference, however, is that I must imaginatively reorient myself to goodness and badness. When playing as Arthur Morgan, *I* still see the killing of innocents as a bad thing. Yet, I can direct Arthur to kill innocent people, for instance, in order to steal someone's horse. How can I do this? I imagine that Arthur knows that killing someone to steal their horse is wrong, that it is a crime, and that his actions could land him in jail or worse. Yet, I also know that it is something I have to do in order to support Dutch and the gang, to maintain my loyalty to their cause, and to further their aims. In these instances, I do all the same moral reasoning that I would do in real life, with the exception that I add a hypothetical premise to my moral reasoning that does not appear in my real-life moral reasoning—that *loyalty to the gang trumps all.*

We *can* make moral judgments in games that differ from our real-world values, and there are also good reasons why players *should want to*. First, some players are *aesthetes*, individuals who are interested in pursuing rich aesthetic experiences. Playing an "evil" character can provide a sense of tension and drama, and it certainly offers an opportunity to try out a form of agency that we normally would not experience. Second, some players are *empaths*, individuals who are interested in seeing the world through another's eyes. Playing an "evil" character allows us a chance to empathize, to look at the value of morality from a different angle. Games like *RDR* and *Grand Theft Auto* (*GTA*), in which the player takes the role of a criminal, are highly lauded in the gaming community and in game criticism for good reason: they offer the player a view of the world that most of us will never see. Finally, some players are *explorers*. Some will play "evil" just to experience all that the game has to offer. Video games are designed to craft aesthetic experiences for us. It seems like a shame to miss out on a part of that crafted experience. Some storylines play out quite differently when I make the "evil" choice. In some games, different alliances and relationships are possible for the evil characters. If you are the kind of player who wants to turn over every rock and unlock every door, then you might also want to leave no moral choices unmade. Playing "evil" characters is a form of exploration, sort of like exploring the entire map in a game, but it is an exploration of choice and consequence.

Think about the different kinds of moral conflicts that players experience. Moral choices in games can be difficult for different reasons. For instance, in some cases, players might be presented with a moral dilemma that creates a tension for the *in-game morality*. These are cases where the player-character is presented with conflicting demands, where any choice that the player makes would be a perfectly valid choice for the player-character, but where one choice excludes another. For instance, in *The Walking Dead*, the player must decide whether to save either Doug or Carly from a zombie attack. From the perspective of the player-character, Lee, either choice is perfectly valid. Lee has just as much reason to save Doug as he has to save Carly. But Lee cannot save them both. In this case, we can imagine that the moral conflict that the player feels is also felt by the fictional player-character. We can think of this as *affective mirroring*, which is when the player's emotional response mirrors the player-character's emotional state. In-game moral conflicts are one sort of case where the player has an affective response to some difficult moral choices.

Other kinds of cases are those where the conflict involves what we could call the *ex-game morality*. These are cases where the game asks the player to do something that conflicts with the player's real-world moral values. In *GTA V*, there is a scene that many players and critics have commented on—a mission called "By the Book," where the player, taking control of Trevor, must torture a man to extract information from him. The torture scene is brutal. The player can choose to waterboard the victim, pull out his teeth, and electrocute him. The mission is also one of the required missions in the main storyline—the player must complete the mission in order to continue in the game. What is interesting about this case is that Trevor's actions are perfectly consistent with Trevor's moral character. Trevor is cruel and uncaring. He should feel no guilt about torturing someone. Instead, the moral dilemma has to do with the conflict between the player and Trevor.[9]

Here is what is interesting about ex-game moral conflicts: they offer a clear demonstration that the player's real-world moral values are engaged while they are playing the game. The reason why the player is conflicted is because they form the moral judgment that Trevor's actions are wrong, and yet the player still has to go along with the action in order to complete the game. The ex-game conflict arises because the player's real-world moral values are at odds with Trevor's fictional actions. It is also worth noticing that this is an interesting case where the game is able to exploit a conflict between the player's goal-seeking attitude and their narrative attitude. As goal-seeking players, we employ our means–ends reasoning to do whatever it takes to complete the game. But as narrative players, I am engaged emotionally with the story and its outcome. I want to complete *GTA V* (goal-seeking) but I don't want to torture someone (narrative). It is because the player is motivated by both attitudes that the conflict arises. We can imagine a player who doesn't care at all about the story. They shouldn't feel any conflict about torturing Trevor's victim. "By the Book" is nothing more than a sequence of button-taps to the purely goal-seeking player. We can also imagine a player who isn't interested in goal-seeking. They might be so upset about the torture scene that they quit playing the game entirely.

From here, we are in a good position to consider what this means for the aesthetic enjoyment of games. Our moral choices, whether real or fictional, have an obvious affective impact on us. When first presented with a moral dilemma, we respond emotionally, often feeling a tension or anxiety toward the unresolved conflict. Through our moral deliberation, we weigh possible outcomes and imagine future possibilities, and we feel that some possibilities are desirable while others are unbearable. Finally, we commit ourselves to a choice, hoping to resolve the dilemma. When we see the actual outcome of our choice, we are relieved when things work out the way we had hoped, and we are horrified when we realize that our choice leads to some tragic or unexpected consequence. This entire process—from dilemma, to deliberation, to action—is fraught with emotion. And this can be a source of aesthetic value. Players can appreciate for its own sake the emotional roller coaster that games provide for us by constructing moving and engaging moral choices. The aesthetic value of moral choice in games comes from the player's enjoyment of the deliberation, emotional tension, and the drama of making difficult choices.

Finally, I take this to further refute aesthetic autonomism: one does not enjoy the aesthetic value of moral choices without actually employing one's moral judgment. Our moral psychology conditions the way that we emotionally respond to moral dilemmas and conflicts. Games are designed to provoke these responses through the construction of dilemmas and conflicts. And part of the fun of playing video games is grappling with the choices that they provide us. Therefore, it cannot be the case, as the aesthetic autonomist would have us believe, that our moral sensibilities have no role to play in our aesthetic responses to games.

3 Criticizing Games

One version of aesthetic autonomism holds that any moral criticism of a work of art is irrelevant to the work's aesthetic value. Works of art can be morally offensive for a variety of reasons. Some works of art glorify violence. Some express offensive political views. Some are sexist or racist. And yet, according to some autonomists, none of these criticisms have anything to do with whether or not the work is aesthetically beautiful. Aesthetic qualities like *beauty, elegance, balance*, or *garishness* describe ways that a work appears. These are qualities that are found in the way that the work looks or sounds. And, unfortunately for morality, it is possible for a work to be both morally offensive and beautiful.

If this is true of works of art generally, then it is certainly also true for video games. Some games glorify violence, express offensive political views, and employ sexist or racist tropes. But, according to the autonomist, so what? These qualities have nothing at all to do with whether the game works, whether the gameplay is challenging, or even whether it is fun to play. Unfortunately for morality, it is possible for a video game to be, for example, sexist while offering fun combat. For example, *Lollipop Chainsaw* is an over-the-top hack-and-slash game where the player takes control of Juliet, a barely clothed cheerleader who fights off zombie hordes with her chainsaw. The tone of the game is tongue-in-cheek, bordering on the absurd. It makes light of the obvious contrast between Juliet's sexy appearance and the violence that she unleashes on the undead. The game takes a third-person perspective, which allows the player to move the camera around independently from the avatar. The player can get an (unprompted) achievement by positioning the camera to look up Juliet's skirt—the "I Swear! I Did It by Mistake!" achievement. The up-skirting achievement was an obvious source of criticism by some fans. But the autonomist would insist that the game's sexism (a moral quality) has nothing to do with whether the gameplay is fun (an aesthetic quality).

Against this view, some philosophers argue that morally offensive works of art are aesthetically flawed. The most prominent version of this theory comes from Berys Gaut (1998), which he calls "ethicism." The argument hinges on the idea that works of art are designed intentionally to elicit some response from their audiences, but some intended responses are "unmerited" by the work. For instance, imagine a romance movie where the main actor gives a poor performance and comes across as unlikable. The intention of the filmmaker is for audience members to swoon over the main actor, but this intention is unmerited by the actor's performance. Gaut's point is that a similar sort of thing can happen with morally problematic works. For instance, imagine a film that depicts a world torn apart by uncontrolled criminality, the crimes are perpetrated by one racial group, and that group is depicted as being inherently violent. The intention of the film is to stoke racial animosity and inspire sympathy for segregation. But viewers recoil at the film, feeling that its depiction presents an unmerited view of both the causes of crime and the nature of race. This moral failure is an *aesthetic* failure in the film because the aim to use an artistic medium to elicit a response is a distinctly aesthetic project. The film is a work of art and the intention of the film is to stoke racial animosity. Yet, the film failed at its intention to elicit this response. And a failed intention in a work of art is one form of artistic failure. So, works of art that contain morally unmerited views are thereby aesthetically flawed. The upshot of this theory is that it is perfectly reasonable for a critic to condemn the moral failings of a work in their appraisal of the work's aesthetic quality.

There are a few further points to notice about ethicism. First, we need to distinguish between immoral ideas that are merely depicted in a work and immoral ideas that are promoted by the work. Works of art often depict characters as having abhorrent attitudes and show horrific acts of cruelty. Yet, viewers know that, no matter how bad the villain behaves, the work is not promoting the villain's actions as something to be condoned or glorified. When we morally criticize works of art, most mature consumers accept that works of art may depict something immoral without thereby promoting it. To know what the work promotes, the consumer needs to be sensitive to the "prescribed" attitude that is built into the work. When watching the *Star Wars* movies, the viewer sees the characters exhibiting certain attitudes in their behaviors. Darth Vader is cruel. Princess Leia is determined and clever. Luke Skywalker is at first uncertain and unserious but later develops into a devoted Jedi. Throughout the films, the viewer is clear about the values and attitudes that are manifested by the characters, which can be read off of their actions and dialogues. But additionally, the films have an unspoken "prescribed" attitude, one that presents certain actions as laudable or condemnable, which colors the viewers' interpretation of events. Viewers are supposed to root for the Rebels and feel dread toward the Sith. At no point does the viewer need to be explicitly told that Darth Vader is the bad guy or that the Rebels are the heroes. Yet, these value judgments are prescribed by the films. According to ethicism, the moral views that are relevant to the aesthetic criticism of a work are those that are promoted or prescribed by the work, and not those that are merely depicted or manifested in the characters' attitudes.

Second, it is easy to overlook the point that the ethical criticism of a work is not an all-or-nothing judgment. Gaut describes ethical criticism as a "pro tanto" judgment, which means that a work is aesthetically flawed *to the extent* that it is morally flawed, no more and no less (1998: 182–3). Some works of art have minor moral flaws while others have more substantial moral flaws. We should not condemn a work totally because of one minor moral flaw. Ethicists are not puritanical in their moral criticism of works. Nonetheless, we also should not ignore minor moral flaws. However small a flaw may be, it weighs proportionally on our aesthetic evaluation of the work. In some cases, the flaw is small enough to be just a single blemish on an otherwise excellent game. It is very common for players to feel conflicted about a game. This can happen when some aspects of the game are enjoyable but where other aspects of the game are cringeworthy. A game might have excellent combat mechanics while also employing offensive racial stereotypes. The combat is one reason to praise the game while the racial stereotypes are one reason to condemn it. An ethicist holds that both of these qualities contribute to the overall aesthetic quality of the work. We do not ignore what is bad about the game for the sake of appreciating what is good.[10] And, ethicism is not just about criticizing works for their moral flaws. It goes the other way too: we also praise works for their positive moral values. Works that align with one's values tend to be admired just that much more.

Finally, ethicism does not force us to accept an absolute or objective view of morality. Even those who believe that morality is personal or subjective can be ethicists. We just need to remember that what is a "merited response" for you might not be a "merited response" for me. Ethicism tells us that we aesthetically evaluate works of art through the lens of our moral values but it does not tell us what moral values we ought to have.

Ethicism is not an uncontroversial theory. It has plenty of detractors (Eaton 2012; Jacobson 1997; Kieran 1997, 2002; Stear 2020, 2022).[11] Nonetheless, ethicism seems to capture something important about the way that we evaluate and engage with video games and works of art generally. The video games that we play tend to align with our moral values. We don't completely dismiss a game that differs from our moral values in a minor way. And players become distinctly uncomfortable when video games force them to commit acts that they judge to be immoral.

How does ethicism apply to video games? In two ways: games present moral viewpoints through their representations and through their choices and actions. Following from the argument in Section 1 above—that video games are value-laden—players morally criticize games for what they represent. The overly sexualized appearance of Juliet warrants the criticism that *Lollipop Chainsaw* employs sexist tropes. The game is aesthetically flawed insofar as the sexualization of the main character counts against it. No matter how fun the gameplay is, my enjoyment of it is marred by its crass exploitation of sexuality. By contrast, *Horizon Zero Dawn* depicts the main character, Aloy, as a powerful and intelligent machine hunter without resorting to overt sexuality. This warrants the praise that *Horizon Zero Dawn* is an enjoyable game. According to ethicism, these are both valid *aesthetic* evaluations of these games.

Some readers might object to my criticism of *Lollipop Chainsaw*. The game is absurd. It is not supposed to be taken seriously. As such, the over-sexualization of Juliet actually serves to heighten the absurdity. In that case, its use of sexist tropes is not a morally negative aspect of the game but rather a morally positive aspect, one that serves the aesthetic aim of absurdity well. The best way to enjoy *Lollipop Chainsaw* is as satire.[12]

This exchange—between my criticism and the objection—is exactly the kind of thing that we often find in popular debates about video games. Looking through online discussion boards, it is not hard to find exchanges like these—where one person says, "That game is sexist," and another person replies, "You're missing the point." What is important for us, however, is this: this objection does not threaten ethicism. If you accept that *Lollipop Chainsaw* is absurdist satire and that its use of sexist tropes actually serves some aesthetic end, then you are thinking like an ethicist![13] The interesting thing about the objection is that it still assumes that moral qualities (sexist tropes) can have an impact on the aesthetic value of a game (absurdist satire). This is in fact *not* an objection to ethicism. Instead, it is an objection to my interpretation of what the sexist tropes are promoting in *Lollipop Chainsaw*. An ethicist can accept that how some moral quality functions in a specific game is open to debate.

Returning to the main discussion now, the second way that ethicism applies to video games has to do with the game's affordances and limitations. We can morally criticize games not only for what they represent but also for what they allow us to do (Sicart 2009). Much of the criticism of the *GTA* games has to do with the actions that they allow. However, we should recognize that what the player is *not* allowed to do is also a choice on the part of the game developer, one that can be morally relevant. Players of the *GTA* games can deal drugs, steal cars, hire prostitutes and kill them to get their money back, and go on murderous rampages. These are affordances—things that the game allows players to do—and they are open to moral examination. But the *GTA* games also limit what the player is able to do. Players cannot escape the thug life, go to community college, and become social workers.[14] While limitations like these are often simply a consequence of the fact that games cannot let players do literally *anything*—it is not a recreation of real life, after all—some limitations are clearly morally relevant choices on the part of the game designer. For instance, in many games, children cannot be harmed. No matter how much I shoot at children in *RDR*, they just scatter and hide. In other games, friendly characters cannot be harmed—like the villagers in *The Legend of Zelda: Breath of the Wild*, the refugees in *Ghost of Tsushima*, or the fellow tribe members in *Horizon Zero Dawn*. This is a morally relevant choice: the games' designers are taking away the possibility that Link, Jin Sakai, or Aloy could be villainous characters.

4 Criticizing Games Externally

Ethicism allows us to criticize individual games for the imagery that they use and the affordances and limitations they employ. However, when we criticize games, we can do more than look at internal qualities like their imagery and gameplay. We can also take external factors into account—that is, factors that cannot be attributed wholly to the game itself. I think this topic is a deeply important one because feminist game criticism is ultimately founded on our ability to make evaluative claims based on broad, external factors.

One of the main complaints that gamers make against feminist game criticism is that we should evaluate games "on their own merits." Whether a game is fun to play or not has to do with qualities that are internal to the game. Feminist game critics often talk about issues that are external to games themselves—like the representation of women in media broadly, or online harassment, or sexism in gaming companies. But the aesthetic quality of a game has nothing to do with other forms of popular media, the fact that there are jerks online, or office politics. Feminism is illegitimate as a form of criticism, these objectors hold, because our aesthetic evaluation of a game should properly focus on just the game. I will argue that this view is wrong, that our aesthetic evaluation of games can look to external factors, and that feminist criticism is an integral part of game criticism.[15] We can start to think about this by looking again at the criticism of sexist tropes in video games and, from there, push further afield to consider what other external factors might be relevant to moral criticism.

Let us return to *Lollipop Chainsaw* for a moment. As mentioned above, some defenders of the game insist that it is satire. But what exactly does that mean? To view a game as satire requires that we look outside of the game itself. The reason why is because satire demands comparison. The "satire defense" holds that the sexualization of Juliet in *Lollipop Chainsaw* should be viewed positively because it is a comment on the absurdity of hyper-sexualized female characters in video games. That defense implies that gamers are aware that female characters are absurdly over-sexualized in other video games. But the player's awareness of what happens in other games cannot be an internal quality of *Lollipop Chainsaw*. If I must compare *Lollipop Chainsaw* to other games in order to appreciate its satire, then I must consider some factors that are external to *Lollipop Chainsaw*. And this is exactly what it means to take external factors into account: some aesthetic qualities of video games can only be appreciated by looking comparatively at other games or by looking broadly at trends in gaming. If we are comfortable with the idea that "satire" is a legitimate aesthetic value, then we must already be comfortable with taking external factors into account when evaluating a game.

Feminist critics often look for trends in gaming. We have already mentioned the trend to employ hyper-sexualized representations of women. Other trends that can be commonly found in games are, for example, playable characters are more often male than female, women are "damsels in distress," women typically play support roles in combat and most often as healers, and violence against women in narrative games often take the form of sexual violence.[16] What is interesting about trends is that the problematic content becomes (more) offensive just because it is repeated so often. Any one game taken in isolation could be forgiven for its use of a problematic trend. Consider the "damsel in distress" trope: it is not unreasonable to think that a woman could be in trouble and require some help. The first time I played *Super Mario Bros.* as a child, it didn't strike me as offensive that the Princess was a damsel in distress. However, after playing video games for decades, it is ridiculous to think of how many times I have had to rescue a damsel, especially considering how rarely I have ever been asked to rescue a "dude in distress."[17]

The fact that trends occur is neither good nor bad. Indeed, some trends are inoffensive. For instance, it is a trend for players to score higher damage points for headshots. Once this idea was introduced in games, it took off and is now nearly universal in combat games. However, trends can become damaging for a few reasons. First, trends are damaging when they are made to serve a narrow group of people and that group becomes viewed as the one whose tastes are worth serving. For instance, one common expectation in gaming is to assume that the typical gamer is a youngish White male.[18] This expectation results in a number of trends. When games allow players to design their avatar, the trend is for the default avatar to be a youngish White male, just like the expected player. Selecting an avatar that deviates from that expectation is something that the player has to actively choose. For the same reason, many games have really bad options for Black hairstyles, because the expectation is that youngish White male players are unlikely to want Black hairstyles (Winslow and Colbert 2023). These are trends that are based on a narrow expectation of who the likely player will be.

Other trends can be damaging when they express harmful viewpoints. Many researchers and critics have noted the trend where female characters are presented in a hyper-sexualized manner (Downs and Smith 2010; Lynch et al. 2016). This trend is harmful to women because it reinforces the idea that women are objects to be looked at and that a woman's value is directly tied to her sex appeal. The damage done by the use of this trend has partly to do with the content of the viewpoint itself, but it also has to do with the way that the repeated use of a trend reinforces its own legitimacy. When an idea is repeated often enough, it becomes familiar and takes on a sense of normalcy. The more it is repeated, the more expected it becomes. If a trend is repeated often enough, it can seem like "that's just the way that games are." Then, games that buck the trend come to seem abnormal and weird. However popular this viewpoint might be, it is one that game designers ought not to capitalize on. Trends become offensive when they are oppressive.

What is a "harmful viewpoint"? Stephanie Patridge (2011) has offered an insightful theory to help identify these in video games. Images have social meanings, some evil and sinister, others comforting and hopeful. For instance, swastikas or scenes of burning crosses are symbols that have social meanings. To say that the meaning of a symbol is "social" is to say that its meaning is not objective or innate. These images get their meaning because of certain facts about our society—specifically, facts about how swastikas and burning crosses are images that are used to terrify particular racial groups. It is because we use these symbols in a certain way that they get their meaning. But we shouldn't take the social nature of meaning to suggest that the meaning of these symbols can be easily changed. No one can change the meaning of these symbols by simply declaring, "I didn't mean anything by it, I just like the way it looks." In this sense, the meaning of these images is "incorrigible."

When video games make use of incorrigible social meanings, the game designer cannot simply dismiss the meaning of their imagery by saying, "Hey, it's just a game, I didn't mean anything by it." It is part of our social reality that women are often reduced to objects-to-be-looked-at. Video games that employ hyper-sexualized representations of women are reproducing not only a trend in gaming but also a harmful part of our social reality. The hyper-sexualization of women in games is not a mere aesthetic choice, one that is somehow detached from the reality that we live in.

In the discussion above, we have used the terms "trend" and "trope." I suggest a terminological distinction between *trends* and *tropes*. We could describe a "trend" as when something appeals to a significant enough group of people and makers attempt to capitalize on that popularity. As the examples above show, trends can be obvious and observable—like hyper-sexualized representations of women in games—but others can be quite broad and abstract. The trend that games are designed with youngish White males in mind is often difficult to directly observe in any particular game, while the lack of decent options for Black hairstyles is the observation of a *lack*. When some specific and identifiable content becomes a trend, critics and academics would often refer to that as a "trope." Trends can be broad and abstract, but tropes are always associated with some identifiable content.

Trends (and tropes) are always relative to a "comparison class." A comparison class is a group of things where relevant comparisons can be made. "Triple-A games" is one comparison class. "First-person shooters" is another. "Zelda games" is yet another comparison class. Some comparison classes are quite large—like "platformer games"—while other comparison classes are fairly small—like "games in the *Dragon Age* series." Researchers will at times make comparisons across large classes and across small classes. Both kinds of comparisons can be quite useful.

Thinking of the claim that games employ hyper-sexualized representations of women, what is the relevant comparison class for this claim? Most researchers who study this trend tend to focus on triple-A games, and to a lesser extent they also focus on action-adventure games. The focus on these sorts of games is for a good reason. "Triple-A action-adventure games" is a large comparison class and one that takes up a significant share of the attention that is paid to video games. It is one of the most visible, widely known, and lucrative classes of games. The trends that appear in games of this class have a way of influencing the styles and expectations for games of other classes. So, what happens in triple-A action-adventure games has a greater cultural relevant than what happens in other comparison classes.

A common mistake that people make when debating trends in video games is to deflect criticism by changing the comparison class. When people make the claim that "video games rely on sexist tropes," the (often unspoken) relevant comparison class is triple-A action-adventure games. A common, but mistaken, reply to this claim is to offer a counterexample from a different comparison class. The exchange goes like this: one person says, "Lots of video games employ sexist tropes," and another defensively says, "That's not true, there are plenty of games that don't, like *Stardew Valley*, *Calico*, and *Agent Alice*." The problem with this defensive reply is that it relies on deflecting the point away from the relevant comparison class (triple-A action-adventure) and redirecting attention to games that fall into very different comparison classes (farming games, café-management games, and hidden-object games, respectively).

When aesthetically evaluating a video game, an ethicist can perfectly well draw on their knowledge of trends and tropes. In Section 3 above, I argued that ethicists can draw on their knowledge of what video games represent and what they allow players to do to draw moral, and therefore aesthetic, judgments. If this sort of real-world knowledge is allowable when evaluating video games, then there is no reason why a knowledge of trends and tropes would be any different. Understanding the representational content of a video game requires the player to draw on their cultural knowledge of symbols and meanings. And, as Patridge's account of incorrigible social meaning shows, some symbols gain their meaning by participating in broader social realities.

Video games are objects that participate in a wider cultural conversation. As such, we cannot pretend that parts of that conversation are somehow off-limits. Video games are a form of cultural expression. They can express ideas about what we value, what we hope for, and what we find fun. They can also unfortunately express ideas about who we hate, they can be insensitive to the troubles that people actually suffer, and they can reproduce and amplify attitudes that are demonstrably harmful. Ethicism links together the ways in which what we think *is good* influences what we find to be *beautiful*.

We should remember also that ethicists needn't be puritanical about their criticism of games. An ethicist would not draw the knee-jerk conclusion that *Lollipop Chainsaw* is utterly without any merit because of its use of sexist imagery. Instead, an ethicist would consider the sexualized representation of Juliet against other aspects of the game and would try to come to a balanced judgment of the game overall. Should we see the game as satire? Is its use of satire effective or shallow? What other qualities of the game make it worth playing? What is important for us here is that the answers to these questions will be bound up in the aesthetic values that we find not only in the goal-seeking, narrative, and dollhouse qualities of the game, but also how our moral sensibilities color our responses to those qualities.

5 Summing Up

The argument in this chapter takes an important step forward for game criticism, even if it is a small one. I have argued that games are value-laden, that moral choices engage our actual moral reasoning abilities, that a game's moral qualities are a legitimate object of aesthetic evaluation, and that games have moral properties when considered both individually and against broader cultural trends. When critics accuse a game of some moral fault, it is untrue to reply that moral judgments have no role to play in aesthetic matters. Of course they do. Players cannot enjoy a game for its own sake when they are held back by feelings of angst over the game's moral faults. To put it another way, players do not stop being people in the real world when they play a game.

7

But, Is It Art?

The central task of this book is to argue that video games are objects of aesthetic value. But does this mean that video games are works of art? Works of art are aesthetic objects, but they are not the only things that are aesthetic objects. Aesthetic pleasure, aesthetic experience, and aesthetic value can be found throughout our everyday lives, not just when we go to art museums (Saito 2007). Food has an aesthetic value. So does nature. Fashion is an aesthetic practice, and having a personal style is one way that we participate in that practice. Riding my bicycle through heavy city traffic and feeling my body effortlessly weave between the cars is an aesthetic experience. And so is watching an exciting soccer match. We can find the aesthetic value in lots of things, not just in art. *Aesthetics* is a broader topic than is *art*. Nonetheless, many people associate *aesthetics* very strongly with *art*. So, a book about the aesthetics of video games needs to say something about their status as art.

Some people are skeptical that video games can be art. These skeptics come in two forms. The typical skeptic is someone who doubts specifically that video games can be works of art, but they accept that other things are works of art. Typically, they will have a theory about art and will argue that video games don't fit their theory. Their reasons for skepticism often have to do with the belief that there is a conflict between the creative, open-endedness of art and the rule-following competitiveness of games. We will look at two versions of this argument in Section 1. Another kind of skeptic is the more extreme belief that "art" is a useless concept. Some of these skeptics believe that *art* is an undefinable concept, while others believe that it is an elitist or culturally chauvinistic concept. Either way, extreme art-skeptics argue that we would be better off without the concept of *art*. In fact, *I* am one of those extreme art-skeptics (Bartel and Kwong 2021). That is the reason why I left this chapter for last—because I don't think that video games *must* be works of art in order for us to think about their aesthetic value. Indeed, nothing that I said in the previous chapters really depends on the art-status of video games. That should be proof enough that the concept *art* isn't doing some important theoretical work.

Still, the question about the art-status of video games can't be dismissed that easily, and perhaps that is for good reason. In fact, I think there are two reasons why even skeptics like me should care about this topic. First, the debate over the art-status of video games is useful because it helps us to understand what is valued about video games. For many philosophers, this debate is posed as a metaphysical question about the *essence of art*. But what they mostly end up talking about is the ways in which we value things. So, one way to approach the debate over the art-status of video games is to read between the lines: it is really a debate about how video games should be valued and whether they can be valued in ways that are similar to paintings, film, animation, and literature. That is what matters to me—the ways in which we value video games.

Second, I think the debate is worthwhile because *art* isn't going away. I think there is good philosophical reason to reject the concept of *art*, but that doesn't mean that we can get rid of the concept easily. *Art* is a concept that is deeply embedded in our culture and even in our legal system. If something counts as a work of art, then it actually has a different legal status—various countries' copyright laws, censorship laws, and taxation laws will treat art differently from other things. As long as the concept of *art* plays these roles, it is worth thinking about what counts and what doesn't.

In this final chapter, we will look at some of the recent debates over the art-status of video games. In Section 1, we will look at arguments against, and in Section 2, we will look at arguments in favor. The theorists who argue against the art-status of video games raise some challenging points about the value of video games, and the theorists who defend their art-status offer some ingenious replies. Finally, in Section 3, I will argue that, if anything gets to be art, then video games should because they are designed to be aesthetic objects. Video games are valued by gamers for the unique aesthetic experiences that they provide and games are designed to do just that.

1 Who Thinks Video Games Can't Be Art?

When we think about "games," we tend to think about competitions, challenges, things that we can win. Some video games are obviously competitions—*Mortal Kombat*, *Gran Turismo*, and *Madden NFL*. We play these games by trying to master their challenges and we know when we've done it by our scores and trophies. When we think about "art," we tend to think about thoughtful, expressive, or emotional experiences, things that can be enjoyed or interpreted but not won or lost. There are some video games that are obviously intended to be works of art—*Proteus*, *Depression Quest*, and *Dear Esther*. We play these games by trying to understand their message or simply by experiencing them, but the player can neither win nor lose. Finally, there are other video games that seem to straddle the line between *art* and *game*, things that can be thoughtfully interpreted just as much as they can be won—games like *This War of Mine*, *Portal*, and *Heaven's Vault*. So, what is the relationship between *games* and *art*? Some people worry that there is a conflict between the nature of games and the nature of art. However, people who hold this worry often give different accounts of it. Here, we will consider two.

Roger Ebert was a renowned film critic whose word on matters of taste reached millions of his followers. So, it carried some weight when he declared that video games categorically can never be art (2007, 2010a,b). On my reading, Ebert makes two serious mistakes but also offers one interesting problem to consider. Ebert's first mistake is he declares that video games categorically cannot be works of art because they do not satisfy his definition of "art," but his definition turns out to be very muddled. His definition is this:

> I thought about those works of Art that had moved me most deeply. I found most of them had one thing in common: Through them I was able to learn more about the experiences, thoughts and feelings of other people. My empathy was engaged. I could use such lessons to apply to myself and my relationships with others. They could instruct me about life, love, disease and death, principles and morality, humor and tragedy. They might make my life more deep, full and rewarding. (2010b)

Ebert argues that no video game can be art on this definition. He says, "No one in or out of the field has ever been able to cite a game worthy of comparison with the great poets, filmmakers, novelists and poets [sic]" (2010a). Two games that are often offered as examples of artistic video games are *Braid* and *Flower*. About *Braid*—a puzzle game that allows players to go back in time to correct past mistakes—Ebert says that the game's narrative is "prose on the level of a wordy fortune cookie" (ibid.). About *Flower*—a game where the player controls the wind, blowing flower petals over a field to pollinate other flowers and bring life back to a dying valley—Ebert says that it offers nothing "more than decorative interest on the level of a greeting card" (ibid.). Video games can be very entertaining, but that is all. He says, "Let me confess I enjoy entertainments, but I think it important to know what they are. ... *Spider-Man 2* is one of the great comic superhero movies but it is not great art" (2007).

As definitions of art go, this isn't a good one. Ebert's definition captures a sentiment that many people share: that a work of art, *for me*, is something meaningful and moving *to me*; and a work is meaningful partly because it taught me something valuable. However, the problem with definitions like this is that there are many things that I accept are *bona fide* works of art even though they don't move me at all. For instance, I recognize that the *Mona Lisa* is a work of art; so too are the compositions of John Cage and the paintings of Kandinsky, but I don't find any of these particularly moving. Also, there are many works of art that are meaningful and moving to me, but I don't attribute any deep or significant lessons to them. I love the music of Parliament Funkadelic and the prints of Hokusai, but not because I learned some valuable lesson from them. Ebert's definition of art is unworkable because it sets the bar too high—only things that are profoundly moving and cognitively valuable count as *art*. In fact, Ebert himself recognizes this problem and thoughtfully rejects his own definition (2010b).

Ebert's second mistake, which is really unforgiveable, is that he admits to never having played many video games. He claims to have only played two: *Cosmology of Kyoto* and *Myst*. If someone is unwilling to see if there is anything worthwhile in video games, then it is certain that they won't find anything. To Ebert's credit, this is a point that he (reluctantly) concedes—that his lack of experience with games leaves him in a poor position to judge. He says, "I would never express an opinion on a movie I hadn't seen. Yet I declared as an axiom that video games can never be Art. I still believe this, but I should never have said so. Some opinions are best kept to yourself" (2010b).

Ebert's writing is hyperbolic, his definition of "art" is unfeasible, and—on top of it all—he's never played many video games. These are all good reasons to dismiss his comments. However, he makes one point, buried among his other comments, that does pose an interesting challenge to the art-status of video games. It is a comment that comes out in his back-and-forth reply to Clive Barker (Ebert 2007). He quotes Barker as saying,

> I think that Roger Ebert's problem is that he thinks you can't have art if there is that amount of malleability in the narrative. In other words, Shakespeare could not have written "Romeo and Juliet" as a game because it could have had a happy ending, you know? If only she hadn't taken the damn poison. If only he'd have gotten there quicker.

Ebert replies,

> He is right again about me. I believe art is created by an artist. If you change it, you become the artist. Would "Romeo and Juliet" have been better with a different ending? Rewritten versions of the play were actually produced with happy endings. "King Lear" was also subjected to rewrites; it's such a downer. At this point, taste comes into play. Which version of "Romeo and Juliet," Shakespeare's or Barker's, is superior, deeper, more moving, more "artistic"?

This comment is very brief, so some charitable interpretation is needed. I think it is best put like this: Ebert worries that there is a conflict between the freedom of gameplay and the artist's creative authority. Games are malleable. When we play a game, we get a different outcome from one playthrough to the next. Sometimes I win, sometimes I lose. This is one of the essential features of games: that the player has some input, that how the game turns out depends on choices that the player makes, and different choices lead to different results.

Art is different according to Ebert. He says, "Video games by their nature require player choices, which is the opposite of the strategy of serious film and literature, which requires authorial control" (2005). When we enjoy a work of art, part of what we appreciate is the artist's choices, reflected in their sense of taste. Many works of art have a message, a story to tell, or a lesson to impart. And these all come from the artist. Indeed, the artist is the person who has the creative authority to invent a fictional world and to decide what is canonical within the world that they invented. So, art is supposed to be the product of the artist's vision, one person who can be attributed creative control. But gameplay gives the player control over how the game turns out, and this robs the artist of their creative authority. The artist's message, then, no longer belongs to the artist. Again, as Ebert says, "I believe art is created by an artist. If you change it, you become the artist" (2007). I cannot really appreciate the artist's work—their message and its meaning—if I can make changes to their work.

This is one part of Ebert's account that has some merit. In fact, many game designers and theorists have commented on how narrative video games suffer from exactly this problem. Stories typically develop along a predeterminate path. To tell a rich and detailed story in a video game, the game must funnel the player along a predictable line, thus taking away some degree of freedom from the player. An example of this is *Max Payne 3*. The story of the game is fixed. It tells its story by giving the player a linear path to follow. However good the battles might be, the player has little input in the story, which makes it feel like a long movie that one simply clicks through. Alternatively, giving the player more freedom to contribute to the narrative results in weak or ambiguous storylines. The need to balance the freedom of play alongside the rigidity of a story is a fundamental tension that many videogame developers have struggled with.[1] So, Ebert is not wrong to worry about this.

This is one possible conflict between games and art. For Brock Rough (2016, 2018a), the conflict is quite different—in fact, it seems almost the opposite of Ebert's issue. Rough's claim is that games cannot be works of art and vice versa because the norms governing the appreciation of video games are inconsistent with the norms governing the appreciation of art.[2] Rough's argument is a rather technical. I will simplify it.

Every game specifies the goal that the player seeks and the means by which they seek it. We can always specify what the goal is independently from the means of achieving the goal. But with art, the goal is simply to appreciate it. Appreciating a work of art means (at least) to pay attention to all of the work's relevant features. If a work of art was also a game, then it would need to exhibit the distinction between the goal and the means in order to be a game, and we would need to pay attention to all of its relevant features in order to appreciate it as a work of art. But these two demands seem to create a dilemma: the means of appreciating an art-game (to understand it) is already captured by its goal (to understand it). Rough interprets this to mean that we cannot separate the means of appreciating the work from the goal of understanding the work; and it is not possible for one object to meet both demands; so, there can be no game-art hybrids (2018b: 15).

Rough's argument ultimately has to do with his understanding of what a game is and his account of what art appreciation demands. There are many places where one could begin picking away at Rough's argument—I would begin by questioning his account of games.[3] But, instead of doing that, I want to recognize a potential issue that we could take from Rough, an issue that is at least inspired by his account even if it cannot be directly attributed to Rough. There may be a potential conflict between the rule-bound nature of games and the rule-free nature of art. When we play a game, we must follow its rules. Games are defined by their rules and players are required to abide by them. If we don't, then we are not really playing *that* game.

Art is different. When we appreciate a work of art, we don't follow rules in the same sense. We engage with art in a more creative and exploratory way. The point of art appreciation isn't to win. The point is instead to understand or aesthetically experience the work. For something to be both a game and a work of art, one would have to both follow its rules while also and at the same time freely engaging with it. And that is impossible. By following rules, I must limit my freedom and my ability to creatively explore a work of art; and by freely exploring, I cannot limit myself with arbitrary rules.[4] So, in the spirit of Rough's criticism, games cannot be works of art because each of these things demands a mode of attention that conflicts with the mode of attention demanded by the other.

2 Who Thinks Video Games Can Be Art?

Among Ebert's comments about the art-status of games, he asks one easily overlooked but important question: "Why are gamers so intensely concerned, anyway, that games be defined as art?" (2010a). Despite its dismissive tone, this is actually a worthwhile question: why does it matter whether games are art? What is at stake? What would be gained if we recognized video games as art? Ebert suggests that gamers want to defend the art-status of games just because they seek validation. Video games are often looked down upon as a waste of time. But if video games are art, then that time cannot be wasted. As many gamers point out, no one thinks that spending hours reading a novel is a waste of time. Gamers just want the same degree of respect. In the end, Ebert accepts that it may be best to simply placate gamers and their hurt feelings, if we must.

It is worthwhile to ask why gamers want to count video games as art and to explore what possible motivations there could be animating their anxieties. However, it is also important to notice that Ebert's question cuts both ways. He asks, "Why do gamers want to define games as art?" But one could just as well ask, "Why does Ebert want to *deny* that games are art?" What is Ebert defending? Why must the boundaries of art be protected? What would Ebert lose if we recognized video games as art?

Some philosophers think that at least some video games can be works of art. Aaron Smuts (2005) offers one of the earliest philosophical defenses of the art-status of video games. Philosophers and art theorists have been debating over the definition of "art" since at least the nineteenth century.[5] Yet there is no consensus about how to define it.[6] There are many competing definitions of art today that one could choose from. Smuts argues that, if we look at the major contending definitions, some video games would surely count.[7] He says, "Video games can be art according to historical, aesthetic, institutional, representational and expressive theories of art. ... If we can agree that all these theories generally track our intuitions about what should be considered art, then when they are all in agreement we have good reason to think that we have successfully picked out an art form" (2005: §1). Smuts' all-encompassing strategy allows us to identify video games as works of art without forcing us to defend any particular definition of art.

Briefly, here are the five theories that Smuts offers. First, some philosophers defend *historical* theories of art, whose central premise is that some object is a work of art if it was made with the intention to be appreciated in some way that a past work of art was appreciated

(Levinson 1990). Smuts argues that many video games would count as works of art on this historical definition as it is clear that many games are designed to share much with film and animation. One small example is the way that many games employ a lens flare effect, as when the player pans around the scene in a third-person-perspective game. This is interesting because lens flare implies the presence of a camera; as it is a video game, however, clearly there was no camera. So, the lens flare is an illusion. The use of lens flare in a video game is clearly a stylistic choice that serves no purpose within the game except to draw on a visual effect that is common in film.

Aesthetic theories of art hold that works of art are meant to serve an aesthetic function (Beardsley 1983; Iseminger 2004). Of course, art can serve lots of functions, but its main function is to provide worthwhile aesthetic experiences according to this theory. Traditionally, these worthwhile experiences would aim for things like beauty, coherence, and unity; but experiences of horror, disgust, sadness, and melancholy can also be worthwhile in art. Video games are clearly often designed with aesthetic aims in mind. Smuts notes that "modern video game designers are deeply concerned with traditional aesthetic considerations familiar to animators, novelists, set designers for theater productions and art directors for films" (2005: §5). So, just as the aesthetic concerns of filmmakers and animators are sufficient to make movies and cartoons art, so too should the aesthetic concerns of game designers suffice to make video games art. Again, Smuts says, "Any aesthetic theory of art that acknowledges the art status of animation would also recognize many contemporary video games, since the intentions of the creators and the variety of aesthetic experience the two art forms admit overlap considerably" (ibid.).

Institutional theories of art hold that something is a work of art if it serves a particular role within the "artworld" (Dickie 1997; Diffey 1969). The "artworld" is an informal social institution where individuals act as creators, curators, critics, buyers, sellers, and collectors. The objects that they create, critique, interpret, buy, and sell are "works of art." On this theory, there is nothing further intrinsically valuable or distinctive about works of art other than the fact that they happen to be the objects that people make, display, and interpret. Video games certainly play this role. Some have been exhibited in recognized art museums, there has been an increase in university programs dedicated to video games, and the development of venues devoted to video game criticism all serve as evidence for the "institutional credibility" of video games as an artform (Smuts 2005: §5).[8]

Representational theories of art emphasize that, whatever else we must say of art, it is the sort of thing that can carry messages and meanings (Danto 1981; Goodman 1976; Langer 1953). Even though some works of art are meaningless, it is central to art, and to our appreciation of art, that we at least expect works of art to possess some meaning. When faced with a perplexing piece of modern art, it is common for viewers to ask, "What is it about?"; and it is just as common to accept a plausible story of what it is about as evidence that the object is, really, a work of art. Some video games are not about anything, but many are. Indeed, the narrative possibilities for video games have increased as the technology has become more sophisticated. Even for those games that are not about anything in some grand sense, games are at least minimally representational in that they have characters, depict identifiable actions and scenarios, and are thus open to interpretation.

Finally, *expressive* theories of art hold that works of art are vehicles for expressing emotion (Collingwood 1938; Tolstoy 1898). What matters here is not so much the arousal of an emotion but rather something like the communication or external embodiment of an emotion. Players often become frustrated by difficult challenges or elated when they overcome a formidable foe; but these sorts of emotional responses are not what interest expressive theorists. While many video games are designed merely to offer some competitive challenge, other games are designed with emotional engagement in mind—for example, it seems clear that moral choice video games rely on emotionally piquing the player's sensibilities.

Smuts offers many reasons to think that at least some games are art; however, he does not defend the art-status of all video games categorically. Some video games should be seen squarely as games, and therefore we benefit little by thinking of them as art. For instance, there is little need to search for meaning in *FIFA 20*. So, it would likely benefit us very little to think of it as art. By contrast, it seems entirely appropriate to search for meaning in games like *Death Stranding*. Treating some video games as art, but not others, seems right. And video games aren't uncommon in this respect. There are other categories where some members are works of art while others are not. For instance, some photographs are works of art—like the works of Julia Margaret Cameron or Sherrie Levine—while other photographs are not—like the picture of me on my driver's license. Similarly, we should not treat the art-status of video games as an all-or-nothing matter.

Both Grant Tavinor (2009) and Dominic McIver Lopes (2010) follows Smuts' lead, arguing that some video games should count as works of art, though both adopt a *cluster theory* of art. According to the cluster theory, there is no single, essential feature that all works of art must share. Instead, there is a cluster of conditions that can make something art. To take one prominent account, Berys Gaut (2000) offers ten criteria that make up the cluster of art-making properties. The sort of properties that make something art are (1) possessing positive aesthetic qualities, (2) being expressive of emotion, (3) being intellectually challenging, (4) being formally complex and coherent, (5) having a capacity to convey complex meanings, (6) exhibiting an individual point of view, (7) being an exercise of creative imagination, (8) being a product of a high degree of skill, (9) belonging to an established artform, and (10) being intended to be a work of art (2000: 28). Both Tavinor and Lopes argue that some video games would clearly satisfy enough of the cluster to count as art. Video games that do not satisfy these conditions are those that we do not suspect as being art. As Tavinor says about classic video games like *Pong*, they often lack "direct pleasure in aesthetic qualities, skill and virtuosity, style, the potential for critical evaluation, expressive individuality, emotional saturation, and intellectual (rather than sensory-motor) challenge, in anything other than a near-vacuous sense of these criteria" (2009: 191).

When looking at contemporary video games, it is fairly easy to find examples of video games that satisfy one of Smuts' definitions of art, or some of the art-making cluster properties that Tavinor and Lopes favor. Many games are aesthetically rewarding, cinematic, and expressive. But one issue that Smuts, Tavinor, and Lopes all face is that properties they identify that make video games works of art rely on traditional artistic qualities—like looking beautiful or telling a compelling story. This would imply that video games are works of art only when they possess these traditionally recognized artistic qualities. But can video games be works of art by virtue of the properties that are unique to them—properties like gameplay and interactivity?

Smuts considers whether the act of playing a game itself could be an artform; however, he ultimately decides not to pursue the possibility (2005: §3). When we look for evidence to prove that video games are art, we tend to look at qualities of the games themselves and not qualities of the experience of playing them. Smuts suggests an interesting reason for this: because the technology of video games evolves so quickly, and also because gamers tend to focus on playing more recent games, it may be that there are no video games that all players (or even most players) would be familiar with. This means that there would be no shared language or common set of experiences that gamers could use to develop a critical language for gameplay. Smuts' has a good point here. Compare this to other artforms. When someone develops an interest in film, music, or painting, it is very common that they would try to familiarize themselves with older, influential works as well as the history of the medium. If we gathered together a diverse group of people who are all film enthusiasts, for instance, there would be a very high chance that all of those people have seen at least one movie in common—perhaps it would be *The Wizard of Oz*, or *Pulp Fiction*, or *The Godfather*. This shared experience gives that group of people a basis to work from to develop the critical language to talk about other films. Now, imagine that we were to gather together a diverse group of gamers. Would there be an equally high chance that all of those people have played at least one game in common? I think the chance would be very small. "Gamer" is a fractured group that doesn't have a lot of shared experiences. Many gamers are loyal to only one brand of console, many only play games that are available on the current generation of consoles, and many will specialize on one particular genre of games. The fact that I am a gamer doesn't guarantee that I will have many shared gaming experiences with some other gamer. Smuts' point here is that it is possible that game criticism has long paid more attention to games themselves than the experience of playing games because of the lack of shared experience among gamers. For that reason, Smuts doesn't reject the possibility that playing could be an artform, but he doesn't pursue the thought further.

Tavinor suggests that some aesthetic and expressive qualities can come from elements of gameplay, though his defense of this claim isn't as strong as one might like. Tavinor comments that the "graceful movements of the characters in *Heavenly Sword*" (2009: 180) or the feeling that cars in *Grand Theft Auto IV* (*GTA IV*) have a sense of "heft" (ibid.: 181) may count as kinesthetic qualities, which places video games closer to artforms like dance. These comments go some way toward defending the artistic relevance of gameplay. However, Tavinor also comments that the competitive nature of many games might count *against* their status as works of art (ibid.: 191–2). Video games might "partially overlap" with art insofar as they possess qualities that are found in traditional artforms, but video games are also distinctive in that they possess "qualities not traditionally seen as crucial to art" (ibid.: 192).

Lopes suggests that games might be art "precisely because of how they work as games" (2010: 115). Specifically, the interactivity of games might offer players aesthetically relevant sources of meaning—"a game can express ideas through the range of possibilities it generates" (ibid.: 117). Taking on this suggestion from Lopes, consider *Gris*, which is a story-driven puzzle platformer. Its graphics are stunningly beautiful, but the puzzles themselves are not particularly challenging. Despite the relative ease of the game, it is still immensely satisfying to play. The puzzles introduce new and unexpected concepts for gameplay (Webster 2018). The pleasure of playing *Gris* has less to do with the satisfaction of overcoming a difficult challenge and more to do with appreciating how the character's unique abilities open up interesting new possibilities for movement. The main character—a girl named Gris—can gently glide, swim, jump, and transform into an immovable block. The player navigates through the different environments in the game by employing these affordances. At one stage, the screen is divided in half where the upper and lower halves each have their own center of gravity. The player must use Gris' abilities in combination with the properties of the environment to navigate the maze. Despite the simplicity of the maze, it is simply enjoyable to be able to move through the space in unexpected ways. In the case of *Gris*, it is not just the visual graphics or the interpretable meaning of the game that would make it art, however beautiful or intriguing they might be. Additionally, it is the gameplay that creates certain aesthetic possibilities—the affordances for movement and properties of the environment create opportunities for gameplay that is elegant, graceful, and clever. Thus, Lopes is generally positive about the prospect that gameplay can itself be an artistic element of video games, though his defense of this claim is very brief.

To sum up these theorists' views from the above two sections, some video games might be art because they possess traditional artistically valued properties, ones that are sufficient to make things like paintings and films works of art (Smuts, Tavinor). Other video games possess meaning and expressiveness because of properties that are unique to video games, like their interactivity (Lopes). Even if we cannot categorically count *all video games* as works of art, it seems clear that at least some should count as art no matter which theory we choose. These are all good reasons to think that some video games are works of art. Nonetheless, there are some interesting conflicts left to resolve. Both Ebert and Rough worry that there is a conflict between the demands of gameplay and the demands of art. For Ebert, that conflict is the possible loss of artistic control; for Rough, it is the conflict of the competing demands of rule following and artistic understanding. My view is that both Ebert's and Rough's concerns can be met if we accept the broad understanding of the aesthetic value of video games that I defended in the previous chapters.

3 Aesthetic Objects as Art

According to the attitudinal theory that I defended in this book, video games are obviously aesthetic objects. From here, I believe there is a possible route open to argue that some video games are works of art. Video games are works of art when they are designed primarily with aesthetic aims in mind, and gameplay itself can be designed to serve aesthetic aims. This argument could satisfy both Ebert's and Rough's criticisms.

First, video games are aesthetic objects. An aesthetic experience is just an experience that is valued for its own sake, as I argued in Chapter 1. So, to describe something as an *aesthetic object* on this account is just to say that, under the right conditions, one's experience of the object can be valued for its own sake. To put it another way, an aesthetic object is whatever object of one's attention it is that one enjoys experiencing for its own sake.

We should make a quick distinction here between *accidental* aesthetic objects and *designed* aesthetic objects. Our broad account of aesthetic value is so broad that almost any object can be valued for its own sake. In that case, lots of things are *accidental* aesthetic objects. When I watch my cats wrestle with each other, I can pay attention to the speed, fluidity, and power of their movements while also noticing how they hold back from actually hurting each other. I don't think that my cats are intentionally putting on a performance for my enjoyment. Or, when I sit on my porch during a storm, I take pleasure in the sound and smell of the rain. I don't think that the weather designed the storm to be enjoyable. These aesthetic experiences are accidental: I appreciate for its own sake my experience of something that wasn't designed to induce that experience.

Other objects are *designed* to be aesthetic objects. Someone put some thought and effort into designing the object so that others can enjoy experiencing it. Songs, films, paintings, theatrical performances, food, landscapes, clothing, jewelry, cars, tea ceremonies, rollercoasters, *and video games*—all of these things are designed, at least partly, to be enjoyed for their own sake. Many of these things have other aims as well. Cars are worthless if they don't work, no matter how pretty they are. So, something can be a designed aesthetic object even while it has some other aim.

One of the interesting things about designed aesthetic objects is that they produce a wide range of aesthetic values. We can take pleasure in the way that the object looks, sounds, smells. But also, because the object is designed, we are able to look for things like meaning, irony, satire, symbolism, allusion, and originality; and each of these can be a distinctive source of aesthetic enjoyment. These sorts of values cannot be found in accidental aesthetic objects. We take pleasure in appreciating for its own sake the satire of *GTA*, the critical allusions to Ayn Rand in *BioShock*, and the irony of *Broforce*. But we don't go looking for irony and symbolism in a thunder storm.

More importantly for our purposes, many video games are aesthetic objects *because* of their gameplay, not *despite* their gameplay, as I argued in Chapter 3. When we take pleasure in gameplay for its own sake, then gameplay becomes the reason why a video game is an aesthetic object for us. This point might be sufficient to counter Rough's claim that games cannot be art. Rough is focused on the fact that we play games by following rules to achieve a predefined outcome. But sometimes, we also play games for the experience of playing them. This is a point that is defended by C. Thi Nguyen (2020): sometimes we enjoy playing a game because we intrinsically enjoy the activity that the game allows us to pursue. I might push myself on my bicycle to beat an opponent up a hill; but sometimes, I push myself just because I enjoy the feeling of my bicycle's speed. Nguyen argues that games are art because they are designed with aesthetic aims in mind. Through gameplay, the player enjoys the feeling of their own agency. And games are designed to offer different forms of agency. For Nguyen, the art of games is the way that agency can be manipulated to produce interesting and worthwhile aesthetic results.[9] We can now add to this that there are other kinds of agency that players value for its own sake—like the agency required to make narrative choices (from Chapter 4) and the agency required to develop our own imaginative stories (from Chapter 5).

So, video games are designed to produce experiences that we value for their own sake. Does that mean that they should count as works of art? Not yet. Nguyen's account provides an answer to Rough's concern by putting gameplay within the scope of designed aesthetic objects, which gets us most of the way there.[10] But what we need is an argument to show that, because gameplay provides aesthetic experiences, games are therefore works of art. The difficulty here is that there are many designed aesthetic objects that are not works of art, and it may just be the case that video games are one of those. Rollercoasters, cars, and food are all designed aesthetic objects, but they are typically not considered works of art. It might be tempting to say that all of these things *should* be art. However, many philosophers worry that, if we took this line, then the concept of art will proliferate to the point of meaninglessness (e.g., Tavinor 2009: 174). If every single object that is designed to have a little touch of flair is a work of art, then "art" seems pretty shallow, trivial, and ordinary. Can we defend the art-status of video games while avoiding the problem of proliferation?

Possibly. Here is an argument for the art-status of video games that might just avoid unprincipled proliferation. The argument has three premises. First, there is a strong intuitive link between *art* and *designed aesthetic objects*.[11] Aesthetic objects count as works of art when they are designed with their aesthetic aim primarily in mind. It is not that every designed aesthetic object is a work of art. Only those aesthetic objects that are *primarily* designed for their aesthetic aim would count. Food, clothing, and cars can have aesthetic aims; but they can still serve their intended function even when they fail to achieve their aesthetic aims. Second, what is distinctive of video games (or, indeed, games generally) is that they are appreciated for their gameplay. A good game is not simply one that sorts winners from losers. A good game is one that is compelling to play. Third, gameplay can be designed with aesthetic aims in mind (whether that gameplay is goal-seeking, narrative, or dollhouse play). This premise is not a categorical claim. It does not say that all gameplay is designed with aesthetic aims in mind, nor that all games are works of art because they all contain gameplay. Instead, the point is that gameplay is a tool that game designers can use to achieve certain aesthetic aims. When game designers use gameplay in this manner, then they are using it like an artistic medium (cf. Nguyen 2020). When gameplay is used as an artistic medium, it allows them to communicate ideas, create meanings, and produce aesthetic effects. So, we shouldn't see gameplay as something distinct from or alien to the artistic elements of a game. Instead, well-designed games can draw aesthetic experiences out of gameplay itself. On this view, some video games (but not all) would count as art.

For example, consider *This War of Mine*, which offers a reflection on the atrocities of war where the player manages the lives of refugees living in a war-torn city. The player is often forced to make difficult choices about whom to save and what to prioritize. Rough suggests that we should think of *This War of Mine* as a work of art but not as a game (2018b: 3). For Rough, we are supposed to engage with the emotionally complex narrative. So, playing the game to win would be a crass misunderstanding of it. He says, "To 'play [*This War of Mine*] to win,' to accumulate the most points, or merely survive, without consideration of the morally ambiguous aspect of the work would be to miss the point and thus to engage with it improperly" (ibid.). In reply, we should notice the complex, interwoven ways in which gameplay contributes to the player's aesthetic experience. Crucially, it is the gameplay that presses the player into a deeper, and more uncomfortable, reflective position. "Playing to win" takes on a different meaning in this game. *Winning* means doing the greatest amount of good for the survivors, but doing the greatest good sometimes comes at a steep emotional cost. A full and rich experience of the game demands that one plays by the rules and tries to win while also struggling with the harsh choices that the greater good sometimes demands. So, in response to Rough, we don't have to choose between *game* and *art*—or between playing to win and engaging with the narrative. Instead, the narrative is bound up in the gameplay and vice versa. This is what an art-game would look like.

This argument offers a version of Lopes' defense of the art-status of video games. Lopes argues that *meaning* can be drawn out of gameplay (2010: 116–18). I think that is correct. Finding *meaning* in gameplay is one kind of experience that is valuable for its own sake. But we might expand on Lopes' point: we can value the experience of gameplay for its own sake for many reasons, not just when we find meaning in it. Think of Tavinor's example of taking pleasure in the feeling that cars in *GTA* have a sense of "heft" (2009: 181). The pleasure Tavinor describes is a kind of aesthetic experience, though not because the heft of the cars is interpreted as having any particular meaning.

This argument avoids unprincipled proliferation.[12] It is not that all aesthetically appealing objects are works of art, nor even all designed aesthetic objects. Rather, it is objects designed primarily with aesthetic aims in mind. And some video games are designed to satisfy these aims. Additionally, this argument can distinguish between *video games that are works of art* and *video games that are not*. As was stated above, *video games* might be a category like *photographs*: some are works of art and some are not. The games that we are tempted to think of as works of art (e.g., *This War of Mine*) are those that are designed with aesthetic aims primarily in mind. And those that we do not think of as works of art (e.g., *Pong*) are those that are not designed with such aims in mind.

So, that means that video games are art, right? For the most part. If you don't accept that there is a strong link between *art* and *objects designed primarily for aesthetic aims*, then this argument won't impress you much. Even worse, if you are skeptical that *art* is a useful concept at all, on general philosophical grounds, then you will have little reason to accept this argument either. However, I think that the designed aesthetic object argument is likely the strongest reason to believe that video games are works of art.

However, even if you do reject the designed aesthetic object argument, or even the usefulness of *art*, the arguments in this book have still fulfilled an important task: at the very least, we have demonstrated that video games are aesthetic objects and that gameplay is central to what makes video games aesthetic objects. I think *this* is what is important.

Video games are, for many people, a source of profound aesthetic delight, which comes in the form of goal-seeking play, narrative play, and dollhouse play. These three forms of play in video games provide an inexhaustible source of aesthetic enjoyment. If you thereby also want to call video games "works of art," then I certainly won't try to stop you.

Notes

1

1 For an introductory overview, see Shelley (2017).
2 This view is widely known as either the *representational theory* of perception or the *intentional theory*. Representational theories have many contemporary defenders (see, for instance, Crane 2001 and Tye 1995) and also many opponents (for instance, Brewer 2011 and Martin 2002). The debate over the nature of perception is fascinating, but it is not the focus of our attention.
3 Iseminger (2006) and Levinson (2013).

2

1 Rami Ali (2022) makes a similar distinction between sporting games, storytelling games, and simulation games.
2 One influential account of play that I will be leaving out is that of Brian Sutton-Smith's (1997). In that book, Sutton-Smith argues that play is ambiguous in the sense that it does not have one single definition. Rather, there are multiple different "rhetorics" of play, each having their own function and discourse. While some of the rhetorics that Sutton-Smith describes evince a psychological account of play, others are not directly relevant to the aesthetics of games.
3 We will examine this in more detail in Chapter 3, pages 51–3.
4 It is an open question whether Huizinga's magic circle is a useful or even plausible idea. See Nguyen (2017) for a helpful overview of the debate. This debate does not concern me. Rather, I draw attention to the "magic circle" for what it indicates about the player's state of mind.
5 One might object that surely some people engage in play for the sake of producing extrinsic goods. Some people take up a sport for the sake of their health, others will join a sport team for the sake of camaraderie, and professional athletes certainly play for high salaries and prize money. But

Caillois' point is that these extrinsic goods cannot explain the value of play. Many people—children, amateur athletes, people who simply love the game—continue to play with no expectation of any extrinsic reward. They do so because they enjoy it. Moreover, Caillois says that professionals who play at their sport *only* for the sake of an extrinsic reward "are not players but workers. When they play, it is at some other game" (2001: 6).

6 Miguel Sicart argues for a similar point in his discussion of "playfulness," which he describes as an attitude, one that appropriates a context that is not intended for play (2014: Ch. 2).

7 I have previously voiced some criticism of the idea that agency is an artistic medium (see Bartel 2021); however, my criticism of that point should not overshadow my agreement with Nguyen's account of the aesthetic value of games.

8 Many accounts of game playing—like those of Suits (2014), Juul (2005), and Nguyen (2020)—offer accounts that are limited to the goal-seeking attitude of play.

9 Thanks to Brandon Polite for allowing me to share his enthusiasm for chocobo breeding.

10 Evidence for this can be found in Juul (2005: 28 and 40) where he exhibits some skepticism about games of chance. It is also worth noticing here that Juul's definition of games is fairly narrow and exclusive. Notably, Juul claims that pen-and-paper games like *Dungeons and Dragons* and simulation games like *SimCity* are not "classic" games (ibid.: 43), meaning that they are borderline cases of games.

11 For details about propositional attitudes, the reader could start with Richard (1990) or Salmon and Soames (1988).

12 This view is very common among analytic philosophers of art and aesthetics. For a representative example, see Carroll's (2009) account of art criticism.

13 Thanks to Nick Wiltshire for pointing this out.

3

1 We might today question whether animals are as arational as Huizinga seemed to accept; however, this is a point that I will not pursue here.

2 These four elements that I take from Caillois' account are not intended to be the limits of the aesthetics of games. Rather, I offer these for two reasons. First, it offers a convenient frame to contextualize some recent work on the aesthetics of games. Second, looking for the ways that video games realize these four elements clearly helps to establish a link between video games and the long history of games.

3 Pronounced "me-hi chik-sent-me-hi."

4 One exception is Braxton Soderman's critical examination in *Against Flow* (2021). Soderman argues that flow theory exploits a feature of our psychology that allows us to be easily manipulated and has itself been further exploited by the gaming industry to get players addicted to games. While this criticism is itself interesting, Soderman's objections to flow theory are not strictly about its plausibility.

5 Readers may think that Nguyen's "harmony of capacity" sounds a lot like Csikszentmihalyi's notion of flow. They are similar, but they are not the same thing. According to Csikszentmihalyi, flow states are those where players become so absorbed in play that they lose their sense of self. But this loss of a sense of self is not part of Nguyen's account of the harmony of capacity. Instead, part of what the player appreciates is that they have developed a certain set of skills, and this requires a degree of self-recognition. It is the experience of realizing "I can do this" when facing a challenge that was previously beyond your abilities.

6 For instance, see Leino (2020), who argues that players cannot pursue a goal while enjoying the aesthetic beauty of the game. For Leino, it seems that we have to split our attention separately between these two.

7 If it sounds weird to describe builds in *Minecraft* as "architectural," then read guidebooks to *Minecraft* builds like that of Birch, Brew, and Moore (2020).

8 For a critical discussion of transmedial games, see Bartel (2018).

9 Similar points apply to other social phenomenon, though these vary by degree. The rules of etiquette can easily be broken if the host and dinner guests agree to suspend the rules. For the rules of the road, rule breaking is allowable in emergencies or when extenuating circumstances are present, like running a red light to get a dying person to a hospital. The enforcement of many traffic laws is often left to the discretion of law

enforcement agents. Alternatively, wartime rules of engagement are one area where one hopes for strict adherence to the rules.
10 See Chapter 6 for further discussion.
11 It is not just the mechanics that are enjoyable here but also the proprioceptive feeling of movement that such gameplay demands (Cf. Artis 2021: 67).
12 I discuss this example in detail in Bartel (2024). However, the focus in that essay concerns the way that gameplay can aide the player in empathizing with the player-character.

4

1 The obvious exception to this would be novels and films that explicitly deal with alternate decision-paths, like choose-your-own-adventure novels or the film *Run Lola Run* (1998).
2 My approach here is inspired by Salen and Zimmerman's, who reject questions like "Are games narratives?" in favor of questions like "What kinds of narrative experiences do games make possible? What is the role of narrative in the design of meaningful play?" (2004: 378).
3 There has been much philosophical discussion how what representation is and how it works. Kendall Walton's (1990) theory of fiction as a form of make-believe is subtitled "On the Foundations of the Representational Arts." For Walton, the notion of fiction and representation run together such that we understand something as a representation by engaging in a fictional pretense. I do not aim to mount a critique of Walton's theory here, and I am open to the possibility that my view is largely consistent with Walton's theory. However, I want to reserve the term "fiction" for a more specific function. As my examples (hopefully) show, I take it that we might sometimes wish to use the concept of *representation* without fully running it together with *fiction*. This is surely the case with signs. A steaming coffee mug sign on a shop door gives information by representing something, but we might not wish to invoke the notion of fiction in order to explain coffee shop signs.

4 Or, if you like, it is at this level of description, above the mere recognition of what symbols might mean, that it becomes meaningful to invoke the notion of *fiction*.
5 This description comes from the game manual.
6 Grant Tavinor (2009) convincingly demonstrates that Walton's account can be applied to fictions in video games too.
7 Tavinor (2009: 23–4) defends a similar distinction.
8 Fisher (2022: 436) proposes a different terminology to capture this distinction. A "work-truth" is "true in all branches of a work," while a "branch-truth" is "true in some but not all branches of the work."
9 Aarseth (2004) strongly resists the idea that video games are "interactive narratives." Aarseth points to the primacy of the ludic elements of video games rather than their stories as definitive of their medium. Given this, Aarseth concludes that video games are better understood as "simulations" (see also Frasca 2003b). He writes,

> Simulation is the key concept, a bottom-up hermeneutic strategy that forms the basis of so many cognitive activities: all sorts of training, from learning to pilot a plane to learning to command troops, but also the use of spreadsheets, urban planning, architectural design and CAD, scientific experiments, reconstructive surgery, and generative linguistics. And in entertainment: computer games. If you want to understand a phenomenon, it is not enough to be a good storyteller, you need to understand how the parts work together, and the best way to do that is to build a simulation. (2004: 52)

For my part, I find "simulation" to be an odd category, one that doesn't really contrast against *fiction* or *narrative* so easily. Aarseth is motivated by the idea that computer games are playable systems of rules. Video games function as simulations because they can map out the rules of a system so well. And what is interesting about simulations is that, because their formal structure is modeled after some real-world process, the simulation will behave in the same way as the real-world process (Frasca 2003b: 223). However, I worry that the reason why some video games are simulations has as much to do with the fictive aspect of what those simulations are supposed to represent as it has to do with the ludic aspect of how their systems work. For an abstract set of rules to be a simulation of something, it must also be a fiction. Otherwise, it is just an abstract set of rules. To take one example, *Microsoft Flight Simulator* both presents the process of flying as well as the fictional representation of flight. So, I don't see "simulation" as an alternative to "interactive narrative" but instead see it as a particular kind of interactive narrative.

10 Certainly, text-based games like *Oregon Trail*, *Colossal Cave Adventure*, and *The Hobbit* were built around their embedded narratives. Nonetheless, if we are looking for storytelling through *action*, then text-based games are the wrong places to look.

11 In two side-quests, the player briefly encounters a member of the Tenakth, described as "reavers from the south" who are reputed to be particularly savage, and a member of the Utaru, a peaceful tribe of farmers. These tribes both become the main focus of the second game, *Horizon Forbidden West*, along with the Quen.

12 The difference between my account of agency and Bettina Bódi's (2023) may only be terminological. I take from Nguyen (2020) the idea that agency is a felt quality; it is something that a player experiences and has some awareness of. Thus, I think it would be appropriate to describe agency as an aesthetic effect, or perhaps as a broad category of aesthetic effects. For Bódi, agency is a quality of an artifact—it is the player's ability to act, which is something that the player has whether they are aware of it or not. Despite this, Bódi's claims about the way in which game design elements shape the players' experience of a game are not at odds with the claims I make here (nor is it incompatible with Nguyen's account for that matter), the main difference being that what Bódi calls "agency" I am calling "interactivity." Indeed, there are many theorists working on video games now who are roughly trying to say similar and compatible things, though we are using different terms for it. Game studies doesn't yet have a settled vocabulary.

13 To be clear, my narrative choices do not matter in these games, but my strategic choices—how I approach a battle and how I respond in the moment—certainly do.

14 See pages 132–3.

15 There has been extensive research on player/character identification in studies of role-playing games. It would push the bounds of this discussion too far to examine that body of research in detail. We need to only restrict

ourselves to role-playing in video games. For a broad overview of the research, see Bowman and Schrier (2018).
16 I have argued this point in more detail elsewhere (see Bartel 2024). The remainder of this paragraph contains a brief recap of my earlier argument.
17 However, see Ramirez, Elliott, and Milam (2021) for a critical discussion of the use of games to provoke empathy. While their account focus on applications in virtual reality, their arguments are general enough to apply to non-VR video games as well.

5

1 To be fair, there are a few exceptions in *Ghost of Tsushima*. Wearing some armor sets will reward the player with special trophies. There are also some places in the game where unique dialog options open up if the player is wearing the right armor. But these are exceptions to the general point. There are dozens of pieces of headwear to collect and only a very small number of them have any impact on the game.
2 See pages 38–9.
3 Video games generally offer users an engaging and entertaining entry point into developing internet and computer literacy skills. When video games are regarded as "boys' things," the opportunity to develop those skills is denied to girls. For a discussion, see Kocurek (2015).
4 For further discussion, see Waszkiewicz and Bakun (2020).
5 Maslow is often incorrectly quoted as claiming that the lower needs must be satisfied before progressing on to the higher needs; however, he in fact claims that the order in which needs are satisfied "is not nearly as rigid as we may have implied," and he goes on to list a variety of ways in which the satisfaction of higher needs might proceed either before or without the satisfaction of some lower needs (1943: 386). The same is true in video games. Agata Waszkiewicz and Martyna Bakun (2020) argue that video games often include isolated moments of coziness, like sitting around the safety of a campfire between battles (e.g., *Dragon Age: Origins*). In these games, survival and safety are not assured, yet the campfire offers a cozy space where the needs of love, esteem, and self-actualization can be pursued.

6 For an interesting discussion, see Bessière, Seay, and Kiesler (2007).
7 The comparison to investing is a point that I heard Elizabeth Cantalamessa make in a presentation on the aesthetics of collecting *Funko Pops!* on the American Society for Aesthetic's Discord channel, March 15, 2023.
8 I take this point from Walter Benjamin. In his essay, "Unpacking My Library, a Talk about Book Collecting," it is clear that part of the joy that Benjamin finds in collecting books is relishing its provenance. "The period, the region, the craftsmanship, the former ownership—for a true collector the whole background of an item adds up to a magic encyclopedia whose quintessence is the fate of the object" (1999b: 62).
9 See pages 109–16.
10 Scholars from theater studies have examined the roles of performance and improvisation in gaming. See Burn (2016) and Nitsche (2016) for a overviews and for other perspectives on role-playing not discussed here.
11 Thanks to Christopher Harrison for this example.
12 Of course, players can make goals like climbing all the mountains of Hyrule *the fastest* into a goal-seeking game, one where they compete with each other by videoing their play and streaming it or posting it online. In that case, *Hyrulean speed climbing* would become an informal game—or a "metagame"—one that is not defined by the video game itself but is instead defined and sustained by the gaming community.
13 See Chapter 4, 95–6.
14 My interest in this topic was inspired by a conference panel on "boring games" by Olli Leino and Sebastian Möring at the Philosophy of Computer Games Conference in Copenhagen, 2018.
15 https://skyhookgames.com/case-study/lawn-mowing-simulator/.
16 Actually, I think what they mean is, "It looks just like a movie."
17 Social realism, in the sense defined here, appears in many other video games. It is not as though video games generally avoid social realism or are incapable of it. For a discussion, see Galloway (2004).
18 My account of "procedural realism" is inspired by Bogost's notion of "procedural rhetoric" (2008).
19 The kind of authenticity that I refer to is quite different from the existential authenticity that Möring (2014) describes about boring games.

6

1. Careful social scientists will avoid making causal claims about violence in video games directly. It is more common for social scientists to make claims of correlation. Nonetheless, there are some areas where social scientists are comfortable making causal claims. For instance, see the discussion of "confirmed" effects in Barlett, Anderson, and Swing (2009).
2. The literature on this topic is vast and there are major points of disagreement among social scientists. See Barlett, Anderson, and Swing (2009) and Ferguson (2007) for reviews, and contrasting views, of the broad trends on studies of media effects.
3. Thanks to Jennifer Courtney-Bartel for suggesting this interpretation.
4. One obvious limitation here must be that the game designer could cheat. A game that is designed to demonstrate the effects of political policies could be rigged such that the policies that the designer favors always happen to have happy endings, while the policies of the opposing party always result in ruin. For such a game to genuinely work, we would need to trust the game designer's programming, or perhaps the relationship between input and output would need to be explained very thoroughly.
5. The thought experiment originally appeared in Philippa Foot's essay, "The Problem of Abortion and the Doctrine of the Double-Effect" (reprinted in Foot 2002: 19–32). It was further developed into the form that is widely discussed today by Judith Jarvis Thomson (1976).
6. See Book 1 of Aristotle's *Nicomachean Ethics*.
7. These numbers do not add up to 100 percent but instead add up to 103 percent. Perhaps the discrepancy is because the reported figures were rounded? Unfortunately, Lange's essay does not report raw data to verify.
8. While I largely agree with Hume that reason is a slave to the passions (*Treatise* II.3.3), I would not go so far as to argue for an emotivist account of morality, like that of Jesse Prinz (2007). Instead, taking lessons from Antonio Damasio (1995), I mean only to acknowledge that reason and emotion both have some role to play in moral decision-making.
9. I discuss this sort of conflict as an instance of an *unwilling player* in Bartel (2020: 85–6).

10 And, I should add that the opposite is also true: we should not ignore what is good about a game and fixate solely on what is bad about it. That would be puritanical.
11 It is not my aim to present a complete defense of ethicism against all is objections here. Interested readers can find my partial defense of ethicism in Bartel (2019, 2020) and Bartel and Cremaldi (2018).
12 It is worth noting that the "satire defense" can be used disingenuously. A point that Anita Sarkeesian (2010) makes about irony in advertising is that calling a representation "ironic" means that advertisers can use offensive and outrageous imagery while avoiding criticism. The same is true of "satire" in video games. If the game offends you, that is your mistake because all the sexist imagery is cleverly wrapped up in satire. The "satire defense" is effectively an ethical cover: players can disguise their enjoyment of sexist tropes behind a veneer of intellectual critique.
13 Some philosophers reject ethicism and argue instead for a position called "immoralism," which is the idea that moral faults can actually be aesthetic merits in some works under the right conditions (Eaton 2012; Kieran 2002; Stear 2022). A common example that immoralists use is the popular appreciation of villainous characters like Walter White in *Breaking Bad* and Thomas Harris' character Hannibal Lecter. Immoralists may then argue that the use of sexist tropes can be a form of satire and therefore aesthetically praiseworthy.

 I have two points in reply. First, I am doubtful that immoralism really delivers on what it promises. We must remember Gaut's distinction between promotion and depiction. Moral faults are those that rise to the level of promotion, not mere depiction. For a moral fault to be an aesthetic merit, it would have to be the case that the viewer recognizes the immoral content as immoral, sees the work as promoting immorality, and yet still aesthetically values both the offensive content and the work's promotion of it. And that is not what is happening in the case of Walter White or Hannibal Lecter. Instead, it seems more like the admiration for Walter White takes the form of a morality tale, while the admiration for Hannibal Lecter is a matter of morbid fascination. If viewers had the sense that *Breaking Bad* or *Hannibal* were promoting the lifestyles of Walter or Hannibal, I think critical response to these works would be very different from what it is. For this reason, I think immoralism doesn't really work on its own (for a similar criticism of immoralism, see Paris 2019). Second, we can view *Lollipop Chainsaw* as satire only if we think that it merely depicts sexist tropes rather than promotes them. Satire works when the player judges the sexist tropes as "morally bad" and also interprets the game as ridiculing the use of these tropes—indeed, that is what would make it satire. But the depiction and ridicule of a sexist trope is not immoralism, it is just ethicism repackaged.

14 I made a similar point previously, in Bartel (2020: 77).
15 I also see feminist game criticism as being grounded in ethicism, or something like it. However, I will not make that argument here.
16 For extensive examples and analyses, see Sarkeesian's series, "Tropes vs. Women in Video Games," on her YouTube channel *Feminist Frequency*.
17 There are not a lot of examples of dudes in distress, but there are some. For instance, Lord Shimura in *Ghost of Tsushima*, King Avad in *Horizon Zero Dawn*, and Dandelion in *The Witcher 3* are all distressed dudes in need of rescue.
18 Demographic studies of gamers over the decades show that this demographic group is still very strong, but they no longer have the dominance in gaming that they once did. The Entertainment Software Association releases an annual "Essential Facts" sheet every year detailing the latest demographic statistics for the United States. As of 2023, the average age of a gamer in the United States is thirty-two years, 53 percent of gamers identify as male, 46 percent identify as female, and 72 percent identify as ethnically White (ESA 2023). Of course, these are only demographic statistics for one country. Considering that there are estimated to be over twice as many gamers in Asia than in Europe and North America combined, the "average gamer" worldwide would be Asian. Meanwhile, the worldwide percentages for male and female gamers are likely around 55 percent and 45 percent, respectively. While that puts female gamers in the minority, this needs to be kept in perspective. According to Exploding Topics, there were 3.22 billion gamers in 2023 (https://explodingtopics.com/blog/number-of-gamers). If that is accurate, then the number of female gamers worldwide is somewhere around 1.5 billion. Female gamers might be in the minority, but that is still a massive demographic.

7

1. For a discussion on this point and more on potential conflicts between the rules of a game and its fiction, see Juul (2005): Chs. 4 and 5.
2. Rough makes a number of concessions, however. Rough allows that some artworks can seem like games, some games can be aesthetically appealing, and that elements of a game could be used to create a work of art and vice versa. Additionally, Rough claims that some things commonly called "video games" in fact do not count as games in the first place; so, it is entirely possible that such things could be works of art (2018b).
3. Rough's argument relies strongly on Bernard Suits' (2014) definition of "games." Suits' definition has been highly influential in the field of philosophy of games and sport; however, it is unclear whether his definition really works for video games.
4. Jesper Juul (2018) offers a similar argument. For him, the problem is that games force players to optimize their actions. We try to achieve the goal of winning as efficiently as we can while still following the rules. By contrast, art demands free exploration and poetic engagement. While Juul does not draw the conclusion that *video games cannot be art*, he instead draws the conclusion that there is a fundamental tension between video games and what he claims are the traditional demands of aesthetics.
5. One can find comments about the nature of art going back many centuries. For instance, Plato and Aristotle had much to say. However, they weren't really trying to define "art." Concerted effort to fix a definition for "art" really begins, I think, among German philosophers following in the wake of Kant (1790) and Hegel (1886).
6. See Bartel and Kwong (2021) for my account of what we should do given this lack of consensus.
7. Tavinor (2009: 175) offers some criticism of Smuts' account, but he also adopts the same strategy in defense of the art-status of video games.
8. But see Tavinor (2009: 190) for a criticism.
9. See the previous discussion of Nguyen's theory in Chapter 3 pages 62–5.
10. Nguyen's own account (2020: Ch. 6) tentatively accepts a cluster theory of art. But he ultimately sidesteps the question, "art games art." Instead, Nguyen says that what really matters is how games are valued. I think that's right. But see Bartel (2021) for a criticial discussion.

11 Both the aesthetic theory of art and the cluster theory agree on this, but they differ in that the cluster theory views the link as one possible art-making property among many. For our purpose, we don't have to choose between these two theories. All we need is the intuitive link between *art* and *designed aesthetic objects*.

12 That being said, this argument would surely also imply that there are many things that are primarily designed to be aesthetic objects that, while they are not considered to be art currently, ought to be art. Many video games would count as art on this argument, and so too would some flower gardens, landscape architecture, jewelry, and perfumes. Is this much proliferation a problem? Not really. The point of the argument is to recognize as art those things that ought to be so recognized. The argument avoids *unprincipled* proliferation, but it would imply that *art* as we currently understand it is missing a few categories.

References

Aarseth, Espen (1997). *Cybertext: Perspectives on Ergodic Literature.* Baltimore: Johns Hopkins Press.

Aarseth, Espen (2004). "Genre Trouble: Narrativism and the Art of Simulation." In Noah Wardrip-Fruin and Pat Harrigan, eds., *FirstPerson: New Media as Story, Performance, and Game.* Cambridge, MA: MIT Press, 45–55.

Aarseth, Espen (2014). "Ludology." In Mark J. P. Wolf and Bernard Perron, eds., *The Routledge Companion to Video Game Studies.* London: Routledge, 185–9.

Ali, Rami (2022). "The Video Gamer's Dilemmas." *Ethics and Information Technology* 24: 18.

Anderson, James, and Jeffrey Dean (1998). "Moderate Autonomism." *British Journal of Aesthetics* 38: 150–66.

Artis, Aderemi (2021). "The Argument from Extreme Difficulty in Video Games." *Journal of Aesthetics and Art Criticism* 79: 64–75.

Barlett, Christopher, Craig Anderson, and Edward Swing (2009). "Video Game Effects—Confirmed, Suspected, and Speculative." *Simulation and Gaming* 40: 377–403.

Bartel, Christopher (2018). "Ontology and Transmedial Games." In Jon Robson and Grant Tavinor, eds., *The Aesthetics of Videogames.* London: Routledge, 9–23.

Bartel, Christopher (2019). "Ordinary Monsters: Ethical Criticism and the Lives of Artists." *Contemporary Aesthetics* 17. https://contempaesthetics.org/2019/11/08/article-869/#FN1 (accessed July 20, 2024).

Bartel, Christopher (2020). *Video Games, Violence, and the Ethics of Fantasy: Killing Time.* London: Bloomsbury Academic.

Bartel, Christopher (2021). "Art, Aesthetics, and the Medium: Comments for Nguyen on the Art-Status of Games." *Journal of the Philosophy of Sport* 48: 321–31.

Bartel, Christopher (2023). "Ethics and Video Games." In James Harold, ed., the *Oxford Handbook of Ethics and Art.* Oxford: Oxford University Press, 474–89.

Bartel, Christopher (2025). "Videogames as Vehicles for Empathetic Perspective Shifting: Imagining Psychosis in *Hellblade*." In Katerina Bantinaki, Efi Kyprianidou, and Fotini Vassiliou, eds., *Empathy and the Aesthetic Mind: Perspectives on Fiction and Beyond*. London: Bloomsbury.

Bartel, Christopher, and Anna Cremaldi (2018). "'It's Just a Story': Pornography, Desire, and the Ethics of Fictive Imagining." *British Journal of Aesthetics* 58: 37–50.

Bartel, Christopher, and Jack M. C. Kwong (2021). "Pluralism, Eliminativism, and the Definition of Art." *Estetika* 58: 100–13.

Beardsley, Monroe (1983). "An Aesthetic Definition of Art." In Hugh Curtler, ed. *What Is Art?* New York: Haven Publications, 15–29.

Benjamin, Walter (1999a). *Selected Writings, Volume 2*. Translated by Rodney Livingstone and others. Edited by Michael W. Jennings, Howard Eiland, and Gary Smith. Cambridge, MA: Harvard University Press.

Benjamin, Walter (1999b). *Illuminations*. Translated by Harry Zorn. Edited by Hannah Arendt. London: Pimlico.

Bessière, Katherine, A. Fleming Seay, and Sara Kiesler (2007). "The Ideal Elf: Identity Exploration in World of Warcraft." *CyberPsychology and Behavior* 10 (4): 530–5.

Birch, Aaron, Simon Brew, and John Moore (2020). *Independent and Unofficial Guide: Minecraft Epic Builds*. New York: Scholastic Inc.

Blom, Joleen (2023). *Video Game Characters and Transmedia Storytelling*. Amsterdam: Amsterdam University Press.

Bódi, Bettina (2023). *Videogames and Agency*. London: Routledge.

Bogost, Ian (2008). "The Rhetoric of Video Games." In Katie Salen, ed., *The Ecology of Games: Connecting Youth, Games, and Learning*. Cambridge, MA: MIT Press, 117–40.

Bogost, Ian (2010). "Cow Clicker: The Making of an Obsession." *Ian Bogost*, July 21, 2010. http://bogost.com/writing/blog/cow_clicker_1/ (accessed July 6, 2022).

Bogost, Ian (2016). *Play Anything*. New York: Basic Books.

Bowman, Sarah Lynne, and Karen Schrier (2018). "Players and Their Characters in Role-Playing Games." In José Zagal and Sebastian Deterding, eds., *Role-Playing Game Studies*. New York: Routledge, 395–410.

Brewer, Bill (2011). *Perception and Its Objects*. Oxford: Oxford University Press.

Burgess, Melinda, KarenDill. S. Paul Stermer, Stephen Burgess, and Brian Brown (2011). "Playing with Prejudice: The Prevalence and Consequence of Racial Stereotypes in Video Games." *Media Psychology* 14: 289–311.

Burn, Andrew (2016). "Role-Playing." In Mark J. P. Wolf and Bernard Perron, eds., *The Routledge Companion to Video Game Studies*. London: Routledge, 241–50.

Caillois, Roger (1961). *Man, Play, and Games*. Translated by Meyer Barash. Chicago: University of Illinois Press, 2001.

Carroll, Noel (1996). "Moderate Moralism." *British Journal of Aesthetics* 36: 223–38.

Carroll, Noel (2006). "Aesthetic Experience: A Question of Content." In Matthew Kieran, ed., *Contemporary Debates in Aesthetics and the Philosophy of Art*. Malden, MA: Blackwell, 69–97.

Carroll, Noel (2009). *On Criticism*. New York: Routledge.

Casamassina, Matt (2005). "GDC 2005: Iwata Keynote Transcript." *IGN*, March 10, 2005. https://www.ign.com/articles/2005/03/11/gdc-2005-iwata-keynote-transcript (accessed July 18, 2024).

Collingwood, R. G. (1938). *The Principles of Art*. New York: Oxford University Press, 1958.

Consalvo, Mia, and Christopher Paul (2019). *Real Games: What's Legitimate and What's Not in Contemporary Videogames*. Cambridge, MA: MIT Press.

Cook, Daniel (2018). "Cozy Games." *Lost Garden*, January 24, 2018. https://lostgarden.home.blog/2018/01/24/cozy-games/ (accessed September 14, 2023).

Costikyan, Greg (2013). *Uncertainty in Games*. Cambridge, MA: MIT Press.

Crane, Tim (2001). *Elements of Mind*. New York: Oxford University Press.

Csikszentmihalyi, Mihaly (1975). "Play and Intrinsic Rewards." *Journal of Humanistic Psychology* 15: 41–63.

Csikszentmihalyi, Mihaly (1990). *Flow: The Psychology of Optimal Experience*. New York: Harper and Row.

Csikszentmihalyi, Mihaly (1997). *Finding Flow: The Psychology of Engagement with Everyday Life*. New York: Basic Books.

D'Agostino, Fred (1981). "The Ethos of Games." *Journal of the Philosophy of Sport* 8: 7–18.

Damasio, Antonio (1995). *Descartes' Error: Emotion, Reason, and the Human Brain*. New York: Avon Books.

Danto, Arthur (1981). *Transfiguration of the Commonplace*. Cambridge, MA: Harvard University Press.

De Lisi, R., and J. L. Wolford (2002). "Improving Children's Mental Rotation Accuracy with Computer Game Playing." *Journal of Genetic Psychology* 163: 272–82.

Dewey, John (1934). *Art as Experience*. New York: Minton, Balch.

Dickie, George (1997). *The Art Circle: A Theory of Art*. Chicago: Spectrum Press.

Dickie, George (2005). "The Triumph in *Triumph of the Will*." *British Journal of Aesthetics* 45: 151–6.

Diffey, Terry (1969). "The Republic of Art." *British Journal of Aesthetics* 9: 145–56.

Dixon, Nicholas (2016). "Internalism and External Moral Evaluation of Violent Sport." *Journal of the Philosophy of Sport* 43: 101–13.

Downs, Edward, and Stacy Smith (2010). "Keeping Abreast of Hypersexuality: A Video Game Character Content Analysis." *Sex Roles* 62: 721–33.

Eaton, A. W. (2007). "A Sensible Antiporn Feminism." *Ethics* 117: 674–715.

Eaton, A. W. (2012). "Robust Immoralism." *Journal of Aesthetics and Art Criticism* 70: 281–92.

Ebert, Roger (2005). "Why Did the Chicken Cross the Genders?" *Roger Ebert*, November 27, 2005. https://www.rogerebert.com/answer-man/why-did-the-chicken-cross-the-genders (accessed July 18, 2024).

Ebert, Roger (2007). "Games vs. Art: Ebert vs. Barker." *Roger Ebert*, July 21, 2007. https://www.rogerebert.com/roger-ebert/games-vs-art-ebert-vs-barker (accessed June 4, 2020).

Ebert, Roger (2010a). "Video Games Can Never Be Art." *Roger Ebert*, April 16, 2010. https://www.rogerebert.com/roger-ebert/video-games-can-never-be-art (accessed June 4, 2020).

Ebert, Roger (2010b). "Okay, Kids, Play on My Lawn." *Roger Ebert*, July 1, 2020. https://www.rogerebert.com/roger-ebert/okay-kids-play-on-my-lawn (accessed June 4, 2020).

ESA (2023). "2023 Essential Facts about the U.S. Video Game Industry." *Entertainment Software Association*. https://www.theesa.com/2023-essential-facts/ (accessed July 18, 2024).

Ferguson, Christopher (2007). "The Good, the Bad, and the Ugly: A Meta-analytic Review of Positive and Negative Effects of Violent Video Games." *Psychiatric Quarterly* 78: 309–16.

Fisher, Alex (2022). "Truth in Interactive Fiction." *Synthese* 200: 436.

Flanagan, Mary (2009). *Critical Play*. Cambridge, MA: MIT Press.

Flanagan, Mary, and Helen Nissenbaum (2014). *Values at Play in Digital Games*. Cambridge, MA: MIT Press.

Foot, Philippa (2002). *Virtues and Vices*. Oxford: Oxford University Press.

Frasca, Gonzalo (2003a). "Ludologists Love Stories, Too: Notes from a Debate That Never Took Place." *Proceedings of the 2003 DiGRA International Conference*, 92–9. http://www.digra.org/digital-library/publications/ludologists-love-stories-too-notes-from-a-debate-that-never-took-place/ (accessed May 14, 2019).

Frasca, Gonzalo (2003b). "Simulation versus Narrative: Introduction to Ludology." In Mark J. P. Wolf and Bernard Perron, eds., *The Video Game Theory Reader*. London: Routledge, 221–35.

Gabbiadini, Alessandro, Paulo Riva, Luca Andrighetto, Chiara Volpato, and Brad Bushman (2016). "Acting Like a Tough Guy: Violent-Sexist Video Games, Identification with Game Characters, Masculine Beliefs, and Empathy for Female Violence Victims." *PLoS ONE* 11: e0152121.

Galloway, Alexander (2004). "Social Realism in Gaming." *Game Studies* 4 (1). https://www.gamestudies.org/0401/galloway/ (accessed July 18, 2024).

Gaut, Berys (1998). "The Ethical Criticism of Art." In Jerrold Levinson, ed., *Aesthetics and Ethics: Ethics at the Intersection*. Cambridge: Cambridge University Press, 182–203.

Gaut, Berys (2000). "'Art' as a Cluster Concept." In Noel Carroll, ed., *Theories of Art Today*. Madison: University of Wisconsin Press, 25–44.

Gaut, Berys (2010). *A Philosophy of Cinematic Art*. Cambridge: Cambridge University Press.

Goodman, Nelson (1976). *Languages of Art*. Indianapolis, IN: Hackett.

Green, C. S., and D. Bavelier (2003). "Action Video Game Modified Visual Selective Attention." *Nature* 423: 534–7.

Griffith, J. L., P. Voloschin, G. D. Gibb, J. R. and Bailey (1983). "Differences in Eye-Hand Motor Coordination of Video-Game Users and Non-Users." *Perceptual and Motor Skills* 57: 155–8.

Grodal, Torben (2000). "Video Games and the Pleasures of Control." In Dolf Zillmann and Peter Vorderer eds., *Media Entertainment: The Psychology of Its Appeal*. London: Routledge, 197–213.

Grodal, Torben (2003). "Stories for Eye, Ear, and Muscles: Video Games, Media, and Embodied Experiences." In Mark J. P. Wolf and Bernard Perron, eds., *The Video Game Theory Reader*. London: Routledge, 129–55.

Hardcastle, Daniel (2019). *Fuck Yeah Video Games*. London: Unbound.
Harold, James (2011). "Autonomism Reconsidered." *British Journal of Aesthetics* 51: 137–47.
Harold, James (2020). *Dangerous Art*. Oxford: Oxford University Press.
Hayes, Elisabeth, and Elizabeth King (2009). "Not Just a Dollhouse: What *The Sims2* Can Teach Us about Women's IT Learning." *On the Horizon* 17 (1): 60–9.
Hegel, G. W. F. (1886). *Introductory Lectures on Aesthetics*. Translated by Bernard Bosanquet. New York: Penguin, 1994.
Huizinga, Johan (1938). *Homo Ludens*. London: Paladin, 1970.
Hume, David (1757). "Of the Standard of Taste." In Stephen Copley and Andrew Edgar, eds., *David Hume: Selected Essays*. Oxford: Oxford University Press, 1993: 133–54.
Iseminger, Gary (2004). *The Aesthetic Function of Art*. Ithaca, NY: Cornell University Press.
Iseminger, Gary (2006). "The Aesthetic State of Mind." In Matthew Kieran, ed., *Contemporary Debates in Aesthetics and the Philosophy of Art*. Malden, MA: Blackwell, 98–112.
Jacobson, Daniel (1997). "In Praise of Immoral Art." *Philosophical Topics* 25: 155–99.
Jung, Carl (1969). "On Psychic Energy." In G. Adler and R. F. C. Hull eds., *Collected Works of C.G. Jung, Volume 8: Structure & Dynamics of the Psyche*. Princeton, NJ: Princeton University Press, 3–66.
Juul, Jesper (2005). *Half-Real*. Cambridge, MA: MIT Press.
Juul, Jesper (2013). *The Art of Failure*. Cambridge, MA: MIT Press.
Juul, Jesper (2018). "The Aesthetics of the Aesthetics of the Aesthetics of Video Games: Walking Simulators as Response to the problem of Optimization." *The Philosophy of Computer Games Conference, Copenhagen*. https://www.jesperjuul.net/text/aesthetics3/ (accessed July 18, 2024).
Kant, Immanuel (1790). *The Critique of Judgement*. Translated by James Creed Meredith. Oxford: Oxford University Press, 1953.
Kieran, Matthew (1997). "Aesthetic Value: Beauty, Ugliness and Incoherence." *Philosophy* 72: 383–99.
Kieran, Matthew (2002). "Forbidden Knowledge: The Challenge of Immoralism." In Sebastian Gardner and Jose Luis Bermudez, eds., *Art and Morality*. London: Routledge, 56–73.

Kirkpatrick, Graeme (2011). *Aesthetic Theory and the Video Game*. New York: Manchester University Press.

Klenk, Michael (2021). "How Do Technological Artifacts Embody Moral Values?" *Philosophy and Technology* 34: 525–44.

Klevjer, Rune (2016). "Cut-scenes." In Mark J. P. Wolf and Bernard Perron, eds., *The Routledge Companion to Video Game Studies*. London: Routledge, 301–9.

Kocurek, Carly (2015). *Coin-Operated Americans: Rebooting Boyhood at the Video Game Arcade*. Minneapolis: University of Minnesota Press.

Lahti, Evan (2012). "Interview: Ken Levine on American History, Racism in BioShock Infinite." *PC Gamer*, December 13, 2012. https://www.pcgamer.com/bioshock-infinite-interview-ken-levine-racism-history/ (accessed January 10, 2024).

Lange, Amanda (2014). "'You're Just Gonna Be Nice': How Players Engage with Moral Choice Systems." *Journal of Games Criticism* 1(1). https://gamescriticism.org/2023/07/14/youre-just-gonna-be-nice-how-players-engage-with-moral-choice-systems/ (accessed August 5, 2022).

Langer, Susanne (1953). *Feeling and Form*. New York: Charles Scribner's Sons.

Langton, Rae (1993). "Speech Acts and Unspeakable Acts." *Philosophy & Public Affairs* 22: 293–330.

Leino, Olli Tapio (2018). "Escape from C-D Road: On the Value of Boredom in Euro Truck Simulator 2 Multiplayer." *The Philosophy of Computer Games Conference, Copenhagen*. https://gamephilosophy.org/wp-content/uploads/confmanuscripts/pcg2018/Leino%20-%202018%20-%20Escape%20from%20CD-Road.pdf (accessed September 5, 2023).

Leino, Olli Tapio (2020). "The Tragedy of the Art Game." Paper presented at the 2020 DiGRA International Conference—Play Everywhere, Tampere, June 3–6. http://www.digra.org/wp-content/uploads/digital-library/DiGRA_2020_paper_232.pdf (accessed February 13, 2022).

Levinson, Jerrold (1990). *Music, Art, and Metaphysics*. Ithaca, NY: Cornell University Press.

Levinson, Jerrold (2013). *Aesthetic Pursuits*. Oxford: Oxford University Press.

Lopes, Dominic McIver (2010). *A Philosophy of Computer Art*. London: Routledge.

Lynch, Teresa, Jessica Tompkins, Irene van Driel, and Niki Fritz (2016). "Sexy, Strong, and Secondary: A Content Analysis of Female Characters in Video Games across 31 Years." *Journal of Communication* 66: 564–84.

MacKinnon, Catherine (1987). *Feminism Unmodified: Discourses on Life and Law*. Cambridge, MA: Harvard University Press.

Martey, Rosa Mikeal, and Jennifer Stromer-Galley (2007). "The Digital Dollhouse: Context and Social Norms in *The Sims Online*." *Games and Culture* 2 (4): 314–34.

Martin, M. G. F. (2002). "The Transparency of Experience." *Mind and Language* 17: 376–425.

Maslow, A. H. (1943). "A Theory of Human Motivation." *Psychological Review* 50: 370–96.

Matravers, Derek (2017). *Empathy*. Malden, MA: Polity Press.

Matthes, Erich Hatala (2022). *Drawing the Line*. Oxford: Oxford University Press.

Melchionne, Kevin (1999). "Collecting as an Art." *Philosophy and Literature* 23 (1): 148–56.

Morgan, William (2012). "Broad Internalism, Deep Conventions, Moral Entrepreneurs, and Sport." *Journal of the Philosophy of Sport* 39: 65–100.

Möring, Sebastian (2014). "Freedom in Games—between Fear and Boredom." *The Philosophy of Computer Games Conference, Istanbul*. https://gamephilosophy.org/wp-content/uploads/confmanuscripts/pcg2014/Moering-2014.-Freedom-in-Games.-PCG2014.pdf (accessed September 5, 2023).

Moss, Richard (2016). "Hitting the Virtual Roads of Euro and American Truck Simulator with Retired Truckers." *Rock Paper Shotgun*, June 23, 2016. https://www.rockpapershotgun.com/american-truck-simulator-real-life-trucker (accessed September 5, 2023).

Murray, Janet (1997). *Hamlet on the Holodeck*. New York: Free Press.

Nitsche, Michael (2016). "Performance." In Mark J. P. Wolf and Bernard Perron, eds., *The Routledge Companion to Video Game Studies*. London: Routledge, 388–95.

Nguyen, C. Thi (2017). "Philosophy of Games." *Philosophy Compass* 12 (8): e12426.

Nguyen, C. Thi (2020). *Games: The Art of Agency*. New York: Oxford University Press.

Nguyen, C. Thi (2021). "The Opacity of Play: A Reply to Commentators." *Journal of the Philosophy of Sport* 48 (3): 448–75.

Paris, Panos (2019). "The 'Moralism' in Immoralism: A Critique of Immoralism in Aesthetics." *British Journal of Aesthetics* 59: 13–33.

Patridge, Stephanie (2011). "The Incorrigible Social Meaning of Video Game Imagery." *Ethics and Information Technology* 13: 303–12.

Peterson, Martin, and Andreas Spahn (2011). "Can Technological Artifacts Be Moral Agents?" *Science and Engineering Ethics* 17: 411–24.

Prinz, Jesse (2007). *The Emotional Construction of Morals*. Oxford: Oxford University Press.

Ramirez, Erick Jose, Miles Elliott, and Per-Erik Milam (2021). "What It's Like to Be a ___: Why It's (Often) Unethical to Use VR as an Empathy Nudging Tool." *Ethics and Information Technology* 23: 527–42.

Richard, Mark (1990). *Propositional Attitudes: An Essay on Thoughts and How We Ascribe Them*. New York: Cambridge University Press.

Robson, Jon, and Aaron Meskin (2016). "Video Games as Self-Involving Interactive Fictions." *Journal of Aesthetics and Art Criticism* 74: 165–77.

Robson, Jon, and Grant Tavinor, eds. (2018). *The Aesthetics of Videogames*. London: Routledge.

Rough, Brock (2016). *Are Videogames Art?* PhD dissertation. University of Maryland, College Park. DOI: 10.13016/M2Q518.

Rough, Brock (2018a). "The Incompatibility of Games and Artworks." *Journal of the Philosophy of Games* 1. https://doi.org/10.5617/jpg.2736 (accessed June 10, 2020).

Rough, Brock (2018b). "Videogames as Neither Video nor Games." In Jon Robson and Grant Tavinor, eds., *The Aesthetics of Videogames*. London: Routledge, 24–41.

Russell, J. S. (1999). "Are Rules All an Umpire Has to Work With?" *Journal of the Philosophy of Sport* 26: 27–49.

Ryan, Marie-Laure (2006). *Avatars of Story*. Minneapolis: University of Minnesota Press.

Salen, Katie, and Eric Zimmerman (2004). *Rules of Play: Game Design Fundamentals*. Cambridge, MA: MIT Press.

Salmon, Nathan, and Scott Soames (1988). *Propositional Attitudes*. New York: Oxford University Press.

Saito, Yuriko (2007). *Everyday Aesthetics*. New York: Oxford University Press.

Sarkeesian, Anita (2010). "Retro Sexism and Uber Ironic Advertising." *Feminist Frequency*, YouTube: 19 September 2010. https://www.youtube.com/watch?v=PD0Faha2gow (accessed September 24, 2016).

Schellekens, Elisabeth (2006). "Towards a Reasonable Objectivism for Aesthetic Judgments." *British Journal of Aesthetics* 46: 163–77.

Schulzke, Marcus (2013). "Simulating Philosophy: Interpreting Video Games as Executable Thought Experiments." *Philosophy and Technology* 27: 251–65.

Seabrook, John (2006). "Game Master." *New Yorker*, October 29, 2006. https://www.newyorker.com/magazine/2006/11/06/game-master (accessed July 18, 2024).

Shelley, James (2017). "The Concept of the Aesthetic." In Edward N. Zalta, ed., *The Stanford Encyclopedia of Philosophy* (Winter 2017 edition). https://plato.stanford.edu/archives/win2017/entries/aesthetic-concept/ (accessed September 5, 2023).

Shepard, Kenneth (2023). "*Baldur's Gate 3* Aims for RPG Fans' Ultimate Character Creator." *Kotaku*, July 18, 2023. https://kotaku.com/baldurs-gate-3-character-creator-races-genitals-options-1850653066 (accessed July 18, 2024).

Sibley, Frank (2001). *Approach to Aesthetics*. New York: Oxford University Press.

Sicart, Miguel (2009). *The Ethics of Computer Games*. Cambridge, MA: MIT Press.

Sicart, Miguel (2014). *Play Matters*. Cambridge, MA: MIT Press.

Simon, Robert (2000). "Internalism and Internal Values in Sport." *Journal of the Philosophy of Sport* 27: 1–16.

Smuts, Aaron (2005). "Are Video Games Art?" *Contemporary Aesthetics* 3. https://digitalcommons.risd.edu/liberalarts_contempaesthetics/vol3/iss1/6/ (accessed June 19, 2020).

Soderman, Braxton (2021). *Against Flow*. Cambridge, MA: MIT Press.

Spaulding, Shannon (2017). "Cognitive Empathy." In Heidi Maibom, ed., *The Routledge Handbook of Philosophy of Empathy*. New York: Routledge, 13–21.

Stear, Nils-Hennes (2020). "Fatal Prescription." *British Journal of Aesthetics* 60: 151–63.

Stear, Nils-Hennes (2022). "Immoralism Is Obviously True: Towards Progress on the Ethical Question." *British Journal of Aesthetics* 62: 615–32.

Stermer, S. Paul, and Melissa Burkley (2015). "SeX-Box: Exposure to Sexist Video Games Predicts Benevolent Sexism." *Psychology of Popular Media Culture* 4: 47–55.

Stueber, Karsten (2006). *Rediscovering Empathy: Agency, Folk Psychology, and the Human Sciences*. Cambridge, MA: MIT Press.

Suits, Bernard (2014). *The Grasshopper: Games, Life, and Utopia*, 3rd ed. Peterborough: Broadview Press.

Sutton-Smith, Brian (1997). *The Ambiguity of Play*. Cambridge, MA: Harvard University Press.

Tavinor, Grant (2005). "Videogames and Interactive Fiction." *Philosophy and Literature* 29 (1): 24–40.

Tavinor, Grant (2009). *The Art of Videogames*. London: Routledge.

Thomson, Judith Jarvis (1976). "Killing, Letting Die, and the Trolley Problem." *The Monist* 59: 204–17.

Tolstoy, Leo (1898). *What Is Art?* Translated by Richard Pevear and Larissa Volokhansky. New York: Penguin Books, 1995.

Tye, Michael (1995). *Ten Problems of Consciousness*. Cambridge, MA: MIT Press.

Van den Hoven, Jeroen (2005). "Design for Values and Values for Design." *Information Age* 4: 4–7.

Vanderhoef, John, and Matthew Thomas Payne (2022). "Press X to Wait: The Cultural Politics of Slow Game Time in *Red Dead Redemption 2*." *Game Studies* 22 (3). https://gamestudies.org/2203/articles/vanderhoef_payne (accessed September 5, 2023).

Verbeek, Peter-Paul (2006). "Materializing Morality: Design Ethics and Technological Mediation." *Science, Technology, & Human Values* 31: 361–80.

Waldow, Anik (2019). "Empathy: Affect, Language and Cognition in the Discovery of the Past." In Derek Matravers and Anik Waldow, eds., *Philosophical Perspectives of Empathy*. New York: Routledge, 13–27.

Walton, Kendall (1990). *Mimesis as Make-Believe*. Cambridge, MA: Harvard University Press.

Waszkiewicz, Agata, and Martyna Bakun (2020). "Towards the Aesthetics of Cozy Video Games." *Journal of Gaming & Virtual Worlds* 12 (3): 225–40.

Webster, Andrew (2018). "Gris Is Like a Stunning Animated Movie That You Can Play." *The Verge*, December 13, 2018. https://www.theverge.com/2018/12/13/18137844/gris-review-nintendo-switch-pc-gaming (accessed June 20, 2020).

Willard, Mary Beth (2021). *Why It's Ok to Enjoy the Work of Immoral Artists*. London: Routledge.

Willis, Marissa (2019). "Choose Your Own Adventure: Examining the Fictional Content of Video Games as Interactive Fictions." *Journal of Aesthetics and Art Criticism* 77: 43–53.

Winslow, Levi, and Isaiah Colbert (2023). "It's About Damn Time Games 'Git Gud' at Black Hair." *Kotaku*, February 28, 2023. https://kotaku.com/black-hair-games-character-creator-options-kinda-funny-1850170200 (accessed July 16, 2024).

Wohlwend, Karen (2017). "Monster High as a Virtual Dollhouse: Tracking Play Across Converging Transmedia and Social Media." *Teachers College Record* 119 (12): 1–20.

Wolf, Mark, ed. (2001). *The Medium of the Video Game*. Austin: University of Texas Press.

Yu, Jeffrey (2021). "Stardew Valley Cup Competition Explained." *Game Rant*, August 28, 2021. https://gamerant.com/stardew-valley-cup-competition-concernedape/ (accessed July 18, 2024).

Zagal, José (2009). "Ethically Notable Videogames: Moral Dilemmas and Gameplay." *Proceedings of DiGRA 2009: Breaking New Ground: Innovation in Games, Play, Practice and Theory*. https://dl.digra.org/index.php/dl/article/view/362 (accessed June 10, 2023).

Zagal, José, and Sebastian Deterding (2018). "Definitions of 'Role-Playing Games.'" In José Zagal and Sebastian Deterding, eds., *Role-Playing Game Studies*. New York: Routledge, 19–51.

Zangwill, Nick (1995). "The Beautiful, the Dainty, and the Dumpy." *British Journal of Aesthetics* 35: 317–29.

Index

Aarseth, Espen 85, 211 n.9
aesthetic autonomism 155–6, 163, 171–2
aesthetics
   accidental vs. designed 200–1
   and art 7, 185, 200–2
   attitudinal theory of 14–15
   definition of 4–5
   diversity of 7, 87, 201
   and experience 10, 200
      as internal vs. external 12–16
   and gameplay 6, 52–7, 197–9, 201, 204
   and moral choice 155, 171, 203
   and moral judgment 172–3
   the narrow sense of 6, 65
   and play 52–3
affordances 43, 72, 78, 107, 176
agency 43–4, 106–7, 201–2, 212 n.12
American Truck Simulator 137–44
Animal Crossing: New Horizons 36–7, 144
art
   and aesthetics 7, 185, 200–2
   definitions of 188–9, 193–5, 219 nn.11, 12
   and gameplay 191–2, 197–9, 201–2, 204
   and rule-following 192
   skepticism about 185–6
Artis, Aderemi 64–5, 77–8
attitudes, propositional 42
avatars
   and identity 110, 113, 115, 127, 132, 212–13 n.15
   and player relationships 112–14, 116

The Banner Saga 83
Batman: Arkham Asylum 84–5

Benjamin, Walter 121, 214 n.8
BioShock 90–1, 152
BioShock Infinite 151–4, 166
Bódi, Bettina 43–4, 212 n.12
Bogost, Ian 26–7, 37–8, 43, 120, 160–1
boredom 139, 142–4
Braid 188

Caillois, Roger 23–5, 51, 53–7, 65–6, 78, 109, 158, 207–8 n.5
Calico 46
Carroll, Noel 12, 160
casual games 37, 39
Civilization 67, 112
chance 54, 65–71
choice
   and limitations 108
   and morality. *See* moral choice
   and narrative 107–8
   as sanctioned 33, 108
Clash Royale 46
collecting 35, 128–31
Combat 98–9
competitive play 54, 57–8, 60
consequence
   and aesthetic value 107–9
   and dialogue 105
Cook, Daniel 123
Costikyan, Greg 66–8
Counter Strike: Global Offensive 126
cozy games 123–4, 213 n.5
creative authority 189–90
Csikszentmihalyi, Mihaly 58–62, 209 n.7
customization. *See* dress-up play
cut-scenes 104–5

D'Agostino, Fred 158
"damsels in distress" 178–9, 217 n.17

Dear Esther 84
Dewey, John 13–14
difficulty 55–6, 60, 65, 78–9
dollhouse play
   and collecting 35, 128–31
   defined 33–7, 119
   and dress-up play 34–5, 122–3, 125–8
   and feminine associations 124
   and freedom 122, 133, 144, 149
   and prescriptive vs. suggestive play 34, 144–5
   and role-playing 36, 127–8, 132–3, 143
Donkey Kong 92, 148
Dr. Mario 91, 97
Dragon Age: Origins 3, 96–7
dress-up play 34–5, 122–3, 125–8
Dungeons & Dragons 2, 67, 208 n.10

Ebert, Roger 187–91, 192–3, 199
Elder Scrolls V: Skyrim 32–3, 34, 46–7, 101, 111, 129
embodiment 112–13, 116
empathy 114–15, 169, 213 n.17
ethicism 172–7, 182–3, 216 n.13
evocativeness 145–6

Farming Simulator 137–8
feminist game criticism 177–8
fiction
   coherent and incoherent 91–3
   definition of 91, 210 n.3
   games as works of fiction 86
   as interactive 97–8, 211 n.9
   as make-believe 93–4, 210 n.3
   as "self-involving" 165–6
   and truth 96–7, 211 n.8
film 50, 83, 197
Final Fantasy 36
flow 49, 59–62
Flower 188
Frasca, Gonzalo 86

freedom 122, 133, 144
   and narrative control 190–1
   and rule-following 192
freeplay 54–5

gameplay
   and aesthetics 6, 52–7, 197–9, 201, 204
   and art 191–2, 197–9, 201–2, 204
   as central to games 50
   as flow 59–62
   as striving play 62–5
games
   as aesthetic objects 200–5
   and arguments against their art-status 187–92, 218 n.2
   and arguments for their art-status 192–9
   defined 25–6
   ontological approaches 43
   value of 62, 148–9
Gaut, Berys 172–4, 196
Ghost of Tsushima 76–77, 102–3, 110, 117–19, 127–8, 134–5, 213 n.1
"girls' games" 120, 124
goals
   different kinds 30–2, 35, 134–5
   and dollhouse play 134–6
goal-seeking play
   and competitive play 57–8
   defined 30–2
   and flow 49, 59–62
   and striving play 62–5
Gran Turismo 7 126
Grand Theft Auto V 170, 176
Gris 198–9
Grodal, Torben 106
Gwent 87–8

Hearthstone 147–8
Hellblade: Senua's Sacrifice 77

Index

Horizon Zero Dawn 91, 95, 100–1, 105, 115, 175, 212 n.11
Huizinga, Johan 22–3, 51–3, 158, 207 n.4
Hume, David 6, 11, 22

incorrigible social meaning 180
interactivity
  and art 198–9
  defined 107, 212 n.12
  and narratives 83–4, 97–8, 106–9
  and moral choice 165–6
Iseminger, Gary 14

Journey Escape 93
Juul, Jesper 26, 38–9, 43, 61, 71–2, 76, 78–9, 92, 120, 138, 208 n.10, 218 n.4

Kant, Immanuel 6, 11, 13

Lawn Mowing Simulator 138–9, 142
The Legend of Zelda: Breath of the Wild 19–20, 77, 134, 135
Leino, Olli Tapio 139, 144, 209 n.8
Levine, Ken 154
Levinson, Jerrold 15
limitations 43, 72, 78, 108, 176–7
Lollipop Chainsaw 172, 175–6, 178, 182–3, 216–17 n.13
Lopes, Dominic McIver 195, 198–9, 204
lore 101–3
ludology 85

Mario Kart 28–9, 49
Maslow, A. H. 123, 213 n.5
Max Payne 3 103, 147, 191
Melchionne, Kevin 130–1
Middle-earth: Shadow of Mordor 101–2
Minecraft 135

moral choice
  and aesthetics 155, 171, 203
  and choosing "evil" 164–5, 168–9
  in fiction 161–2, 167, 170
  as genuine 161–2, 163–71
moral judgment 156, 161
  internal vs. external 156, 177
moral psychology 161–2, 166–7, 215 n.8

narrative
  and action 98–100
  defined 94–8
  embedded and emergent 95–7, 136
  and interactivity 83–4, 97–8, 106–9
  and passive media 50, 83, 101, 190
  and open-world games 103, 122
narrative play
  and consequence 83–4, 107–9
  defined 32–3, 82–3
  and games that lack a narrative 87–8, 95
  importance of 85
  and lore 101–3
  and role-playing 109–16
  and worldbuilding 100–1
narrative structures 103–4
narratology 86, 210 n.2
Nguyen, C. Thi 27–9, 58, 62–5, 106, 133, 201–2, 209 n.7, 212 n.12, 218–19 n.10

open-world games 103, 122

Pajares-Tosca, Susana 86
Patridge, Stephanie 180
persistence 147

play
  and aesthetics 52–5, 62, 112
  characteristics of 22, 23–4, 29
  diversity of 53–4, 87
  and motivation 27–8, 44–5, 51–2, 60, 62, 112
play attitudes 21, 24–5, 29–30, 40–5, 56
  and game design 45–7
  vs. ontological approaches 43
playthroughs 96–7
Pokémon 129
procedural realism 141–3
procedural rhetoric 161
proprioception 64–5, 198
Proteus 39

racism 151–4, 173, 179
"real" games 37, 39, 41, 120
realism 76–7, 138, 140–1, 143
Red Dead Redemption 81–2, 87
Red Dead Redemption 2 111, 133, 168
representation 90–1, 210 n.3
responsiveness 146–7
Robson, Jon and Aaron Meskin 165–6
role-playing
  and decision-making 112
  defined 110
  and dollhouse play 36, 127–8, 132–3, 143
  and empathy 114–16
  and narrative play 109–16, 132
  and perspective-taking 110–15, 127–8, 133, 143, 167–8
Rough, Brock 191–2, 199, 201, 203, 218 n.2
rules
  as arbitrary 26, 63, 71
  defined 74–5
  and difficulty 55–6
  and formalism 71–3

  vs. freeplay 54–5
  vs. mechanics 74–6

Salen, Katie, and Eric Zimmerman 66, 68, 70, 72, 73–4, 210 n.2
sandbox games 122
Sarkeesian, Anita 216 n.12
satire 176, 178, 216 n.12, 216–217 n.13
Schellekens, Elisabeth 9
Schulzke, Marcus 161–2
sexism 172, 175, 178–80, 213 n.3
Shelley, James 11–12
A Short Hike 61, 146
Sicart, Miguel 162, 208 n.6
simulation 137–144, 211 n.9
skill 21, 38–9, 53–4, 59–60, 64–5, 79, 138, 141
Smuts, Aaron 193–8
Soderman, Braxton 209 n.4
Star Wars 173–4
Stardew Valley 32, 44–5, 98, 124
striving play 62–5
storytelling 3, 6, 79, 88, 98–105, 133, 212 n.10
Suits, Bernard 25–6, 62, 218 n.3
Super Mario Odyssey 85
Sutton-Smith, Brian 207 n.2

Tavinor, Grant 196, 198, 204, 218 n.7
Tetris 45–6, 91, 144, 145
The Sims 136
This War of Mine 203
Thomas Was Alone 99–100
toys 121, 145–147
transgressive play 44–5
trends 178–82
tropes 180–2

uncertainty 66–71
Unpacking 123

value-laden 157–62
Vanderhoef, John and Matthew Thomas Payne 139–40
violence 159, 215 n.1 and n.2

The Walking Dead 84, 108, 169

Walton, Kendall 93–4, 210 n.3
Willis, Marissa 96–7
The Witcher 3: Wild Hunt 104, 109, 217 n.17
World of Warcraft 104
Wright, Will 120, 122
worldbuilding 100–1